THE FULL RIDE SCHOLARSHIPS BOOK:

Attend College Debt-Free

Chrisnuel Publishing

The Full Ride Scholarships Book: Attend College Debt-free by Chrisnuel Publishing.

Published by Chrisnuel publishing.

Distributed by Amazon LLC.

Credits: Quality research was done during the production of this book. We wish to acknowledge some highly helpful platforms from which accurate data was sourced – US news (*college data*), and Wikipedia (*general inquiries*). Also credits to Convertful for the abstract illustration used on the book cover.

Printed and bound in the United States of America.

Table of Contents

Table of Contents

Dedication

This book is dedicated to Almighty God and to all scholars – both U.S. and International scholars – who wish to attend college on a full ride scholarship and graduate debt-free.

May Your Dreams Come True!

Introduction

In today's world, education is a key to unlocking a world of opportunities. However, the rising costs of higher education can often place a heavy financial burden on students and their families. As a result, many deserving and talented individuals find themselves facing significant obstacles in pursuing their academic aspirations.

This book, "The Full Ride Scholarships Book" aims to address this issue by providing comprehensive information and guidance on securing scholarships/financial aids to make higher education more accessible to all. It comprises of Full Ride scholarships, Full Tuition Scholarships and Other Scholarships with a minimum of value of $5,000 up to full tuition specifically for undergraduate studies. Additionally, we explore various tips and other essential financial aid application processes, equipping students with the knowledge to access the support they need.

This is a comprehensive resource designed to empower individuals to pursue their educational dreams without the burden of overwhelming financial stress.

Introduction

The scholarships listed here have been curated for students from virtually all backgrounds. This helps to promote diversity in the classroom by making education more accessible to students from a variety of backgrounds. Scholarships help to recognize and reward academic achievement, which can encourage students to continue working hard and pursuing their goals..

Feel free to explore and leverage the wealth of scholarship information inside this book!

CHAPTER 1

FULL RIDE INSTITUTIONAL $CHOLARSHIP$

1 Alabama A&M University

Location: Huntsville, Alabama
Setting: Urban (1,173 Acres)
Undergraduate Enrollment: 5,206
Type: Public

AAMU Presidential Scholarship: Full tuition, room, board, fees and $1000 book allowance per semester.

Requirements: High School GPA of 3.75 or above | Act Score of 28 or above/ Sat score of 1310 or above | Citizen or legal resident of United States.

Application Deadline: January 15

Application Link:
https://www.aamu.edu/admissions-aid/financial-aid/scholarships/index.html

2 University of Alabama in Huntsville

Location: Huntsville, Alabama
Setting: City (432 Acres)
Undergraduate Enrollment: 7,169
Type: Public

National Merit Awards: Full tuition, room, board, and course fees stipend (up to $500 per academic year) and a one time $3,000 UAH led summer study-abroad allowance.

Requirements: National Merit Finalists, National Achievement Finalists, National Hispanic Recognition Program Scholars.

Application Deadline: December 15

Application Link:
https://www.uah.edu/admissions/undergraduate/financial-aid/scholarships/freshmen

3 University of Montevallo

Location: Montevallo, Alabama
Setting: Rural (160 Acres)
Undergraduate Enrollment: 2,215
Type: Public

Montevallo Ambassador Scholarship: Full tuition, fees, room and board.

Requirements: High School GPA of 3.5 or above | ACT Score of 30 or above / SAT score of 1360 or above

Application Deadline: February 1

Application Link:
https://www.montevallo.edu/admissions-aid/undergraduate-admissions/scholarships/

4 Troy University

Location: Troy, Alabama
Setting: Rural (1,836 Acres)
Undergraduate Enrollment: 11,297
Type: Public

The Scholars PLUS Award: Full tuition, full housing and meal plan.

The Scholars Award: Full tuition, room and board.

Requirements: 30-36 ACT, 1360 - 1600 SAT | 3.7 GPA

Application Deadline: Check the website for more details.

Application Link:
https://www.troy.edu/scholarships-costs-aid/scholarships/undergraduate-scholarships.html

5 Alabama State University

Location: Huntsville, Alabama
Setting: City (172 Acres)
Undergraduate Enrollment: 3,296
Type: Public

Presidential Academic Scholarship: Full tuition, books, required fees, on-campus room & board for four years of undergraduate study.

Requirements: ACT Score of 26 or SAT score of 1240-1270 | High school GPA of 3.76

Academic Excellence Scholarship: Full tuition, books and required fees.

Requirements: ACT Score of 22 or SAT score of 1240-1270 | High school GPA of 3.51-3.75

Application Deadline: February 15

Application Link: https://www.alasu.edu/admissions/undergrad-admissions/asu-academic-scholarships

6 University of Alabama in Tuscaloosa

Location: Tuscaloosa, Alabama
Setting: Suburban (1,143 Acres)
Undergraduate Enrollment: 32,458
Type: Public

National Merit Finalist: Full tuition, four years on-campus room, $3,500 stipend per year, $2000 study abroad stipend, $2000 book scholarship.

Requirements: ACT Score of 32 or SAT score of 1420 | High school GPA of 3.8

Academic Elite Scholarship: Full tuition, one year on-campus room, $8,500 stipend per year, $2000 book scholarship + plus more

Requirements: ACT Score of 32 or SAT score of 1420 | High school GPA of 3.8

Application Deadline: December 15

Application Link: https://afford.ua.edu/scholarships/

7 Tuskegee University

Location: Tuskegee, Alabama
Setting: Rural (5,000 Acres)
Undergraduate Enrollment: 2,100
Type: Private

Distinguished Presidential Scholarship: Full tuition, room, board, and $800 book allowance.

Requirements: High School GPA of 3.7 or above | SAT score of 1390+ or ACT equivalent.

Application Deadline: May 1

Application Link:
https://www.tuskegee.edu/programs-courses/scholarships/freshman-scholarships

8 Faulkner University

Location: Montgomery, Alabama
Setting: Suburban (84 Acres)
Undergraduate Enrollment: 1,939
Type: Private

National Merit Finalist: Full tuition, room, board, and mandatory fees.

Requirements: National Merit Finalists.

Application Deadline: March 2

Application Link:
https://www.faulkner.edu/admissions/scholarships/

1 University of Arkansas at Little Rock

Location: Little Rock, Arkansas
Setting: Urban (250 Acres)
Undergraduate Enrollment: 6,357
Type: Public

Donaghey Scholars Program: Full tuition, fees, $6,000-$10,000 yearly stipend, study abroad funding, laptop, housing subsidy, up to four year Awarded.

Requirements: Average GPA usually is 3.9 | Average Act Score usually is 30 | US citizens or permanent residents. There are other scholarships available for out-of-state students.

Application Deadline: February 1

Application link: https://ualr.edu/scholarships/freshmen/

2 Harding University

Location: Searcy, Arkansas
Setting: City (350 Acres)
Undergraduate Enrollment: 3,523
Type: Private

National Merit Scholarship: Full tuition, standard room & board, technology fee.

Requirements: National Merit Finalist.

Application Deadline: Check site for more details.

There are scholarships available for International Students.

Application link: https://www.harding.edu/admissions/scholarships

3 Philander Smith College

Location: Little Rock, Arkansas
Setting: Urban (9 Acres)
Undergraduate Enrollment: 710
Type: Private

Presidential Scholarship: Full tuition, fees, books, room & board.

Requirements: High School GPA of 3.4 or above | SAT score of 1200+ or 25+ ACT equivalent

Application Deadline: March 1

Application link: https://www.philander.edu/admissions/paying-for-college/scholarships

4 University of Arkansas at Pine Bluff

Location: Pine Bluff, Arkansas
Setting: City (318 Acres)
Undergraduate Enrollment: 2,182
Type: Public

Chancellor's Scholarship: Awards a Full Ride Scholarship (tuition, fees, room and board, books)

Requirements: A minimum SAT score of 1250 (Math and CR only) or ACT composite score of 28 or Valedictorian or Salutatorian of high school class | Be an entering first-time freshman | 3.5 GPA or above.

University Scholarship: Full tuition, fees, room and board, books.

Requirements: A minimum SAT score of 1050 (Math and CR only) or ACT composite score of 23 | Be an entering first-time freshman | 3.5 GPA or above.

UAPB ARMY ROTC Scholarship: Full tuition, fees, room and board, books and up to $16,000 allowances.

Requirements: U.S. citizen | Cumulative GPA of 2.5; ACT score of 19 | Pass the Army physical fitness test.

Application Deadline: Check the website for more details.

Application Link:
https://www.uapb.edu/administration/enrollment_management/office_of_recruitment/scholarships.aspx

5 Hendrix College

Location: Conway, Arkansas
Setting: Subruban (175 Acres)
Undergraduate Enrollment: 1,130
Type: Private

President's & Madison Murphy Scholarship: Full tuition, board, half the room.

Requirements: ACT Score of 32 or SAT score of 1430 | High school GPA of 3.6

Hays Memorial Scholarship: Full tuition, fees, room, board.

Requirements: ACT Score of 32 or SAT score of 1430 | High school GPA of 3.6

Application Deadline: November 15

Application Link:
https://www.hendrix.edu/financialaid/scholarships/

1

Grand Canyon Univerity

Location: Phoenix, Arizona
Setting: Urban (100 Acres)
Undergraduate Enrollment: 65,870
Type: Private

ROTC Scholarships: Full tuition, the option of room and board in place of tuition, additional allowances for books and fees, monthly living allowances for each school year, worth up to $500.

Application Deadline: Check the website for more details.

Students Inspiring Students: Full tuition and fees per academic year, except for room and meal charges. Renewable for up to 8 semesters.

Additional Information: Students who receive this scholarship are required to complete 50 hours per semester in the GCU Learning Lounge.

Fostering Futures Scholarship: This award covers the cost of tuition, fees, room and meal plan to help qualified Arizona students ***experiencing foster care*** achieve their academic goals.

Eligibility: Applicants must be a U.S. citizen an Arizona resident, Must be in state care at age 17 and enrolled in the Volunteer Foster Care Program Agreement at 18 years of age.

Application Deadline: December 31

Application Link: https://www.gcu.edu/financial-aid/scholarships-grants/additional

1 California State University – Long Beach

Location: Long Beach, California
Setting: Urban (322 Acres)
Undergraduate Enrollment: 33,605
Type: Public

President's Scholarship: Full tuition, campus housing allowance, and subsidies for textbooks, internship, travel abroad, plus more.

Requirements: Top Applicants.

Application Deadline: November 1

Application Link:
https://www.csulb.edu/financial-aid-and-scholarships/scholarships

2 California Institute of Technology

Location: Pasadena, California
Setting: Suburban (124 Acres)
Undergraduate Enrollment: 987
Type: Private

The majority of financial aid awarded to Caltech undergraduates comes from grants. They are all need-based, as the institute does not have a merit aid program. Undergraduate students who fill out a financial aid application will be automatically considered.

Please refer to this site for more details...

Application Link:
https://www.finaid.caltech.edu/TypesofAid/grants

3 University of Southern California

Location: Los Angeles, Carlifornia
Setting: Urban (226 Acres)
Undergraduate Enrollment: 20,699
Type: Private

Mork Family Scholarship: Full tuition, $5,000 Housing stipend per year.

Eligibility: Application is open to incoming freshmen through the USC Office of Admission. Candidates are selected from an extremely competitive pool.

There are scholarships available for International students.

Application Deadline: December 1

Application Link: https://financialaid.usc.edu/undergraduate-financial-aid/admitted-and-continuing-students/scholarships/

4 Soka University

Location: Aliso Viejo, Carlifornia
Setting: Suburban (103 Acres)
Undergraduate Enrollment: 435
Type: Private

Soka's Global Merit Scholarship: Covers the entire cost of attendance, full tuition, room and board, travel, personal expenses, books, and supplies.

Soka's Makiguchi scholarship: Covers the entire cost of attendance, full tuition, room and board, travel, personal expenses, books, and supplies.

Soka's Ikeda Scholarship: The most Prestigious Scholarship at Soka University. Covers the entire cost of attendance, full tuition, room and board, travel, personal expenses, books, and supplies.

N.B: Awarded for the duration of one academic year.

Eligibility: This is determined by the dean of enrollment services based on your admissions application. All admitted students are given equal consideration for this award.

Application Deadline: January 15

Application Link: https://www.soka.edu/financial-aid-tuition/aid-undergraduate-students/undergraduate-types-aid

1 Colorado State University

Location: Fort Collins, Colorado
Setting: City (4773 Acres)
Undergraduate Enrollment: 25,362
Type: Public

Monfort Scholars Scholarship: Full tuition, fees, books, room & board.

Requirements: Upper 5% of graduating class [#1 or #2 if class is fewer than 40], evidence of scholastic ability, leadership etc. , 1300 or higher on SAT(or ACT Equivalent)

Application Deadline: February 1

Application Link:
https://financialaid.colostate.edu/scholarships/

2 Colorado College

Location: Colorado Springs, Colorado
Setting: City (100 Acres)
Undergraduate Enrollment: 2,241
Type: Private

El Pomar Scholarship: Full tuition and fees, room & board and meal Plan.

Requirements: Coloroda Resident, High school senior, top applicants, eligible for need-based financial aid.

Application Deadline: November 1

Application Link:
https://www.coloradocollege.edu/admission/financialaid/scholarships.html

1 University of Connecticut

Location: Storrs, Connecticut
Setting: Rural (4,076 Acres)
Undergraduate Enrollment: 18,983
Type: Public

Stamps Scholars Award: Full support scholarship (tuition, room and board, fees, books, transportation, miscellaneous. Funding for enrichment experiences (up to $12,000 per student)

Requirements: Connecticut Resident | Must qualify for the Nutmeg or Day of pride scholarship.

Nutmeg Scholarship: Full Scholarship (Includes direct and Indirect cost of attendance)

Requirements: Connecticut Resident | All Semifinalist/Finalist in the National Hispanic Recognition program or the National Merit competition semifanlists are eligible for nomination | Nominations are made by the Guidance Counselor's office at each Connecticut secondary school.

Day of Pride Scholarship: Full Scholarship (Includes direct and Indirect cost of attendance). Awarded to outstanding Connecticut secondary school seniors from disadvantaged backgrounds.

Requirements: Nominations are made by the Guidance Counselor's office at each Connecticut secondary school.

Application Deadline: October 25

Application Link:
https://admissions.uconn.edu/cost-aid/scholarship/

2 Western Connecticut State University

Location: Danbury, Connecticut
Setting: Urban (398 Acres)
Undergraduate Enrollment: 3,165
Type: Public

President-to-President Scholarship: In-state tuition and fees for 2 years.

Requirements: Awarded to an outstanding graduating Naugatuck Valley Community College student who has been accepted to WSCU | A minimum 3.3 GPA.

Application Deadline: March 1

Application Link:
https://www.wcsu.edu/waterbury/scholarship/

1 University of Delaware

Location: Newark, Delaware
Setting: Suburban (1,996 Acres)
Undergraduate Enrollment: 18,883
Type: Private-Public

ROTC Scholarships

U.S. Air Force ROTC: There are three different types of scholarships under this category.

This award covers full tuition and authorized fees, plus a monthly living expense stipend and an annual book stipend.

Requirements: U.S. citizens | SAT composite score of 1240 or ACT composite score of 26 | A minimum cumulative unweighted GPA of 3.0 | Applicant must be physically fit.

Application Deadline: January 14

Application Link:
https://www.udel.edu/students/student-financial-services/undergraduate/

2 Delaware State University

Location: Dover, Delaware
Setting: Suburban (706 Acres)
Undergraduate Enrollment: 4,399
Type: Public

Full Scholarship: Full tuition, fees, room and board, text books and school materials.

This scholarship is available to both in-state and out-of-state students.

Eligibility: U.S. citizens | This scholarship is awarded by the office of admissions to entering full-time, first-year freshmen.

Application Deadline: March 15

Application Link:
https://www.desu.edu/admissions/financial-aid/scholarships

1 Lynn University

Location: Boca Raton, Florida
Setting: Suburban (123 Acres)
Undergraduate Enrollment: 2,792
Type: Private

Presidential Scholarship: Award covers Full tuition, housing and food.

Eligibility: 3.65 high school GPA or higher (on a 4.0 Scale) if test scores were not considered by admission | 3.50 high school GPA or higher (on a 4.0 Scale) if test score were considered for admission | A minimum SAT score of 1050 or ACT score of 20 is required.

Application Deadline: February 1

Application Link:
https://www.lynn.edu/admission/tuition-aid/financial-aid/presidential-scholarship

2 Bethune-Cookman University

Location: Daytona Beach, Florida
Setting: Urban (82 Acres)
Undergraduate Enrollment: 2,513
Type: Private

Presidential Scholarship: Full tuition, room, board, and $500 per semester book Scholarship.
Requirements: SAT 1240 OR ACT Composite 26 | 3.75 GPA | Must be a Resident on Campus | Enrollment Fee (Non-Refundable)

Application Deadline: March 1

Application Link:
https://www.cookman.edu/financial_aid/Receiving_Aid/Scholarships/Presidential.html

3 Stetson University

Location: DeLand, Florida
Setting: Suburban (185 Acres)
Undergraduate Enrollment: 2,561
Type: Private

J. Ollie Edmunds Distinguished Scholarship: This scholarship pays for all undergraduate expenses.

Requirements: A minimum SAT score of 1350 (critical reading and math) or an ACT composite score of 30 | A minimum GPA of 3.5

Application Deadline: January 8

Application Link:
https://www.stetson.edu/administration/financial-aid/scholarships/

4 Florida A&M University

Location: Tallahassee, Florida
Setting: City (422 Acres)
Undergraduate Enrollment: 7,301
Type: Public

Presidential Special Scholarship: This scholarship cover fees associated with tuition, but minus the postal fee and the $35 orientation fee, it covers charges for room and board, but minus fines.

Requirements: U.S citizen or permanent resident | Have 1260 on the redesigned SAT or 27 on the ACT | Have a 3.5 FAMU recalculated GPA.

Medical Scholars Program: Full scholarship for both in-state and out-of-state students, Full tuition and fees, double occupancy room rate, and board plus other benefits.

Requirements: 3.5 GPA or higher | 1290 or better SAT score / 29 or better ACT score

Application Deadline: Contact fran.scott@famu.edu for more information.

Army ROTC, Air Force ROTC, Navy-Marine ROTC Scholarship programs all awards Full tuition, room and board, stipends for books, supplies and equipments, etc.

Application Deadline: September 4

Application Link:
https://www.famu.edu/students/scholarships/index.php

5 University of Florida

Location: Gainesville, Florida
Setting: Suburban (2,000 Acres)
Undergraduate Enrollment: 34,881
Type: Public

Machen Florida Opportunity Scholars Program: Awards full grant and scholarship financial aid package to ensure students thrive at UF.

Requirements: Florida Residents | Neither parent may have earned a bachelor's degree | Total family income is less than $40,000 and total family assets, other than home, are less than $25,000.

Application Deadline: October 1

Application Link:
https://admissions.ufl.edu/cost-and-aid/scholarships

6 University of South Florida

Location: Tampa, Florida
Setting: Urban (1,646 Acres)
Undergraduate Enrollment: 33,077
Type: Public

USF Tradition of Excellence Awards: Award covers the full cost of attendance.

Requirements: Applicant must be a National Merit Scholar Finalist.

P.S: Semi-finalists are awarded $20,000 ($5,000 per year) until they are officially classified as a National Merit Finalist and select USF as their first-choice school.

Application Deadline: March 1

Application Link:
https://www.usf.edu/admissions/freshmen/admission-information/cost-of-attendance/scholarships.aspx

7 Barry University

Location: Miami Shores, Florida
Setting: Urban (124 Acres)
Undergraduate Enrollment: 3,122
Type: Private

Stamps Scholars Program: Full tuition, room and board, books, and travel over four years, plus additional $6,000 award for study abroad or other extraordinary learning experience.

Requirements: 3.5 GPA or higher (International equivalent accepted) P.S: It is Open to U.S. and International Freshmen.

Application Deadline: January 15

Application Link: https://www.barry.edu/en/stamps-scholars-program/

8 Webber International University

Location: Babson Park, Florida
Setting: Rural (110 Acres)
Undergraduate Enrollment: 821
Type: Private

Bright Futures Academic Scholarship: 100% average state university tuition – approx. $211 per credit hour + $300 Book stipend.

Requirements: 1330 SAT/ 29 ACT | 3.50 High school GPA.

Application Deadline: August 1

Application Link: https://www.webber.edu/

9 Rollins College

Location: Winter Park, Florida
Setting: Suburban (80 Acres)
Undergraduate Enrollment: 2,145
Type: Private

Alfond Scholars program: Full tuition, fees, room and board.

Requirements: 1450 or higher (Evidenced Based Reading and Math) or ACT's of 32 or higher.

Application Deadline: November 1

Application Link: https://www.rollins.edu/scholarships-aid/scholarships/

10 Florida Institute of Technology

Location: Melbourne, Florida
Setting: Suburban (174 Acres)
Undergraduate Enrollment: 3,374
Type: Private

Farmers Scholars Programs *(Available only to Florida Residents)*

Farmer Scholarship: Full tuition, room and board, and fees.

Requirements: Top applicants.

Application Deadline: February 1

Application Link: https://www.fit.edu/admission/applying/first-year/

11 Florida International University

Location: Miami, Florida
Setting: Urban (344 Acres)
Undergraduate Enrollment: 45,442
Type: Public

FIU National Merit Finalist: Award covers Full tuition, Fees, plus a book stipend, 100% housing with meal plan, Laptop (with demonstration of financial need)

Requirements: Applicant must be recognised as a National Merit Scholar Finalist | U.S citizen, a U.S. lawful permanent resident or an international student with intention of receiving the F-1 visa to study in the United States.

Presidential Merit Scholarship: Awards Full tuition and fees, plus a book stipend.

Requirements: A minimum SAT score of 1370 or 30 ACT or Top 5% of a Florida High School Graduating Class | 4.0 GPA | U.S citizen, a U.S. lawful permanent resident or an international student with intention of receiving the F-1 visa to study in the United States.

FIU College Board Recognition Program Scholarship: Awards Full tuition, fees, book stipends, plus a $1,000 meal plan stipend per semester.

Requirements: Applicant must be awarded one of the recognition awards from the College Board | 4.0 weighted HS GPA | 1370 or SAT or 30 ACT.

Application Deadline: January 31

Application Link:
https://scholarships.fiu.edu/browse-scholarships/merit-scholarships/

12 University of Miami

Location: Coral Gables, Florida
Setting: Suburban (239 Acres)
Undergraduate Enrollment: 12,504
Type: Private

Stamps Scholarship: Award covers the full cost of attendance (includes tuition and fees, on-campus housing, a meal plan, University health insurance, textbooks, a laptop allowance, and access to a $12,000 enrichment fund which may be used for other educational purposes)

Requirements: Top Applicants.

George W. Jenkins Scholarship: Award covers the full cost of attendance which includes tuition and fees, on-campus housing, a meal plan, University health insurance, and a laptop allowance. Students may also receive a stipend for books, transportation, and personal expenses.

Criteria: To be considered for this scholarship, students must be nominated by their guidance counselor.

Application Deadline: November 1

Application Link:
https://admissions.miami.edu/undergraduate/financial-aid/scholarships/freshman/index.html

13 University of Central Florida

Location: Orlando, Florida
Setting: Suburban (1,415 Acres)
Undergraduate Enrollment: 60,075
Type: Public

Benacquisto Scholarship: Awards full institutional cost of attendance for an in-state student minus the sum of Bright Futures and the National Merit award. Out-of-state students will receive an award equal to the in-state cost of attendance minus their National Merit award. These students are exempted from paying out-of-state tuition and fees.

Application Link:
https://www.ucf.edu/financial-aid/types/scholarships/benacquisto/

Florida Academic Scholars: Award amount equal to 100% of tuition and applicable fees in fall, spring and summer.

Eligibility: Eligibility and application criteria are available from your high school guidance office, or the Florida Bright Futures Program website.

Application Deadline: August 31

Application Link:
https://www.ucf.edu/financial-aid/types/scholarships/florida-bright-futures/

14 New College of Florida

Location: Sarasota, Florida
Setting: Suburban (110 Acres)
Undergraduate Enrollment: 632
Type: Public

Florida Freshmen

Florida Education Fund Brain Bowl Scholarship: Awards Full scholarship (tuition, room, and board)

Criteria: This scholarship is awarded to first-place team members of the statewide competition in mathematics and also first place team members in history and culture.

Out-of-State Freshmen

Benacquisto Scholar Award: Out-of-state students who qualify for the Benacquisto scholarship will receive an award equal to the in-state on-campus cost of attendance for New College, minus their National Merit award. Such students are exempt from paying the out-of-state fees. This scholarship covers the full cost of attendance.

Eligibility: Applicant must be recognised as a National Merit Finalist.

Application Deadline: April 1

Application Link:
https://www.ncf.edu/admissions/financial-aid/scholarships/

15

University of West Florida

Location: Penascola, Florida
Setting: Suburban (1,600 Acres)
Undergraduate Enrollment: 9,325
Type: Public

Pace Presidential Scholarship: Full tuition, mandatory fees, a meal plan, on-campus housing, an $800 per-semester textbook stipend, and a one time paid summer research or study abroad experience valued up to $1,500.
Requirements: Students are automatically considered for invitation once they are offered admission.

National Merit Finalist Scholarship: Full tuiton and mandatory fees, a meal plan, on-campus housing, an $800 per-semester textbook stipend, and a one-time paid research or study abroad experience valued at up to $1,500.

Requirements: Awarded to National Merit Finalist.

Argo Spirit Scholarship: Full tuition, on-campus housing, a meal plan, and an $800 per-semester book stipend.

Requirements: Available to Pell Grant-eligible, first-time-in-college Florida resident students who have shown strength of character, or the "Argo Spirit".

P.S: Check the website for more details.

Application Deadline: January 15

Application Link: https://uwf.edu/admissions/undergraduate/cost-and-financial-aid/awards-and-scholarships/presidents-scholarship-competition/

1 Emory University

Location: Atlanta, Georgia
Setting: City (631 Acres)
Undergraduate Enrollment: 7,101
Type: Private

Robert W. Woodruff Scholarship: Full tuition, room and board, lots more . . .

George W. Jenkins Scholarship: Full tuition, fees, on-campus room and board, and a stipend each semester, lots more . . .

Requirements: Top applicants.

Application Deadline: November 15

Application Link:
https://studentaid.emory.edu/undergraduate/types/grants-scholarships/index.html

2 University of Georgia

Location: Athens, Georgia
Setting: City (767 Acres)
Undergraduate Enrollment: 30,166
Type: Public

While there are no available full ride scholarships at the University of Georgia, there are many other scholarships that could be highly beneficial to incoming freshmen.

Application Link:
https://www.admissions.uga.edu/afford/scholarships/

3 Agnes Scott College

Location: Decatur, Georgia
Setting: Urban (100 Acres)
Undergraduate Enrollment: 1,063
Type: Private

Marvin B. Perry Presidential Scholarship: Full tuition, room and board.

Goizueta Foundation Scholarship: Full tuition, room and board.

Requirements: Top scholars.

Application Deadline: January 15

Application Link:
https://www.agnesscott.edu/admission/undergraduate-admission/scholarships-financial-aid/

4 LaGrange College

Location: LaGrange, Georgia
Setting: Rural (120 Acres)
Undergraduate Enrollment: 607
Type: Private

The Presidential Learning and Living Scholarship: Award covers Full tuition, fees, room and board.

Requirements: Top students

Application Deadline: January 1

Application Link:
https://www.lagrange.edu/ADMISSIONS/COST%20AND%20AID/Scholarships.html

5 Spelman College

Location: Atlanta, Georgia
Setting: Urban (39 Acres)
Undergraduate Enrollment: 2,374
Type: Private

Dovey Johnson Roundtree Scholarship: Full tuition, fees and on-campus room and board for four years.

Presidential Scholarship: Full tuition, fees and on-campus room and board for four years.

Requirements: A minimum SAT score of 1330 or 31 ACT | A minimum High school GPA of 3.8 (weighted)

Application Deadline: February 1

Application Link:
https://www.spelman.edu/admissions/financial-aid/scholarships

6 Point University

Location: West Point, Georgia
Setting: Suburban (54 Acres)
Undergraduate Enrollment: 1,916
Type: Private

Founders Scholarship: Awards Full tuition, fees, room and board.

P.S: Scholarship covers 15 – meal plan. Student will be required to pay difference if 19 – meal plan is selected.

Requirements: A minimum GPA of 3.5 | A combined SAT score of 1310 (Evidence-Based Reading and Writing, and Math) and an ACT score of 27 | Applicant should provide a written essay about why a Point University education is important and why he or she desires to attend the University.

P.S: Scholarships are awarded on a rolling basis, and decisions will be made the semester before your start date.

Application Deadline: Check the website for more details.

Application Link:
https://point.edu/admissions/tuition-aid/financial-aid/scholarships/

7 Wesleyan College

Location: Macon, Georgia
Setting: Suburban (200 Acres)
Undergraduate Enrollment: 695
Type: Private

Peyton Anderson Scholarship: Full tuition plus room and board.

Eligibility: This is an annual scholarship for students from the Middle Georgia area who are committed to teaching in the middle Georgia area after graduation.

Requirements: Commitment to teach in Middle Georgia for five years | A minimum High school GPA of 3.6

Lovick P. and Elizabeth T. Corn Scholarship: Full tuition plus room and board.

Eligibility: This is an annual scholarship for students who demonstrate leadership in service to their schools, churches, or communities, and exemplify the qualities of leadership, character, and personal achievement.

Requirements: Applicant must be a graduate from any high school in Columbus, GA, or the greater Chattahoochee area | A minimum GPA of 3.20 (3.00 for Girls Inc.)

Application Deadline: February 15

Application Link:
https://www.wesleyancollege.edu/admission/invitation-scholarships.cfm

8 Morehouse College

Location: Atlanta, Georgia
Setting: Urban (66 Acres)
Undergraduate Enrollment: 2,152
Type: Private

Morgan Stanley Student Success Scholarship: Award varies and scholars will receive funding for the ***full cost of attendance*** that is not already covered by other scholarships and financial aid.

Eligibility: Applicant's must be Incoming freshmen and Demonstrate financial need | 3.5 GPA | 1200+ SAT / 25+ ACT | Quality of submitted essay.

Dr. Michael L. Lomax Student Success Scholarship: Award will cover the ***full cost of enrollment*** and vary based on financial need.

Requirements: ACT 28+ / SAT 1000+ | A minimum cumulative high school GPA of 3.0 | Demonstrate low Expected Family Contribution (EFC) as illustrated on the Free Application for Federal Student Aid (FAFSA) and confirmed by the College's Office of Financial Aid.

SMASH Alumni Scholarship: Award covers the entire cost of enrollment (tuition, room and board expenses) after all Federal and State grants as well as private scholarships have been applied.

Eligibility: SMASH Alumnus | STEM Major | 2.5 GPA | Demonstrated Need (FAFSA required)

Application Deadline: April 14 / May 14

Application Link:
https://morehouse.edu/admissions/financial-aid-and-scholarships/scholarships/

9

Mercer University

Location: Macon, Georgia
Setting: City (150 Acres)
Undergraduate Enrollment: 4,941
Type: Private

Macon Impact Scholarship: Awards Full tuition, room and board.

Eligibility: High school seniors with demonstrated financial need who live in the Bibb County school district and have been enrolled in an accredited Bibb County Public School since the ninth grade.

Besse Willingham Tift Scholarship: Awards Full tuition, room and board.

Eligibility: Awarded to Female high school seniors who are residents of the State of Georgia.

Fabian Distinguished Music Scholars Program: Awards Full tuition, room and board, and a $4,000 enrichment stipend.

Eligibility: Awarded to High school seniors interested in ***studying music*** at Mercer University.

P.S: Applicants must participate in an audition with the School of Music to be considered for the Fabian Distinguished Music Scholars Program.

Stamps Scholars Program: Award covers Full tuition, fees, room and board, Apple iPad and up to $16,000 Enrichment stipend (to support Study Abroad, Undergraduate Research, Unpaid Internships, Conference Fees and Travel, etc.)

Requirements: Top applicants | Applicant must be a U.S. citizen or a permanent resident.

Application Deadline: November 1

Application Link: https://undergrad.mercer.edu/mercer-scholarships/#module-standard-content-scholarship

10 Georgia Institute of Technology

Location: Atlanta, Georgia
Setting: Urban (400 Acres)
Undergraduate Enrollment: 18,415
Type: Public

Stamps President's Scholars Program: Full tuition, mandatory fees, housing, meal plan, books, and academics supplies, personal expenses, stipend for laptop, lots more. . .

Requirements: Semifinalist average SAT is 1450 - 1560 and ACT 33-35 | UK & US Citizens only.

Godbold Family Foundation: Godbold Scholars receive 100% of their financial need. The need is met with Institute gift aid that is matched with a Godbold Scholarship in combination with a $2,500 work study opportunity.

Requirements: Applicant must be an entering freshman from specific counties in South Carolina, Florida, North Carolina, and Tennessee | A minimum SAT score of 1500 (combination of math and verbal scores only) | Demonstrate financial need.

Gold Scholars Program: Awards Full tuition and fees *(to Georgia residents)*, a tuition waiver for *Out-of-State students*, Priority housing during your first year, plus a lot of other benefits.

P.S: *The package assumes the scholar has received the Zell Miller Scholarship independently from the state of Georgia.*

Criteria: This scholarship is offered annually to the top two percent of first-year students. Recipients are selected based upon holistic excellence and potential within the program's four pillars: Scholarship, Leadership, Progress, and Service.

Application Deadline: October 15

Application Link: https://finaid.gatech.edu/undergraduate-types-aid/scholarships/institutional-scholarships

1

University of Hawaii

Location: Honolulu, Hawaii
Setting: Urban (320 Acres)
Undergraduate Enrollment: 14,198
Type: Public

The Regents and Presidential Scholarships covers the cost of tuition, and includes a $4000 stipend per year.

Eligibility: Regents Scholarships are awarded to outstanding freshmen who has a minimum SAT total score of at least 1340 or ACT combined score of at least 29 | A minimum High school GPA of 3.5

Application Deadline: January 15

Application Link: https://www.hawaii.edu/offices/student-affairs/regents-and-presidential-scholars-program/

1 University of Idaho

Location: Moscow, Idaho
Setting: Rural (810 Acres)
Undergraduate Enrollment: 8,809
Type: Public

National Merit Scholarship: This award covers basic registration fees/tuition and the university defined cost for room and board as long as you live in a U of I residence hall.

Requirements: Achieve Finalist standing with the National Merit Scholarship Corporation.

Application Deadline: May 31

ROTC Military Scholarships:

United States Army ROTC: This program offers 3.5 year, 3 year, 2.5 year and 2 year on campus scholarships that will pay for in/out state tuition and fees, pay $510 for books annually, and give at least $250 per month as a stipend while in school.

Call: University of Idaho Army ROTC for application at 208-885-6528

United States Air Force ROTC: This program offers scholarships to students who have at least two years remaining towards their bachelor degree when the scholarship starts. Awards full tuition, books, fees, and a monthly stipend during the academic year.

Call: University of Idaho Unit Admissions Officer, AFROTC Detachment 905, at 208-885-6129 or 800-622-5088.

United States Navy/Marine ROTC: This program offers scholarships to students selected through national competition. It covers college tuition, lab fees, books, uniforms, and includes a monthly stipend.

Call: University of Idaho, Commanding Officer, Naval Science Department at 208-885-6333.

Application Link: https://www.uidaho.edu/financial-aid/scholarships/undergraduate

1 Western Illinois University

Location: Macomb, Illinois
Setting: Rural (1,050 Acres)
Undergraduate Enrollment: 5,309
Type: Public

Presidential Scholarship: Full tuition, fees, a double residence hall room and meal plan.

Requirements: 3.6+ GPA | 1300+ SAT or 28+ ACT.

Application Deadline: December 1

Application Link:
https://www.wiu.edu/student_success/scholarship/

2 Southern Illinois University Carbondale

Location: Carbondale, Illinois
Setting: Rural (1,136 Acres)
Undergraduate Enrollment: 8,000
Type: Public

Chancellor's Scholarship: Covers in-state tuition, mandatory fees, room and board.

Requirements: 3.8+ GPA | Top applicants

Application Deadline: December 1

Application Link:
https://scholarships.siu.edu/types/freshmen-students.php

3 University of Illinois

Location: Urbana-Champaign, Illinois
Setting: City (1,783 Acres)
Undergraduate Enrollment: 35,120
Type: Public

Stamps Scholarship: Awards up to the full cost of attendance.

James Hunter Anthony & Gerald E. Blackshear Endowment: Awards up to full tuition and fees for an academic year.

Requirements: Illinois Resident who have graduated from an Illinois high school | Top applicants.

Application Deadline: December 1

Application Link:
https://www.admissions.illinois.edu/invest/scholarships-all

4 University of Chicago

Location: Chicago, Illinois
Setting: Urban (217 Acres)
Undergraduate Enrollment: 7,470
Type: Private

University Merit Scholarships: The University Scholarship goes towards the full cost of attendance.

Uchicago Evans Scholarship: Awards full housing and tuition.

Requirements: Top scholars.

Application Deadline: December 1

Application Link:
https://collegeadmissions.uchicago.edu/financial-support/scholarships

5 University of Illinois at Chicago

Location: Chicago, Illinois
Setting: Urban (244 Acres)
Undergraduate Enrollment: 21,807
Type: Public

President's Award Program (Honors Scholars Program): Awards Full tuition and housing, a week-long Summer College orientation Program, and a new laptop computer ***(Illinois Resident's)***

Eligibility: Top applicants | Applicants must be Incoming freshmen and Demonstrate financial need | From an Illinois county with low representation in the University system.

Application Deadline: December 1

Application Link:
https://aes.uic.edu/programs/presidents-award-program.html

6 Illinois Institute of Technology

Location: Chicago, Illinois
Setting: Urban (120 Acres)
Undergraduate Enrollment: 3,125
Type: Private

Duchossois Leadership Scholars Program: Full tuition, room and board.

Eligibility: ACT/SAT scores in the top 10% nationally | A minimum 3.5 high school GPA.

Application Deadline: November 15

Application Link:
https://www.iit.edu/admissions-aid/tuition-and-aid/scholarships

7 Trinity International University

Location: Deerfield, Illinois
Setting: Suburban (111 Acres)
Undergraduate Enrollment: 571
Type: Private

There are scholarships available for undergraduate studies at the Trinity International University.

Check the website for more details.

Application Link:
https://www.tiu.edu/divinity/tuition-aid/scholarships/

8 Loyola University Chicago

Location: Chicago, Illinois
Setting: Urban (105 Acres)
Undergraduate Enrollment: 11,703
Type: Private

Dreamer Scholarship: Award covers Full tuition, on campus room and board, and mandatory student fees.

Eligibility: Applicants must exhibit excellence.

ROTC Scholarships

Air Force ROTC Scholarship: Full tuition and Mandatory fees.

Army ROTC Scholarship: Full tuition and fees, $1,200 per year for books, plus a stipend ranging from $350 - $500 per school month. Additionally, Army ROTC Scholarship students receive $3,500 a semester toward on-campus housing from Loyola University.

Navy ROTC Scholarship: Full tuition and fees.

P.S: Students who receive full ROTC scholarships are also awarded a $3500 per semester ROTC On-Campus Housing Grant from Loyola University.

Application Deadline: December 1

Application Link:
https://www.luc.edu/finaid/scholarships/undergraduate/

9 Southern Illinois University Edwardsville

Location: Edwardsville, Illinois
Setting: Suburban (2,660 Acres)
Undergraduate Enrollment: 9,321
Type: Public

Meridian Scholarship: Full tuition, fees, room and board. This scholarship is available to both U.S citizens and International students.

Eligibility: Cumulative 3.5 high school GPA (4.0 scale) | A minimum SAT ERW + M of 1260 or ACT 27.

The SIUE Commitment: Awards Full tuition, mandatory fees and course-specific fees.

Check the website for more details.

Application Deadline: November 15

Application Link:
https://www.siue.edu/financial-aid/types-of-aid/scholarships.shtml

1 Purdue University

Location: West Lafayette, Indiana
Setting: City (2,468 Acres)
Undergraduate Enrollment: 37,949
Type: Private

Beering Scholarship: Awards full ride scholarship to top applicants.

Eligibility: Determined by the dean of enrollment services based on your admissions application.

Application Link: https://engineering.purdue.edu/Engr/AboutUs/News/Announcements/10-incoming-engineering-students-receive-fullride-scholarships

2 University of Southern Indiana

Location: Evansville, Indiana
Setting: Suburban (330 Acres)
Undergraduate Enrollment: 5,539
Type: Public

Presidential Scholarship: Full tuition, room and board and book stipends.

Requirements: Indiana Residents | A minimum SAT score of 1200 / ACT score of 27 | Ranked first or second in their senior class.

Global Ambassador Scholarship: Full tuition, on-campus room and board.

Requirements: This scholarship is awarded to international students | A minimum of 3.5 High school GPA.

Application Deadline: December 4

Application Link: https://www.usi.edu/admissions/scholarships/indiana-freshman-scholarships

3 University of Notre Dame

Location: Notre Dame, Indiana
Setting: Suburban (1,265 Acres)
Undergraduate Enrollment: 8,971
Type: Private

Glenna R. Joyce Scholarship: Full cost of attendance for four years.

Requirements: Top applicants | Must be residents of some specified states.

Western Golf Association Evans Foundation Scholarship: Awards Full tuition, mandatory fees and housing.

Requirements: Top applicants.

Application Deadline: November 1

Application Link: https://scholars.nd.edu/awards/list-of-awards/

4 Ball State University

Location: Muncie, Indiana
Setting: Suburban (1,282 Acres)
Undergraduate Enrollment: 14,416
Type: Public

Whitinger Scholarship: Full tuition, mandatory fees, on-campus room and board.

Presidential Scholarship: Full tuition, fees, room and board.

Ball State Scholars Award: Full tuition, fees, room and board.

Distinction Scholarship: Full tuition, fees, room and board.

Harold Ellison Scholarship: Full tuition, room and board.

P.S: This scholarship is available only to first-time freshmen who have graduated from schools in Delaware County, Indiana.

Applicants must be nominated by their high school guidance counselor and only if they have already been awarded the Ball State Presidential Scholarship.

The deadline to apply is **February 1** of each year.

Requirements: Scholars must demonstrate a high degree of excellence.

Application Deadline: November 15

Application Link:
https://www.bsu.edu/admissions/financial-aid-and-scholarships/types/scholarships

5 University of Indiana

Location: Bloomington, Indiana
Setting: City (1,953 Acres)
Undergraduate Enrollment: 35,660
Type: Public

Wells Scholars Program: Guarantees the full cost of attendance for a period of eight semesters of undergraduate study.

Award covers full tuition, mandatory and course-related fees, as well as living stipends during the fall and spring sufficient to cover the cost of a standard double dorm room contract and a standard meal plan in the residence halls.

P.S: Students receive the same stipend whether they choose to live on or off campus.

Requirements: Top applicants

21st Century Scholarship Convenant:
Available to scholars who demonstrate unmet financial need. Covers the cost of tuition and mandatory fees. Provides additional funding to assist with budgeted room and board, books, and supplies.

Requirements: Check the website for more details.

Application Deadline: November 1

Application Link:
https://scholarships.indiana.edu/future-scholars/index.html

6

Wabash College

Location: Crawfordsville, Indiana
Setting: City (94 Acres)
Undergraduate Enrollment: 835
Type: Private

Wabash College Lilly Award: Full tuition, standard fees, on-campus room and board.

Requirements: A minimum GPA of 3.5 (4.0 scale) | An SAT score of at least 1240 or an ACT composite of 26 | Rank within the top 10 percent of your senior class.

Army ROTC Scholarship Program: Awards Full tuition, on-campus room and board as well as all costs associated with ROTC courses.

Scholarship Cadets are also given a book allowance of $600 per semester along with a $420 per month, tax free stipend allowance during each school year.

Requirements: Applicant must be a U.S citizen | A minimum cumulative high school GPA of 2.50 | Score minimum of 1000 on the SAT or 19 on the ACT | Meet the minimum physical standards of the Army physical fitness test.

Trustee International Scholarships: Awards Full tuition, fees, and on-campus room and board (***to international students***).

Requirements: Top Applicants.

Application Link: https://www.wabash.edu/admissions/international/scholarships

P.S: All international students with a complete admissions application on record by February 15 will be reviewed for the Trustee Scholarship Awards.

Application Deadline: January 6

Application Link: https://www.wabash.edu/admissions/finances/sources

7

Valparaiso University

Location: Valparaiso, Indiana
Setting: City (350 Acres)
Undergraduate Enrollment: 2,349
Type: Private

Lilly Community Foundation Scholarship: Awards full tuition, fees, standard on-campus room and board plus a $900 per year stipend for required books and equipment.

Eligibility: **Indiana residents attending an Indiana high school.**

Requirements: Top students in application pool.

Army ROTC Scholarship Program: Awards Full tuition, fees, standard on-campus room and board, a book stipend and a monthly stipend.

P.S: Applicant must be a U.S citizen | Must apply to ROTC by December 1

Requirements: Top scholars.

Air Force ROTC Scholarship Program: Awards Full tuition, fees, standard on-campus room and board, a book stipend and a monthly stipend.

Requirements: Top applicants.

Application Deadline: March 1

Application Link: https://www.valpo.edu/student-financial-services/planning/scholarships/other/

1 Grand View University

Location: Des Moines, Iowa
Setting: Urban (25 Acres)
Undergraduate Enrollment: 1,694
Type: Private

Immigrant Iowan Scholarship: Award covers full tuition, room charges if the recipient lives on campus, plus some specified fees.

Eligibility: Applicant must be born of an immigrant parent or an immigrant himself or herself | Graduating from an Iowa high school | High school GPA of 3.0 or higher | Not in the U.S. on a student visa.

Presidential Scholarship aspirant's may compete for full tuition and additional $5,000 awards.

Application Deadline: March 1

Application Link:
https://www.grandview.edu/admissions/financial-aid/scholarships-grants

2 Grinnell College

Location: Grinnell, Iowa
Setting: Rural (120 Acres)
Undergraduate Enrollment: 1,759
Type: Private

Laurel Scholarship and Mentorship Program: This is a Chicago-based, small mentorship program that offers pre-arrival programming, a full-tuition scholarship, and additional need-based financial aid to assist with the cost of room and board.

Eligibility: Applicant's Home address must be in the city of Chicago or Cook County, IL | Black or Afro-descendant | U.S. citizen or permanent resident.

Application Deadline: December 1

Application Link:
https://www.grinnell.edu/admission/financial-aid/types-aid/scholarships

1 University of Saint Mary

Location: Leavenworth, Kansas
Setting: Rural (200 Acres)
Undergraduate Enrollment: 903
Type: Private

Jubilee Scholarship: Awards full tuition, room and board.

Requirements: A minimum ACT score of 26 or SAT equivalent | Have a 3.7 cumulative high school GPA (unweighted on a 4.0 scale) | Be ranked in the top 10 percent of your graduating high school class.

Application Link:
https://www.stmary.edu/jubilee

The Sister Joanna Bruner Nursing Scholarship: Assists with educational expenses such as tuition, fees, room, board, and books.

Eligibility: A minimum ACT composite score of 21 or SAT equivalent | Applicant must be accepted to USM's Bachelor of Science-Nursing Program | Must live on campus | Must demonstrate financial need by completing the FASA.

Application Deadline: December 1

Application Link:
https://www.stmary.edu/scholarships/index

2 Fort Hays State University

Location: Hays, Kansas
Setting: Rural (200 Acres)
Undergraduate Enrollment: 11,402
Type: Public

Schmidt Foundation Scholars: The award amount covers 30 hours of tuition and fees for fall and spring courses, books, and room and board. This scholarship aims to support FHSU students, with preference given to students from Kansas and first-generation college students.

Requirements: Top scholars.

Miss Kansas Scholarship: Awards Full tuition and fees.

Eligibility: Check the website for more details.

P.S: Military Scholarships are also available for qualified personnel's.

Application Deadline: November 15

Application Link:
https://www.fhsu.edu/admissions/scholarships/freshmen

1 Campbellsville University

Location: Campbellsville, Kentucky
Setting: Rural (95 Acres)
Undergraduate Enrollment: 5,880
Type: Private

Presidential Excellence: Full tuition, room and board.

Eligibility: Open to students who have 33-36 on ACT/ 2170-2400 SAT & 3.5 GPA.

Application Deadline: November 1

Application Link:
https://www.campbellsville.edu/admission-and-aid/scholarships-and-grants/

3 Bellarmine University

Location: Louisville, Kentucky
Setting: City (145 Acres)
Undergraduate Enrollment: 2,343
Type: Private

Bellarmine Scholar Award: Full ride scholarship plus study abroad stipend and enrollment into Bellarmine's Honors Program.

Requirements: An essay with the topic "Describe an incident or situation in your life which piqued your intellectual curiosity" | A minimum SAT score of 1390/ACT 30 & 3.5 GPA.

Application Deadline: February 1

Application Link:
https://www.bellarmine.edu/financial-aid/institutional/

2 Center College

Location: Danville, Kentucky
Setting: City (178 Acres)
Undergraduate Enrollment: 1,357
Type: Private

Grissom Scholars: Award covers the full cost of attendance, plus additional aid to cover any remaining financial need. $5,000 enrichment funds.

Eligibility: All first-generation college students who apply for admission by January 15 will be considered automatically for the Grissom Scholars Program.

Brown Fellows: Covers full cost of attendance, including tuition, room and board, $10,000 in enrichment funds.

Requirements: 3.95 GPA | Graduating at or very near the top of their high school class.

N.B: Test scores are not required.

Application Deadline: February 1

Application Link:
https://www.centre.edu/admission-aid/scholarships-fellowships

4 Kentucky Wesleyan College

Location: Owensboro, Kentucky
Setting: Suburban (67 Acres)
Undergraduate Enrollment: 780
Type: Private

Kentucky Wesleyan Rogers' Fellows Scholarship: Full tuition, fees, room and board.

Requirements: A minimum 2.5 cumulative high school GPA | Applicant must be a graduate of the Clark Country School District in Las Vegas, Nevada.

Application Deadline: March 1

Application Link: https://kwc.edu/admissions/financial-aid/scholarships/

5 University of Louisville

Location: Louisville, Kentucky
Setting: Urban (287 Acres)
Undergraduate Enrollment: 15,921
Type: Public

National Merit Finalist: Full in-state tuition, $8,000 educational allowance.

Martin Luther King Scholars Program: Full tuition, $8,000 educational allowance.

Requirements: 3.5 GPA | 26 ACT or 1230 SAT | Black/African-American and Hispanic/Latino students.

Mentored Scholarships for out-of-state students:

Brown Fellows Program: Full tuition, plus additional education allowance.

Requirements: 29 ACT or 1330 SAT | 3.5 GPA

Application Deadline: December 15

Application Link: https://louisville.edu/admissions/cost-aid/scholarships

6 University of Kentucky

Location: Lexington, Kentucky
Setting: City (918 Acres)
Undergraduate Enrollment: 22,735
Type: Public

Otis A. Singletary: Full tuition + Housing Stipend. This scholarship is available to both in-state and out-of-state Residents.

Requirements: 33 ACT/1450 SAT | 3.8 GPA

Application Deadline: December 1

Application Link: https://www.uky.edu/financialaid/scholarships

7 Kentucky State University

Location: Frankfort, Kentucky
Setting: City (916 Acres)
Undergraduate Enrollment: 1,610
Type: Public

Commonwealth Scholarship: Full tuition, course fees, room and board, provides a stipend for books and supplies per semester.

Requirements: Residents of Kentucky | A minimum GPA of 3.2 (4.0 Scale) | Rank in 10% of graduating class.

Presidential Scholarship: Full tuition, course fees, room and board, provides a stipend for books and supplies per semester.

Requirements: A minimum SAT score of 1170/ACT 26 | 3.5 GPA or higher.

John Henry Jackson Scholarship: Full tuition and mandatory fees, standard housing, meals and books.

Requirements: A minimum 3.5 cumulative high school GPA | A minimum 25 ACT or SAT equivalent.

Application Deadline: February 15

Application Link:
https://www.kysu.edu/finance-and-administration/financial-aid/scholarships.php

8 Lindsey Wilson College

Location: Columbia, Kentucky
Setting: Rural (200 Acres)
Undergraduate Enrollment: 1,753
Type: Private

Begley Scholarship: Awards full tuition, fees, room & board. If a student chooses to commute, the scholarship will cover tuition and fees only.

Requirements: A minimum high school GPA of 3.0 | A minimum ACT composite score of 24.

P.S: A typewritten essay (one to two pages in length) on a topic chosen by the scholarship committee is required.

Application Deadline: Check the website for more details.

Application Link:
https://www.lindsey.edu/admissions/cost-and-financial-aid/Academic-Scholarships.cfm

9 Murray State University

Location: Murray, Kentucky
Setting: Rural (253 Acres)
Undergraduate Enrollment: 7,756
Type: Public

National Merit Finalist Scholarship: Awards Full tuition, On-campus housing (double occupancy) and Meal plan.

Requirements: Awarded to National Merit Finalists.

Presidential Fellowship: Awards Full tuition, On-campus housing (double occupancy) and Meal plan.

Requirements: A minimum of 28 ACT composite score (or minimum of 1300 SAT Verbal and Math Combined Score) | A 3.7 cumulative high school GPA on a 4.0 scale.

Marvin D. Mills Scholarship: Awards Full tuition (equal to Kentucky cost of tuition), On-campus housing (double occupancy) and a Meal plan.

Requirements: A minimum of 24 ACT composite score or SAT equivalent | A 3.2 cumulative high school GPA on a 4.0 scale.

Application Deadline: December 1

Application Link: https://www.murraystate.edu/admissions/scholarships/newfreshmen.aspx

1 Dillard University

Location: New Orleans, Louisiana
Setting: City (55 Acres)
Undergraduate Enrollment: 1,224
Type: Private

University Scholarship: Full tuition, room and board and mandatory fees.

Requirements: A minimum 3.8 cumulative high school GPA (4.0 scale) | A minimum 27 ACT composite score or 1220 SAT combined score.

Application Deadline: March 15

Application Link:
https://www.dillard.edu/financialaid/institutional-scholarships.php

3 Louisiana Tech University

Location: Ruston, Louisiana
Setting: Rural (2,277 Acres)
Undergraduate Enrollment: 10,083
Type: Public

National Merit Scholarship: Full tuition, fees, on-campus housing, and meals.

Awarded to National Merit Finalists.

Requirements: A minimum 3.0 cumulative high school GPA (4.0 unweighted scale)

Application Deadline: Apply for admission according to National Merit deadlines.

Application Link:
https://www.latech.edu/admissions/freshman-scholarships/

2 Louisiana Sate University

Location: Baton Rouge, Louisiana
Setting: Urban (2,000 Acres)
Undergraduate Enrollment: 30,952
Type: Public

Stamps Scholarship: Full tuition, fees, room & board, books, supplies, etc. A potential $14,000 for enrichment experiences | The opportunity to earn up to an additional $1,550 per year by participating in the President's Future Leaders in Research program. | A one-time use $1,100 laptop stipend.

The President's Alumni Scholars Award: Full tuition, fees, room & board, books, supplies, etc. A $2,000 study abroad stipend | The opportunity to earn up to an additional $1,550 per year by participating in the President's Future Leaders in Research program.

Requirements: Top Applicants.

Application Deadline: December 15

Application Link:
https://www.lsu.edu/financialaid/types_of_scholarships/entering_freshman_scholarships/top-merit-based-scholarships.php

4 Xavier University

Location: New Orleans, Louisiana
Setting: Urban (66 Acres)
Undergraduate Enrollment: 2,696
Type: Private

Board of Trustees Scholarship: Awards full tuition, fees, and room & board to top applicants.

Presidential Scholarship: Full tuition and fees.

Saint Katharine Drexel Scholarship: Awards full tuition and fees to students who attend a Catholic high school within the United States and are the Valedictorian or Salutatorian of their high school graduating class.

Norman C. Francis Scholarship: Awards full tuition and fees to students who attend a public high school within Orleans or Jefferson Parishes and are the Valedictorian or Salutatorian of their high school graduating class.

Requirements: A minimum 3.3 GPA | 22 ACT/1140 SAT.

Application Deadline: January 31

Application Link:
https://www.xula.edu/financialaid/scholarships/index.html

5 Tulane University of Louisiana

Location: New Orleans, Louisiana
Setting: Urban (110 Acres)
Undergraduate Enrollment: 7,350
Type: Private

Stamps Scholarship: Award covers the total cost of attendance and provides an enrichment fund to support endeavours such as study abroad, undergraduate research, academic or co-curricular conferences, and unpaid internships.

P.S: Select Stamps Finalists will be invited to interview in early spring.

John Hainkel Louisiana Scholars Award: Full tuition, room and board plus a stipend for books and other expenses.

Eligibility: Students who finish in the top 5% of their class while taking an honors or AP course load are eligible for this scholarship.

P.S: To be eligible, students must submit for early admission and submit the Dean's scholarship application and have a sealed scholarship recommendation from one of their educators.

Application Deadline: January 15

Application Link:
https://admission.tulane.edu/tuition-aid

1 University of Southern Maine

Location: Portland, Maine
Setting: City (142 Acres)
Undergraduate Enrollment: 5,956
Type: Public

The Promise Scholarship: This Scholarship is designed to help students overcome financial and academic barriers. Awards will ensure any gaps are met to cover the full cost of tuition and fees.

Eligibility: Student must demonstrate a high financial need.

Preferences Include: Students referred from a Promise Partner Youth Development Organization and First-generation students.

Application Deadline: March 15

Application Link:
https://usm.maine.edu/scholarships/

2 University of Maine

Location: Orono, Maine
Setting: Rural (660 Acres)
Undergraduate Enrollment: 9,774
Type: Public

Scholarship Programs for *Maine Residents*

UMaine National Merit Award: Awards Full tuition, fees, standard room and board.

Eligibility: Applicant should be a Semi-finalist with the National Merit Scholarship Corporation.

Scholarship Programs for *Out-of-State Residents*

Presidential Flagship: Award range from $20,000 to Full tuition and fees.

Requirements: Top applicants.

P.S: *Semi-finalists with the National Merit Scholarship Corporation are eligible for the highest awards in this category,* ***including: 100% Tuition and fees, up to 15 credits per semester, & standard room and board.***

Application Deadline: December 1

Application Link:
https://go.umaine.edu/apply-2022/scholarships/

1 Coppin State University

Location: Baltimore, Maryland
Setting: Urban (38 Acres)
Undergraduate Enrollment: 1,757
Type: Public

Presidential Scholarship: Awards Full tuition, room, board, fees, insurance fee, and up to $2,000/year for books.

Requirements: A weighted high school cumulative grade point average of 3.5 or above | A minimum 1200 SAT score or an ACT composite score of 25.

Fanny Jackson Coppin Scholarship: Awards Full tuition, room, board, and up to $1000/year for books.

Requirements: A weighted high school cumulative grade point average of 3.3 or above | A minimum 1140 SAT score or an ACT composite score of 23.

Army ROTC Scholarship: Awards full tuition, required educational fees, and provides a specified amount for books, supplies, and equipment. Each scholarship also includes a monthly stipend of $300 to $500 depending on your academic classification.

Requirements: A minimum 2.5 cumulative high school GPA | A minimum 920 SAT or composite 19 ACT score no later then November of the year you apply.

Application Deadline: October 1

Application Link:
https://www.coppin.edu/tuition-and-aid/scholarships-and-scholars-programs

2 Washington College

Location: Chestertown, Maryland
Setting: Rural (112 Acres)
Undergraduate Enrollment: 955
Type: Private

Washington Scholars Program: Awards full tuition and fees, as well as room and board.

P.S: Applicant must demonstrate financial need.

Eligibility: Prospective Washington Scholars must be nominated by their high school counselors, community-based organization leaders, teachers, or their admissions counselors in order to be considered.

Application Deadline: January 15

Application Link:
https://www.washcoll.edu/admissions/admitted/available-scholarships.php

3 University of Maryland

Location: College park, Maryland
Setting: Suburban (1,340 Acres)
Undergraduate Enrollment: 30,353
Type: Private

Banneker/key Scholarship: Awards full tuition, mandatory fees, room & board, and book allowance each year for eight undergraduate consecutive semesters.

Requirements: Top applicants.

Application Deadline: November 1

Application Link: https://academiccatalog.umd.edu/undergraduate/fees-expenses-financial-aid/merit-based-financial-assistance/

5 McDaniel College

Location: Westminster, Maryland
Setting: Suburban (160 Acres)
Undergraduate Enrollment: 1,762
Type: Private

The Dorsey Scholars Program: Awards full tuition, room and board. In addition, Dorsey scholars also receive a stipend for books (up to $600 per semester), technology (up to $2000), and travel to McDaniel College Europe in Budapest (up to $2000).

Requirements: Student must exhibit excellence.

Application Deadline: December 15

Application Link: https://www.mcdaniel.edu/admissions-cost/cost-financial-aid/types-financial-aid/mcdaniel-scholarships

4 Loyola University Maryland

Location: Baltimore, Maryland
Setting: Urban (80 Acres)
Undergraduate Enrollment: 3,977
Type: Private

Army ROTC Scholarship: Awards Full tuition, fees, books and supplies. Recipients also receive a tax-free subsistence allowance each month that the recipient attends classes (up to 10 months each year)

Requirements: Top applicants.

Application Deadline: January 15

Application Link: https://www.loyola.edu/department/financial-aid/undergraduate/programs/scholarships

1 Boston College

Location: Newton, Massachusetts
Setting: Suburban (405 Acres)
Undergraduate Enrollment: 9,484
Type: Private

Trustee Scholarship: Full tuition and fees.

Requirements: Top Students | Complete the Trustee scholarship essay.

The Gabelli Presidential Scholars program awards full tuition and fully funded scholarships.

Application Deadline: December 1

Application Link:
https://www.bu.edu/admissions/tuition-aid/scholarships-financial-aid/first-year-merit/

2 Northeastern University

Location: Boston, Massachusetts
Setting: Urban (73 Acres)
Undergraduate Enrollment: 16,302
Type: Private

Torch Scholars Program: Full tuition, fees, room and board as well as significant personal and academic support.

Eligibility: Students must be nominated by an education professional, such as a guidance counselor.

Application Deadline: January 1

Application Link:
https://admissions.northeastern.edu/academics/honors-scholars-programs/

3 Simmons University

Location: Boston, Massachusetts
Setting: Urban (12 Acres)
Undergraduate Enrollment: 1,789
Type: Private

Simmons Distinguished Scholar Award: Full tuition, room and board, plus an additional $3000 for academic pursuits such as study abroad, research support, and more.

Requirements: A minimum SAT score of 1300/ACT 28 | 3.3 GPA or higher.

Application Deadline: December 1

Application Link:
https://www.simmons.edu/undergraduate/admission-and-financial-aid/tuition-financial-aid/types-financial-aid/scholarships

4 Clark University

Location: Worcester, Massachusetts
Setting: Urban (50 Acres)
Undergraduate Enrollment: 2,389
Type: Private

Presidential LEEP Scholarship: Full tuition, on-campus room and board for all four years, regardless of a family financial need.

Requirements: Top applicants | Applicant's must submit two additional scholarship essays.

Application Deadline: December 1

Application Link:
https://www.clarku.edu/offices/financial-aid/prospective-students/u-s-students/first-year-scholarships/

5 University of Massachusetts - Lowell

Location: Lowell, Massachusetts
Setting: City (142 Acres)
Undergraduate Enrollment: 12,391
Type: Public

Tsongas Scholarship: Awards Full tuition, fees and standard room/board.

P.S: Applicants are selected by Lowell High School & the UMass Lowell committee.

Eligibility: Open to Massachusetts residents and Lowell High School graduates.

Application Deadline: November 5

Application Link:
https://www.uml.edu/thesolutioncenter/financial-aid/scholarships/freshmen.aspx

6 Framingham State University

Location: Framingham, Massachusetts
Setting: City (77 Acres)
Undergraduate Enrollment: 2,970
Type: Public

The Mancuso English, Humanities, and social & Behavioral Sciences Scholarships: 100% of Day Division tuition, fees and room and board for Mancuso Scholars.

Eligibility: Applicant must graduate from a Massachusetts High School | Apply to the English major or specified FSU Humanities/Social & Behavioral Sciences major on the application for admissions | Have a minimum GPA of 3.5 at the time of application.

Application Deadline: November 15

Application Link:
https://www.framingham.edu/admissions-and-aid/financial-aid/types-of-aid/scholarships/index

1 Central Michigan University

Location: Mount Pleasant, Michigan
Setting: Rural (480 Acres)
Undergraduate Enrollment: 10,421
Type: Public

Centralis Scholar Award: Full tuition, fees, room and board, books, and a $500 allowance toward the cost of books and supplies. Plus a $5,000 study away award.

Requirements: A minimum 3.7 high school GPA | 1260 SAT or 27 ACT.

Application Deadline: December 1

Application Link:
https://www.cmich.edu/offices-departments/office-scholarships-financial-aid/scholarships/

2 Eastern Michigan University

Location: Ypsilanti, Michigan
Setting: City (460 Acres)
Undergraduate Enrollment: 11,617
Type: Public

Presidential Scholarship: Full tuition, room and board.

Requirements: A minimum 3.5 cumulative high school GPA | 1200+ SAT/ 25+ ACT (highest composite)

Application Deadline: December 1

Application Link:
https://www.emich.edu/admissions/scholarships/index.php

3 Michigan State University

Location: East Lansing, Michigan
Setting: Suburban (5,192 Acres)
Undergraduate Enrollment: 39,201
Type: Public

Alumni Distinguished Scholarship: Full tuition, fees, room and board, and $1,000 annually.

Requirements: Scholars are expected to exhibit all-round excellence.

Application Deadline: November 1

Application Link:
https://admissions.msu.edu/cost-aid/scholarships/first-year

4 Lawrence Technological University

Location: Southfield, Michigan
Setting: Suburban (107 Acres)
Undergraduate Enrollment: 2,298
Type: Private

Donley Scholarship: Full tuition, room, board, books and fees for 4 years.

Requirements: High School GPA of 3.5 or higher | Major in the College of Engineering | Demonstrate high Financial need by means of the FAFSA.

Application Deadline: February 1

Application Link:
https://www.ltu.edu/financial-aid/scholarships-freshmen

5 Kalamazoo College

Location: Kalamazoo, Michigan
Setting: City (60 Acres)
Undergraduate Enrollment: 1,210
Type: Private

Heyl Scholarship: Provides support for students graduating from Kalamazoo Public Schools. This scholarship covers full tuition, room, fees, and provides a book allowance.

P.S: It does not cover board. It covers tuition and fees for study abroad programs.

Requirements: Top scholars in application pool.

Application Deadline: October 14

Application Link:
https://admission.kzoo.edu/cost-value/

6 Northern Michigan University

Location: Marquette, Michigan
Setting: City (360 Acres)
Undergraduate Enrollment: 6,434
Type: Public

Presidential Scholars competition: Awards full ride scholarships to graduating high school seniors.

Requirements: To apply for the scholarship competition, students must be admitted and have an ACT composite score of 24 or higher or an SAT minimum score of 1160 and a minimum 3.5 GPA (4.0 scale)

Harden Scholarship: Full tuition, room and board, mandatory fees, and MacBook Pro fee (Art and Design majors)

Requirements: Top students in application pool

Presidential Scholarship: Full tuition, mandatory fees, and MacBook fee (Art and Design majors)

Requirements: Top Applicants

Application Deadline: October 15

Application Link:
https://nmu.edu/financialaid/nmugrants

7 Albion College

Location: Albion, Michigan
Setting: Suburban (574 Acres)
Undergraduate Enrollment: 1,454
Type: Private

Kalamazoo Promise: Students may have up to 100% of their financial need met to cover tuition, fees, housing and food costs.

Eligibility: Available to students who have the Kalamazoo Promise scholarship.

Application Deadline: February 15

Application Link:
https://www.albion.edu/offices/financial-aid/aid-scholarships/scholarships/

9 Michigan Technological University

Location: Houghton, Michigan
Setting: Rural (925 Acres)
Undergraduate Enrollment: 5,710
Type: Public

Leading Scholar Award: *Value for Michigan Resident's:* Full tuition, room and board, and $1,000 to put towards fees and other expenses.

Value for Non-Michigan Resident's: Full tuition.

Requirements: Top applicants.

Application Deadline: October 15

Application Link:
https://www.mtu.edu/finaid/types/scholarships/

8 University of Michigan

Location: Ann Arbor, Michigan
Setting: City (3,207 Acres)
Undergraduate Enrollment: 32,695
Type: Public

Stamps Scholarship: Awarded to incoming U-M students, the College of LSA nominates a select number of incoming LSA students to receive this award.

Award amounts can go up to the full cost of attendance plus additional funding of up to $5,000 to support study abroad, community service, research, and internships.

Requirements: Top students in applicants pool.

Application Link:
https://lsa.umich.edu/scholarships/prospective-students/merit-scholarships.html

10 Lake Superior State University

Location: Sault Ste. Marie, Michigan
Setting: Rural (115 Acres)
Undergraduate Enrollment: 1,655
Type: Public

Laker Gold Scholarship Competition

Laker Premium: Full Ride (12-16 credits tuition + base rate room & board)

Requirements: A minimum 3.5 cumulative high school GPA | Top Applicants.

Application Deadline: December 15

Application Link:
https://www.lssu.edu/financial-aid/types-of-aid/scholarships/

12 Davenport University

Location: Grand Rapids, Michigan
Setting: Suburban (77 Acres)
Undergraduate Enrollment: 4,352
Type: Private

Gerald R. Ford Memorial Scholarship: Awards Full tuition, books, fees, a study abroad experience, on-campus housing and meal plans.

Requirements: A minimum 3.75 cumulative high school GPA | A minimum 1430 SAT or 31 ACT.

Application Deadline: December 15

Application Link:
https://www.davenport.edu/financial-aid/scholarships

11 Wayne State University

Location: Detroit, Michigan
Setting: Urban (190 Acres)
Undergraduate Enrollment: 16,116
Type: Public

Wayne Med-Direct Scholars: Awards Full tuition, room and board, plus other benefits.

P.S: Awarded to students who wishes to pursue a career in Medicine.

Requirements: A minimum 3.5 cumulative high school GPA | A minimum 1310 SAT or 28 ACT score | Applicant must be a U.S. citizen or permanent resident.

Application Deadline: December 1

Application Link:
https://wayne.edu/scholarships/freshmen

1 Concordia College

Location: Moorhead, Minnesota
Setting: Urban (115 Acres)
Undergraduate Enrollment: 1,827
Type: Private

Community Achievement Scholarship: Awards Full tuition, comprehensive fees, room, and board.

Requirements: Top students.

P.S: This scholarship is open to first-generation college-bound students from ethnically and socioeconomically diverse backgrounds who *live in Fargo-Moorhead* or the surrounding area and have a desire to achieve a four-year degree.

Application Deadline: February 28

Application Link:
https://www.concordiacollege.edu/tuition-aid/scholarships/concordia-scholarships/

2 University of Minnesota Twin Cities

Location: The Twin Cities of Minneapolis and Saint Paul, Minnesota
Setting: Urban (1,204 Acres)
Undergraduate Enrollment: 39,248
Type: Public

College of Science and Engineering

Clifford I. and Nancy C. Anderson Scholarship: Award covers the full cost of attendance.

Criteria for consideration is based on financial need.

Sezzle Scholarship: Award covers the full cost of attendance.

Criteria for consideration is based on financial need.

P.S: Preference for students interested in computer science, computer engineering, and data sciences | Preference for students from MN, North Dakota, South Dakota, and Wisconsin.

Application Deadline: November 1

Application Link:
https://admissions.tc.umn.edu/cost-aid/scholarships

1 Rust College

Location: Holly Springs, Mississippi
Setting: Rural (126 Acres)
Undergraduate Enrollment: 755
Type: Private

Honor's Track Scholarship: Awards Holistic Full Scholarships

Requirements: A minimum 3.50 high school GPA.

Application Deadline: December 1

Application Link: https://www.rustcollege.edu/prospective-students/financial-aid/scholarships/

3 Mississippi State University

Location: Starkville, Mississippi
Setting: Rural (4,200 Acres)
Undergraduate Enrollment: 18,305
Type: Public

Presidential Scholarship Award: Full tuition, fees, room and board, research fellowships, and books for four years.

Non-resident students may also receive a scholarship to cover up to 100% of the out-of-state portion of tuition.

Requirements: A minimum 1330 SAT/ 30 ACT | 3.75 High school GPA or higher.

Application Deadline: December 1

Application Link: https://www.honors.msstate.edu/scholarships/

2 Mississippi Valley State University

Location: Itta Bena, Mississippi
Setting: Rural (450 Acres)
Undergraduate Enrollment: 1,654
Type: Public

University Scholarship: This scholarship covers ½ tuition and fees and a book allowance of $200.

Requirements: 3.0 GPA or higher | ACT score of 20-21 or SAT equivalent.

Presidential Scholarship: Full tuition, room, board, fees and a book allowance of $500

Requirements: A minimum ACT score of 24 or SAT equivalent | 3.0 GPA

Vice President's Scholarship: Full tuition and fees and a book allowance of $300.

Requirements: A minimum ACT score of 22-23 or SAT equivalent | 3.0 GPA

Application Deadline: February 1

Application Link: https://www.mvsu.edu/prospective-students/scholarships

4 Jackson State University

Location: Jackson, Mississippi
Setting: Urban (220 Acres)
Undergraduate Enrollment: 4,763
Type: Public

Presidential Academic Scholarship: Award covers Full tuition, fees, room & board, and $750 per semester for books (campus only)

Requirements: ACT score of 28 or above or the SAT score of 1300 and above | 3.50 high school GPA.

Provost Academic Scholarship: Award covers Full tuition, room & board (campus charges only)

Requirements: ACT score of 25-27 or SAT score of 1200-1290 | 3.25 high school GPA.

Application Deadline: February 15

Application Link:
https://sites.jsums.edu/scholarships/

5 University of Southern Mississippi

Location: Hattiesburg, Mississippi
Setting: Suburban (1,090 Acres)
Undergraduate Enrollment: 10,258
Type: Public

Presidential National Merit Finalist Scholarship: Award covers full tuition (and nonresident fees, if applicable), campus housing, a semester book stipend, and a meal plan for four years. Finalists will further receive a $4,000 study-abroad scholarship to participate in a Southern Miss study abroad program of their choice.

Eligibility: National Merit Finalist.

Presidential Scholarship: Award covers full tuition (and nonresident fees, if applicable), campus housing, a semester book stipend, and a meal plan for four years.

Requirements: A minimum 3.0 cumulative high school GPA | A minimum ACT composite score of 30 or a combined SAT score of 1330 excluding the written portion of the SAT.

Application Deadline: January 15

Application Link:
https://catalog.usm.edu/content.php?catoid=9&navoid=515

6 University of Mississippi

Location: Oxford, Mississippi
Setting: Rural (3,693 Acres)
Undergraduate Enrollment: 17,302
Type: Public

Stamps Scholarship: Awards up to the full cost of attendance after other awards. The package includes a $12,000 stipend for educational activities outside the classroom, including study abroad, research, and other enrichment pursuits.

Requirements: Entering freshmen with exceptional academic and leadership records.

Application Deadline: January 5

Academic Excellence Scholarship National Merit Semifinalist/Finalist Award: Awards full tuition, standard cost of a double occupancy room in a campus residence hall, covers full non-resident fee if applicable.

Eligibility: Entering freshmen with National Merit Semifinalist/Finalist status and a 3.0 or higher GPA.

Application Deadline: Follows National Merit announcement timeline.

Ole Miss Opportunity Program:

Eligible Mississippi resident students will receive financial aid support to cover the average cost of tuition, residence hall housing, and an allowance for meals.

Eligibility: Applicant must be a Mississippi resident and a U.S citizen | A minimum 3.0 high school GPA.

Application Link: https://finaid.olemiss.edu/scholarships/

1 Williams Wood University

Location: Fulton, Missouri
Setting: Rural (200 Acres)
Undergraduate Enrollment: 882
Type: Private

Amy Shelton McNutt: Full Tuition, room and board for 4 years.

Requirements: A minimum ACT score of 31 or SAT 1420 | 3.75 GPA.

Application Deadline: February 15

Application Link:
https://www.williamwoods.edu/admissions/undergraduate/scholarships/index.html

2 Park University

Location: Parkville, Missouri
Setting: Suburban (700 Acres)
Undergraduate Enrollment: 7,387
Type: Private

Presidential Honors Scholarship: Full tuition, room and board.

Requirements: Two letters of recommendation from high school teachers | GPA 3.8+ | ACT 32/ SAT 1450 Recommended – Not Required | 300-500 word personal statement as described within application.

Application Deadline: November 1

Application Link:
https://www.park.edu/academics/honors-academy/scholarships/

3 Truman State University

Location: Kirksville, Missouri
Setting: Rural (210 Acres)
Undergraduate Enrollment: 3,622
Type: Public

General John J. Pershing: Awards Full Tuition, on-campus room and meal plan annually, plus a one-time $4,000 study abroad stipend.

Requirements: Applicants should be in the top 3% of their HS class with ACT or SAT scores in the top 3% nationally.

Application Deadline: January 15

Application Link:
https://www.truman.edu/admission-cost/cost-aid/scholarships/

4 Lindenwood University

Location: Saint Charles, Missouri
Setting: Suburban (285 Acres)
Undergraduate Enrollment: 4,808
Type: Private

Sibley Scholarship: Awarded in a range and could cover up to full tuition, room and board.

Requirements: A minimum cumulative unweighted 3.50 high school GPA (on a 4.0 scale) | Submit a resume and a personal essay.

Application Link:
https://www.lindenwood.edu/admissions/student-financial-services/scholarships-grants/

5 Missouri State University

Location: Springfield, Missouri
Setting: City (225 Acres)
Undergraduate Enrollment: 18,419
Type: Public

Presidential Scholarship: Awards $15,000 per year ($7,000 for tuition and $8,000 for on-campus housing).

P.S: Non-Missouri residents will also receive a full waiver of nonresident fees for fall and spring semesters.

Requirements: A minimum 3.90 high school GPA at 6th semester | 31 ACT or 1390 SAT

Application Deadline: December 1

Application Link:
https://www.missouristate.edu/FinancialAid/Scholarships/Freshman.htm

6 University of Missouri, Columbia

Location: Columbia, Missouri
Setting: City (1,262 Acres)
Undergraduate Enrollment: 23,752
Type: Public

Stamps Scholars Award: Awards full scholarship (up to estimated cost of attendance) plus a one-time award of $16,000 for academic development and leadership.

Requirements: 32-36 ACT or 1420-1600 SAT | 3.5 core HS GPA.

National Merit Finalist & Semifinalist Scholarship: Awards full tuition and fees, a $3,500 additional stipend plus a $10,964 one year on-campus housing and dining, a one time payment of $2,000 for research/study abroad and a $1,000 for tech enrichment.

Eligibility: Applicant must be deemed a National Merit Finalist or Semifinalist by the National Merit Scholarship Corporation (NMSC) | Awarded to ***Missouri residents***.

Application Deadline: December 1

Application Link:
https://admissions.missouri.edu/costs-aid/scholarships/

7 Maryville University

Location: St. Louis, Missouri
Setting: Suburban (130 Acres)
Undergraduate Enrollment: 5,809
Type: Private

Presidential Scholarship: Full tuition, room and board.

Requirements: A minimum 3.75 cumulative high school GPA | 1290+ SAT / 27+ ACT

Dr. Donald M. Suggs Scholarship: Full tuition, room and board.

Eligibility: African American students from the St. Louis metropolitan area who have a minimum GPA of 3.25 | 1040+ SAT / 23+ ACT.

Application Deadline: December 1

Application Link:
https://www.maryville.edu/admissions/financial-aid/scholarships/

8 University of Missouri – Kansas City

Location: Kansas City, Missouri
Setting: Urban (150 Acres)
Undergraduate Enrollment: 10,190
Type: Public

Trustees Scholars Program: Awards Full tuition and fees, $500 towards books, on-campus room and board for a standard double room in Oak Street Residence Hall, and a $2,000 stipend toward living expenses in years three and four.

Requirements: A minimum 3.5 cumulative high school GPA in 17-class core curriculum | A minimum ACT composite score of 30 | Rank in the top 5% of your high school graduating class.

Eligibility: U.S. citizen or permanent residents.

Application Deadline: December 1

Application Link:
https://finaid.umkc.edu/financial-aid/scholarships/

1 Montana State University

Location: Bozeman, Montana
Setting: City (956 Acres)
Undergraduate Enrollment: 14,668
Type: Public

Army ROTC Scholarship: Full tuition and mandatory fees or $10,000/year for room and board, a yearly book allowance ($1,200/year) and a tax free monthly stipend ($425/month)

Eligibility: Award is based on college performance (academics, physical fitness and standing in program)

Application Link:
https://www.montana.edu/admissions/scholarships/additional.html

2 University of Providence

Location: Great Falls, Montana
Setting: City (44 Acres)
Undergraduate Enrollment: 665
Type: Private

Institutional Scholarships

The generous merit and athletic scholarships range from $7,500 – ***Full Ride***.

Merit scholarship amounts for freshmen are determined by each student's high school academic performance.

Athletic scholarships are determined by the coach of each sports team and take the place of a merit scholarship on a financial aid offer.

Application Link:
https://www.uprovidence.edu/financial-services/scholarships/

1

Nebraska Wesleyan University

Location: Lincoln, Nebraska
Setting: City (50 Acres)
Undergraduate Enrollment: 1,545
Type: Private

Huge-NWU Scholarships: Full tuition, fees, room and board over four years.

Requirements: Have a cumulative high school GPA of 3.75 or higher (4.0 scale) | Hold an ACT >27 or SAT >1260.

Application Deadline: December 1

Application Link: https://www.nebrwesleyan.edu/admissions/financial-aid-office/undergraduate-aid/first-year-scholarships

1 University of Nevada

Location: Las Vegas, Nevada
Setting: Urban (358 Acres)
Undergraduate Enrollment: 25,365
Type: Public

Army ROTC Scholarship: Awards full tuition plus mandatory fees or applied toward room and board, a $1,200 per year book allowance and a tax-free stipend based on academic status during the academic year.

Requirements: Applicant must be a U.S. citizen | Have a minimum high school GPA of 2.5 | Score a minimum of 920 on the SAT or a 19 composite on the ACT, not including the written portion of the test.

Application Deadline: January 10

Application Link:
https://www.unlv.edu/rotc/finaid

2 Nevada State College

Location: Henderson, Nevda
Setting: Urban (510 Acres)
Undergraduate Enrollment: 7,115
Type: Public

Nevada's Otto Huth Scholarship: Award covers tuition, on-campus housing, meal plans, and textbooks for up to $40,000 total.

P.S: It's intended for **youth who've aged out of foster system** and wish to attend an accredited two-year trade school or four-year university.

Requirements: Applicant must Apply before their 20th birthday | Attend a school in Nevada | Begin their post high school education within 12 months of being awarded the scholarship | Have a minimum GPA of 2.0 and plan on attending school full time.

Application Deadline: April 15

Application Link:
https://nevadastate.edu/community/cedi/scholarships/

1 University of New Hampshire

Location: Durham, New Hampshire
Setting: Suburban (2,600 Acres)
Undergraduate Enrollment: 11,480
Type: Public

Army ROTC Scholarship: Awards full tuition and fees; grant funds toward room and board; annual book benefit of $1,200; monthly tax-free stipend.

Requirements: Top applicants.

Air Force ROTC Scholarship: Awards full tuition and most lab fees; a textbook allowance; monthly cash stipend.

Application Deadline: November 15

Application Link: https://www.unh.edu/financialaid/types-aid/scholarships

1 Kean University

Location: Union, New Jersey
Setting: Urban (240 Acres)
Undergraduate Enrollment: 10,845
Type: Public

William Livingston Full Scholarship: Awards up to $50,000. This covers the total cost of attendance.

Requirements: Top Applicants.

Application Deadline: January 1

Application Link:
https://www.kean.edu/offices/financial-aid/scholarship-services/merit-scholarships-new-incoming-students

3 New Jersey Institute of Technology

Location: Newark, New Jersey
Setting: Urban (48 Acres)
Undergraduate Enrollment: 9,019
Type: Public

National Merit Scholarship: Awards full tuition and fees to students who have been selected by the National Merit Scholarship Corporation (NMSC)

Requirements: To enter the competition, applicant must be either a U.S. citizen or a U.S. lawful permanent resident.

Application Deadline: September 30

Application Link:
https://www.njit.edu/financialaid/merit-based-scholarships

2 Saint Elizabeth University

Location: Morris Township, New Jersey
Setting: Suburban (200 Acres)
Undergraduate Enrollment: 737
Type: Private

College of Saint Elizabeth International Scholarships: Awards full tuition, room & board, and fees to ***international students***.

Requirements: Applicant must have a TOEFL score of at least 173 (computer based), SAT 1200 and an outstanding academic record.

P.S: Only students applying to the Women's College division of the College of Saint Elizabeth are eligible.

Application Deadline: March 1

Application Link:
https://www.internationalscholarships.com/scholarships/543/College_of_Saint_Elizabeth_International_Scholarships

1 University of New Mexico

Location: Albuquerque, New Mexico
Setting: Urban (769 Acres)
Undergraduate Enrollment: 15,914
Type: Public

Freshman New Mexico Resident Scholarships:

Regents' Scholarship: Award approximately $20,000 per year – covers base tuition, fees, and housing.

Requirements: A minimum 3.90 cumulative high school GPA.

National Merit Finalist Scholarship: Award approximately $20,000 per year – covers base tuition, fees, and housing.

Requirements: Awarded National Merit Finalist.

Application Deadline: December 1

Application Link:
https://scholarship.unm.edu/

2 Eastern New Mexico University

Location: Portales, New Mexico
Setting: Rural (360 Acres)
Undergraduate Enrollment: 4,465
Type: Public

In-State Freshman Scholarship

Green and Silver Presidential Scholarship:

Awards Full tuition, fees and residence hall charges plus $1500 per semester.

Requirements: Applicant must be a New Mexico resident | Be a New Mexico high school graduate, New Mexico General Education Development (GED) recipient, or New Mexico High School Equivalency Test (HiSET) recipient | A minimum 3.0 high school GPA | ACT composite score of 27 (or 1260 – 1290 SAT Evidence – Based Reading and Writing, Math) **OR** 3.5 GPA and ACT composite of 25 (or 1200 – 1220 SAT Evidence – Based Reading and Writing, Math)

Application Deadline: March 1

Application Link:
https://www.enmu.edu/admission/scholarships

3

New Mexico Highlands University

Location: Las Vegas, New Mexico
Setting: Rural (175 Arces)
Undergraduate Enrollment: 1,699
Type: Public

Debt Free Four Year Education: Highlands University offers Debt-Free-Four-Year Education to Students from partner High Schools (Santa Fe Public Schools, Denver Public Schools, and most of the schools in the Northeast Regional Education Cooperative, including Mora, Santa Rosa, Wagon Mound, West Las Vegas, and Las Vegas City school districts

Requirements: A minimum 3.0 high school GPA.

Regent's New Mexico scholars Scholarship: Awards full tuition and fees plus $500 per semester.

Eligibility: Applicant must rank in the top 5 percent of graduating class or 25 ACT, family income of $60,000 or less.

Application Deadline: March 1

Application Link: https://www.nmhu.edu/financial-aid-2/scholarships/

1 University of Rochester

Location: Rochester, New York
Setting: Urban (707 Acres)
Undergraduate Enrollment: 6,767
Type: Private

Alan and Jane Handler Endowed scholarship:

Handler students will receive assured, complete financial support (tuition, fees, room, board, books, personal expenses and transportation), plus $5,000 in guaranteed funding to support academic or professional enrichment as well as individual and group opportunities, for the duration of the regular four year academic program.

Requirements: Top applicants.

Application Link: https://admissions.rochester.edu/handler-scholarship/

2 Oswego State University, New York

Location: Oswego, New York
Setting: Rural (700 Acres)
Undergraduate Enrollment: 5,985
Type: Public

Possibility Scholars Program: Award when combined with existing need-based aid covers the total cost of attendance.

P.S: New York state students entering STEM fields (Science, Technology, Engineering or Math) are eligible for consideration, with priority given to high-achieving students with significant financial need.

Requirements: Student should exhibit a high degree of excellence.

Application Deadline: November 15

Application Link: https://www.oswego.edu/financial-aid/scholarships

3 Roberts Wesleyan College

Location: Rochester, New York
Setting: Suburban (188 Acres)
Undergraduate Enrollment: 1,052
Type: Private

The Max and Marian Farash Charitable Foundation's First in the Family Scholarship Program: Award covers all additional funds needed to *completely pay* for the Farash Scholar's tuition, room and board, textbooks, and mandatory fees.

Eligibility: Freshman from Monroe or Ontario County (New York) who will be the first in his/her family (parents, step-parents, or siblings) to have attended any college/university.

Application Deadline: February 14

Application Link: https://www.roberts.edu/undergraduate/tuition-and-aid/grants-scholarships/merit-scholarships/farash-scholarship/

4 Alfred University

Location: Alfred, New York
Setting: Rural (600 Acres)
Undergraduate Enrollment: 1,347
Type: Private

Army ROTC Scholarships: This scholarship provides full financial assistance (full tuition, mandatory fees or can be used for room and board expenses of $10,000 per school year, plus a tax free subsistence allowance for up to 10 months of $420 per month and $1,200 annually for textbooks, classroom supplies and equipment.

Application Link:
https://www.alfred.edu/student-life/military-affairs/grants-financial-aid.cfm

5 Canisius College

Location: Buffalo, New York
Setting: Urban (72 Acres)
Undergraduate Enrollment: 1,788
Type: Private

The Army ROTC Scholarship can be used for either full tuition & fees, or as room and board scholarship. It provides a book stipend, and a subsistence (living allowance) while enrolled in college.

Application Deadline: January 10

Application Link:
https://www.canisius.edu/admissions/scholarships-tuition-aid/scholarships-financial-aid/scholarships/freshmen-scholarships

6 Fordham University

Location: New York City, New York
Setting: Urban (93 Acres)
Undergraduate Enrollment: 10,098
Type: Private

Cunniffe Presidential Scholarship: Award covers tuition, room, board, and fees. It is renewable for 4 years. Recipients are also eligible for a maximum of $20,000 over four years to use for academic enrichment experiences.

Requirements: Check the website for more details.

Application Deadline: November 1

Application Link:
https://www.fordham.edu/undergraduate-admission/apply/scholarships-and-grants/

7 Adelphi University

Location: Garden City, New York
Setting: Suburban (75 Acres)
Undergraduate Enrollment: 5,055
Type: Private

Athletic Grants: Awards up to Full tuition, fees, room and board.

Requirements: Applicants athletic performance/record | Top applicants.

Application Deadline: October 1

Application Link:
https://www.adelphi.edu/aid/scholarships/institutional/additional-awards/

8 Syracuse University

Location: Syracuse, New York
Setting: City (721 Arces)
Undergraduate Enrollment: 15,421
Type: Private

Haudenosaunee Promise Scholarship: Award covers tuition, housing and meals (on campus, up to the amount allotted through the cost of attendance) and mandatory fees.

Eligibility: Applicant must be a certified citizen of one of the historic Haudenosaunee nations (Mohawk, Oneida, Onondaga, Cayuga, Seneca, or Tuscarora) | Have resided on one of the Haudenosaunee nation territories listed for a minimum of four years prior to and during their enrollment at Syracuse University.

Requirements: Top applicants.

Check the website for eligible *Haudenosaunee Territories...*

Application Deadline: November 15

Application Link: https://financialaid.syr.edu/scholarships/su/

9 Pratt Institute

Location: Brooklyn, New York
Setting: Urban (25 Acres)
Undergraduate Enrollment: 3,702
Type: Private

President's Wallace Augustus Rayfield Scholarship: Awards Full ride scholarships *(to students from New York City and New York State)*

Eligibility: Awarded to students in five degree-granting schools of Architecture, Art, Design, Information, Liberal Arts and Sciences.

Requirements: Top applicants.

Kathryn and Kenneth Chenault Scholarship: Awards tuition, room and board, fees, books and supplies.

P.S: This Scholarship is established to support ***diversity in the school of Architecture***.

Requirements: Top applicants

Balenciaga and The Black Alumni of Pratt: Award covers full undergraduate attendance – including tuition, fees, room and board, books and supplies.

Eligibility: Awarded to students in the School of Design, School of Art, and School of Architecture.

P.S: This scholarship will support diversity within these schools and their professional fields.

Requirements: Top applicants

Application Deadline: November 1

Application Link: https://catalog.pratt.edu/undergraduate/financial-aid/scholarships/

1 Lees-McRae College

Location: Banner Elk, North Carolina
Setting: Rural (935 Acres)
Undergraduate Enrollment: 855
Type: Private

Shelton Scholarship: Awards Full tuition, room and board for four years.

Requirements: A minimum 3.75 high school GPA | 1150 SAT score (or ACT equivalent)

Application Deadline: December 1

Application Link: https://www.lmc.edu/admissions/financial-aid/types-of-aid.htm

3 Elizabeth City State University

Location: Elizabeth City, North Carolina
Setting: Rural (154 Acres)
Undergraduate Enrollment: 2,033
Type: Public

Chancellor's Academic Scholarship: A fully funded four year scholarship (full tuition, student fees, university housing, meals and textbooks.)

Requirements: Applicant must be a U.S. citizen or a permanent resident | Have a minimum 3.5 unweighted cumulative GPA.

Application Deadline: January 15

Application Link: https://www.ecsu.edu/financial-aid/types-of-aid.php

2 Gardner Webb University

Location: Boiling Springs, North Carolina
Setting: Rural (240 Acres)
Undergraduate Enrollment: 1,983
Type: Private

The Tucker Heart, Soul, Mind, and Strength Scholarship: Full tuition, room and board.

Requirements: Ministers, teachers and community leaders can nominate a worthy student for a chance at this top scholarship.

Application Deadline: Nominations should be submitted before the end of October.

The Andrews Scholarship: Award covers Full tuition, room and board, and $800 per year for books.

Requirements: Top applicants | Applicant Must have demonstrated financial need | Must be a first generation college student | Must have a demonstrated commitment to diversity | Must be a ***male*** | Must ***not*** be a student athlete.

Application Deadline: April 1

Application Link: https://gardner-webb.edu/admissions-aid/scholarships-and-grants/

4 North Carolina State University

Location: Raleigh, North Carolina
Setting: City (2,140 Acres)
Undergraduate Enrollment: 26,254
Type: Public

Park Scholarship: A fully funded four year scholarship (full tuition, fees, room and board, books and supplies, travel, personal expenses and lot's more.)

Requirements: Top scholars in the applicant pool

Application Deadline: November 1

Application Link: https://studentservices.ncsu.edu/finances/scholarships-and-financial-aid/types-of-financial-aid/scholarships/

5 North Carolina Wesleyan College

Location: Rocky Mount, North Carolina
Setting: Suburban (200 Acres)
Undergraduate Enrollment: 1,249
Type: Private

Founder's Award: Full tuition, room (double only), board & books.

Requirements: 4.0 weighted GPA / 3.75 unweighted | 1240 SAT / 26 ACT.

Application Link: https://ncwu.edu/scholarships/

6 Saint Augustine's University

Location: Raleigh, North Carolina
Setting: Urban (122 Acres)
Undergraduate Enrollment: 937
Type: Private

Presidential Scholarship: The award covers a full direct cost of attendance.

Requirements: High School GPA of 3.8 (on a 4.0 scale) or higher | A minimum 1100 SAT score or a 22 ACT score.

Application Deadline: May 3

Application Link: https://www.st-aug.edu/admissions/financial-aid/types-of-aid/incoming-freshmen-scholarships/

7 East Carolina University

Location: Greenville, North Carolina
Setting: City (1,600 Acres)
Undergraduate Enrollment: 21,688
Type: Public

EC Scholars Program: Award covers in-state tuition for eight continuous semesters, Living arrangements Ballard Residence Hall, the newest residence on campus located on College Hill, Priority course registration to guarantee your needed classes and preferred times, $5,000 stipend to support a required Study Abroad experience, and a lot of other benefits.

Requirements: Top scholars in the applicants pool.

Application Deadline: October 1

Application Link:
https://brinkleylane.ecu.edu/

8 Meredith College

Location: Raleigh, North Carolina
Setting: Urban (225 Acres)
Undergraduate Enrollment: 1,322
Type: Private

Meredith Legacy Scholarship: Awards Full tuition, on campus room and board, college-wide fees (four academic years), books, supplies, international study, and other academic enrichment programs.

Requirements: An average SAT/ACT 1510/34 | Weighted GPA of 4.65, demonstrated leadership and service to others.

Application Deadline: January 15

Application Link:
https://www.meredith.edu/financial-assistance/financial-assistance-undergraduate-scholarships/

9 Salem College

Location: Winston-Salem, North Carolina
Setting: City (57 Acres)
Undergraduate Enrollment: 364
Type: Private

Salem College Promise: Full tuition and fees.

Eligibility: Applicant must be a North Carolina resident | Pell-eligible, with an estimated family contribution of $0-$5,000 (per FASFA)

Outstanding applicants may receive scholarships covering the full cost of attendance through named awards. P.S: Check the website for more details.

Application Deadline: November 1

Application Link: https://www.salem.edu/admissions/scholarships

10 UNC, Chapel Hill

Location: Chapel Hill, North Carolina
Setting: Suburban (729 Acres)
Undergraduate Enrollment: 20,210
Type: Public

Kenan Music Scholarship: This generous scholarship offers the opportunity to combine musical studies with coursework (or a second major) and a four year, full-tuition scholarship (including student fees, room & board).

Requirements: Interested students must submit a scholarship audition request directly to the Department of Music to be considered for this opportunity.

Reserve Office Training Corps (ROTC) Scholarship: Awards full tuition and fees, a $600 per-semester book allowance, and a monthly stipend between $300 and $500, depending on the student's year at the University. Upon graduation, cadets may become officers in the active Army or remain in the Army Reserve.

Application Deadline: March 1

Application Link: https://studentaid.unc.edu/incoming/what-aid-is-available/scholarships/

11 Davidson College

Location: Davidson, North Carolina
Setting: Suburban (841 Acres)
Undergraduate Enrollment: 1,927
Type: Private

Nomination Scholarships:

You must be nominated for consideration.

John M. Belk Scholarship: Full tuition, fees, room and board plus special study stipends that allow you great flexibility in the on and off-campus opportunities you choose to explore.

Lowell L. Bryan Scholarship: Full tuition and fees.

Requirements: Applicant must be a Scholar athlete.

Charles Scholarship: Full tuition, fees, room and board, Book and personal expense allowance, Travel allowance (three roundtrips to Chicago), A new laptop once during a scholar's Davidson career, Special study opportunity funds.

Competition Scholarships:

William Holt Terry Scholarship: Full tuition and fees annually, and a one-time $3,000 special opportunity stipend.

There are lot's of full ride scholarship opportunities available at the Davidson College.

Application Deadline: December 1

Application Link: https://www.davidson.edu/admission-and-financial-aid/financial-aid/scholarships

12 North Carolina A&T

Location: Greensboro, North Carolina
Setting: Urban (800 Acres)
Undergraduate Enrollment: 11,833
Type: Public

National Alumni Scholarship: Full tuition, related fees, room & board.

Eligibility: Applicant must be a U.S. citizen | A minimum 3.5 GPA (4.0 scale) | ACT and SAT score are optional for the 2021-2022 year.

Lewis and Elizabeth Dowdy Scholarship: Full tuition, related fees, room & board.

Eligibility: A minimum 3.75 cumulative GPA (weighted) | Minimum SAT score of 1270 or 27 ACT (test optional for the 2021 applicants) | Applicant must be a U.S. citizen or eligible non-citizen.

Application Deadline: December 15

Application Link: https://www.ncat.edu/admissions/financial-aid/types-of-aid/scholarships/freshmen-scholarships.php

13 Wake Forest University

Location: Winston-Salem, North Carolina
Setting: Suburban (340 Acres)
Undergraduate Enrollment: 5,447
Type: Private

Guy T. Carswell Scholarship: Full tuition, fees, room and board, and includes an allowance for books and personal expenses. Scholars may receive up to $5,000 at least one summer for approved travel or study projects.

Requirements: Top Applicants.

Joseph G. Gordon Scholarship: Full tuition, fees, room and board, and includes an allowance for books and personal expenses. Scholars may receive up to $5,000 at least one summer for approved travel or study projects.

Leadership and Character Scholarship: Full tuition, fees, room and board, and includes an allowance for books and personal expenses.

Graylyn Scholarship: Full tuition, room and board, plus $3,400 for personal expenses.

Requirements: Top Applicants.

Nancy Susan Reynolds Scholarship: Full tuition, room and board, plus $3,400 for personal expenses.

Requirements: Top Applicants.

P.S: Scholars are encouraged to apply for up to $5,000 for a research, study, or travel project during each of the three summers between the first and senior years.

Application Deadline: November 15

Application Link: https://financialaid.wfu.edu/types-of-aid/scholarships/

14 Duke University

Location: Durham, North Carolina
Setting: Suburban (8,693 Acres)
Undergraduate Enrollment: 6,640
Type: Private

Duke University gives out a number of prominent full-ride merit scholarships, including the Benjamin N. Duke (B.N.) Scholars, Angier B. Duke (A.B.) Scholars, David M. Rubenstein Scholars, Reginaldo Howard Memorial Scholars, Trinity Scholars, University Scholars, Robertson Scholars, etc. These scholarships give full monetary assistance to the recipients, typically in addition to programmatic resources and professional assistance.

Karsh Intentional Scholarship: Full tuition, mandatory fees, room and board, plus generous funding for domestic and international summer experiences, etc.

Eligibility: Top **International** undergraduate applicants.

Application Deadline: February 1

Application Link: https://medschool.duke.edu/education/health-professions-education-programs/doctor-medicine-md-program/curriculum/third-year-45

15 Appalachian State University

Location: Boone, North Carolina
Setting: Rural (1,200 Acres)
Undergraduate Enrollment: 18,558
Type: Public

Chancellor's Scholarship: Award covers full institutional costs for up to 4 years; including tuition and fees, room and board, book rental, plus study abroad opportunities, numerous classroom and experiential research opportunities and academic mentoring in the living–learning community of the Honors College.

P.S: Recipients must be accepted into the Honors College.

Requirements: Top students in the applicants pool.

Murray Family ACCESS Scholarship Program: Awards Full tuition, fees, room and board and book rental.

P.S: The Murray Family Appalachian Commitment to a College Education for Student Success (ACCESS) Scholarship Program ensures 50 students from low-income families in North Carolina can attend Appalachian debt-free.

Requirements: Students must demonstrate or have a track record of being excellent.

Application Deadline: November 15

Application Link: https://scholarships.appstate.edu/signature-scholarships

16

University of North Carolina, Charlotte

Location: Charlotte, North Carolina
Setting: Urban (1,000 Acres)
Undergraduate Enrollment: 23,461
Type: Public

Albert Engineering Leadership Scholars Program: Award covers –

- ✓ An annual renewable merit scholarship, including tuition, fees, room and board ($21,500 a year)
- ✓ Membership in the University Honors Program
- ✓ Automatic acceptance into the Engineering Leadership Academy
- ✓ A $6,000 stipend to support housing and meals during a summer internship
- ✓ A $2,500 stipend for study abroad
- ✓ A Laptop or comparable technology purchase
- ✓ Research and Professional development opportunities, and lots more...

Requirements: An unweighted high school GPA of 3.50 – 4.00 or Weighted high school GPA of 3.80 – 5.00 | SAT 1320/1600 or ACT 28/36 | Applicants must be U.S. citizens or permanent residents | Applicants are expected to submit a list of activities, two academic letters of recommendation, one leadership recommendation, and two thoughtfully considered essays.

Application Deadline: November 1

Application Link: https://honorscollege.charlotte.edu/albertscholars.uncc.edu

1 University of North Dakota

Location: Grand Forks, North Dakota
Setting: City (521 Acres)
Undergraduate Enrollment: 9,928
Type: Public

National Merit Scholars

This scholarship is awarded to National Merit Scholar Finalist or Semi-Finalist from North Dakota or Minnesota.

Awards Full tuition and mandatory student fees. This scholarship is in addition to other UND scholarships and waivers you're eligible to receive (up to the full cost of attendance)

Requirements: National Merit Finalist/Semi-Finalist | Applicant must select UND as first choice on the National merit application.

Application Deadline: December 15

Application Link: https://und.edu/one-stop/financial-aid/scholarships.html

1 Miami University

Location: Oxford, Ohio
Setting: Rural (2,100 Acres)
Undergraduate Enrollment: 16,865
Type: Public

Presidential Fellows Program: Full tuition & fees, room and board, plus a one-time $5,000 academic enrichment stipend.

Requirements: Top scholars.

Application Deadline: December 1

Application Link:
https://miamioh.edu/admission-aid/majors-minors-programs/honors-programs/presidential-fellows-program.html

2 University of Toledo

Location: Toledo, Ohio
Setting: Urban (1,037 Acres)
Undergraduate Enrollment: 11,965
Type: Public

Presidential Scholarship: Full tuition, room and board, general fee, a one-time $3,000 stipend for a summer experience.

Requirements: Minimum high school cumulative GPA of 3.8 | 30 ACT or 1360 SAT.

Application Deadline: December 1

Application Link:
https://www.utoledo.edu/admission/freshman/tuition/

3 Marietta College

Location: Marietta, Ohio
Setting: Suburban (90 Acres)
Undergraduate Enrollment: 1,109
Type: Private

John G. McCoy Scholarship: Awards Full tuition, fees, standard room and board.

Requirements: Top scholars in the applicants pool.

Application Deadline: February 15

Application Link:
https://www.marietta.edu/scholarships

4 University of Mount Union

Location: Alliance, Ohio
Setting: City (123 Acres)
Undergraduate Enrollment: 1,889
Type: Private

ROTC Scholarship:

Air Force and Army ROTC Scholarship:

Awards Full tuition, free on-campus housing and board.

Requirements: Top Applicants in the applicants pool.

Check the website for more details...

Application Deadline: November 8

Application Link:
https://www.mountunion.edu/admission/tuition-and-aid/scholarships-and-grants

5 Ohio State University

Location: Columbus, Ohio
Setting: Urban (1,714 Acres)
Undergraduate Enrollment: 46,123
Type: Public

Land Grant Opportunity Scholarship: Award covers the full cost of attendance. This scholarship is awarded to students who are Pell-eligible and demonstrate academic merit.

Eligibility: Applicant MUST be an Ohio resident.

Eminence Fellows Program and Scholarship: Awards up to full cost of attendance, plus an enrichment grant valued at $3,000 accessible after the first year of successful study.

Criteria: Only U.S. citizens and permanent residents are eligible to apply | Finalist are selected based on the strength of their Common Application.

Morrill Scholarship Program

Awards Levels: ***Distinction*** (the value of the cost of attendance)

Requirements: Top Applicants.

Application Deadline: December 1

Application Link:
http://undergrad.osu.edu/cost-and-aid/merit-based-scholarships

6 University of Cincinnati

Location: Cincinnati, Ohio
Setting: Urban (254 Acres)
Undergraduate Enrollment: 29,989
Type: Public

Cincinnatus Scholarship Program: Ranges from $1,500 annually up to full tuition, room and board, and a book allowance.

Requirements: Qualifying students will be determined based on their overall admission application.

Marian Spencer Scholarship: Awards Full tuition, room and board, and a book allowance.

P.S: Specifically reserved for CPS students in the top 10% of their senior class.

Requirements: This scholarship is awarded to top 10% students in each Cincinnati public school (CPS) who exemplify the spirit of Spencer.

Application Deadline: December 1

Application Link:
https://www.uc.edu/about/financial-aid/aid/scholarships.html

7 Case Western Reserve University

Location: Cleveland, Ohio
Setting: Urban (267 Acres)
Undergraduate Enrollment: 6,017
Type: Private

Joan C. Edwards Scholarship: Awards full tuition, room, board, fees, books and personal expenses, as well as conditional admission to the Case Western Reserve University School of Medicine; a medical school scholarship in the amount of tuition and a $20,000 per year stipend!

Criteria: This scholarship is awarded to students in the Cleveland Metropolitan School District with an interest in becoming a physician.

The Army & Air Force ROTC Program also provides significant college scholarships that cover tuition, books, fees, and monthly stipends for those that compete for the opportunity.

Application Deadline: January 15

Application Link:
https://case.edu/admission/tuition-aid/scholarships

8 Cleveland State University

Location: Cleveland, Ohio
Setting: Urban (85 Acres)
Undergraduate Enrollment: 9,950
Type: Public

Honors Program: Full tuition and fees.

Requirements: A minimum ACT composite score of 30 OR SAT score of 1380 | Rank in the top 10% of high school class.

Jack, Joseph and Morton Mandel Honors College

Awards full tuition scholarship at the in-state tuition rate and other associated fees.

Eligibility: International Student's.

Sullivan-Deckard and Helen Packer Scholarship: Award covers Financial aid for tuition, books, fees, and instructional resources. Year – round housing with an approved meal plan. Academic coaching and institutional support services plus a lot of other benefits.

Eligibility: This Scholarship is ***designed for youth who are aging out of foster care or experienced foster care*** and aspire to pursue an undergraduate degree.

Application Deadline: January 15

Application Link:
https://www.csuohio.edu/financial-aid/new-incoming-freshman

1 University of Oklahoma

Location: Norman, Oklahoma
Setting: City (3,326 Acres)
Undergraduate Enrollment: 21,294
Type: Public

National Merit Finalist Scholarship: Awards $68,500 to Resident Freshmen and $121,500 to Non-resident applicant's. This amount covers the total cost of attendance for undergraduate studies at the University of Oklahoma.

Criteria: National Merit Finalist.

Military Scholarships are also available for incoming students.

Application Deadline: December 15

Application Link: https://www.ou.edu/admissions/affordability/scholarships

2 Oklahoma Christian University

Location: Edmond, Oklahoma
Setting: Urban (200 Acres)
Undergraduate Enrollment: 2,003
Type: Private

National Merit Scholar Award

Award amount: OC award + federal grants + state grants + National Merit Award finalist = up to 17 credit hours per semester of full tuition, mandatory fees, cost of room and meal plan.

Requirements: Applicant must select OC as your first-choice university to the National Merit Corporation.

Application Deadline: December 1

Application Link: https://www.oc.edu/admissions/financial-services/scholarships

3 Cameron University

Location: Lawton, Oklahoma
Setting: City (160 Acres)
Undergraduate Enrollment: 3,133
Type: Public

The Incoming freshmen PLUS scholarship: The scholarship will provide recipients with a full tuition waiver for up to 18 hours per semester, a room waiver to cover the scholar's portion of a double room in Shepler Center, and a $400 stipend per semester.

Requirements: Applicant must be a resident of Oklahoma | A minimum high school GPA of 3.0 (unweighted) OR 2.8 and be in the top 25% of the graduating senior class | Achieve ACT minimum composite score of 20 (or SAT equivalent)

Application Deadline: February 3

Application Link: https://www.cameron.edu/plus/incoming-freshman-plus-scholarship

4 Langston University

Location: Langston, Oklahoma
Setting: Rural (40 Acres)
Undergraduate Enrollment: 1,894
Type: Public

1890 USDA Scholar Program: Full tuition, room and board.

Requirements: Top applicants

McCabe Scholarship: The McCabe Scholarship covers the costs of tuition, fees, room and board (designated campus housing only), and $500 per semester for books.

Regents' Scholarship: Covers the costs of room and board in campus housing only.

N.B: This scholarships goes out by e-mail invitation only to students with good academic records.

Application Deadline: May 15

Application Link: https://www.langston.edu/langston-university-scholarships

5 Oklahoma City University

Location: Oklahoma City, Oklahoma
Setting: Urban (104 Acres)
Undergraduate Enrollment: 1,361
Type: Private

Clara Luper Scholarship: Block tuition, standard room & board, and membership in the prestigious President's Leadership Class.

Requirements: Top Applicants | High school GPA of 3.0 or higher.

American Indian Scholarship: Block tuition, standard room & board, and membership in the prestigious President's Leadership Class.

Requirements: Top applicants | High school GPA of 3.0 or higher.

The Mary Ellen & George R. Randall Endowed Great Plan Scholarship for Pre-Med and Science: Full tuition, basic room & board, and fees.

This scholarship is awarded to a graduating high school senior who plans to study pre-medicine at OCU.

Criteria: Study pre-medicine or science.

Application Deadline: February 1

Application Link: https://www.okcu.edu/financialaid/types-of-assistance/scholarships/freshmen

1 University of Oregon

Location: Eugene, Oregon
Setting: City (295 Acres)
Undergraduate Enrollment: 19,565
Type: Public

Stamps Scholarships

Oregon resident Stamps Scholars receive UO resident tuition, fees, room, and board for four years of undergraduate study. *Out-of-state* recipients receive non-resident tuition and fees. All recipients benefit from up to $12,000 in enrichment funds to be used over four years to help pursue study abroad, unpaid internships, or other experiences.

Requirements: A minimum 3.85 cumulative high school grade point average on a 4.0 scale | A minimum 1300 SAT or 28 ACT (no test scores required for Fall 2021 Applicant)

Application Deadline: November 16

Application Link: https://financialaid.uoregon.edu/stamps_scholarship

1 Saint Vincent College

Location: Latrobe, Pennsylvania
Setting: Suburban (200 Acres)
Undergraduate Enrollment: 1,375
Type: Private

Wimmer Scholarship Competition: Awards Full tuition, room and board.

Requirements: A minimum cumulative high school GPA of 3.75 | SAT (ERW and Math) score of 1300 or above, a minimum ACT score of 28 or a CLT of 86.

Application Deadline: March 1

Application Link:
https://www.stvincent.edu/admission-aid/undergraduate-students.html

2 Elizabethtown College

Location: Elizabethtown, Pennsylvania
Setting: Suburban (203 Acres)
Undergraduate Enrollment: 1,737
Type: Private

Stamps Scholarship: Award covers full tuition as well as an enrichment fund which is funded by the Strive Foundation and Elizabethtown College.

Requirements: Top students.

Application Deadline: January 15

Application Link:
https://www.etown.edu/admissions/financial-aid/index.aspx

3 Temple University

Location: Philadelphia, Pennsylvania
Setting: Urban (406 Acres)
Undergraduate Enrollment: 24,106
Type: Public

Athletic Scholarships: Awards Full and partial tuition scholarships plus room and board and book allowances.

Eligibility: Participants in all varsity sports will be considered for scholarships.

P.S: Army ROTC and Air Force ROTC Scholarships are also available.

Application Deadline: February 1

Application Link:
https://sfs.temple.edu/financial-aid-types/scholarships/scholarship-opportunities-temple/new-incoming-students

4 Susquehanna University

Location: Selinsgrove, Pennsylvania
Setting: Rural (325 Acres)
Undergraduate Enrollment: 2,199
Type: Private

Reserve Officers' Training Corps (ROTC): Awards Full tuition, room (double only) and board.

Eligibility: Cadets of the Bison Battalion Army ROTC

Application Deadline: December 1

Application Link:
https://www.susqu.edu/admission-and-aid/tuition-and-financial-aid/financial-aid-options/scholarships/

5 Villanova University

Location: Villanova, Pennsylvania
Setting: Suburban (260 Acres)
Undergraduate Enrollment: 6,989
Type: Private

Presidential Scholarship: Full tuition, room, board (up to 21 meals per week plan), general fee, and the cost of textbooks for eight consecutive semesters.

Criteria: In order to be considered for the Presidential scholarship, students must first be nominated by the chief academic officer of their high school (principal, president, headmaster), secondary school counselor, or an official school designee.

St. Martin de Porres Scholarship: Full tuition and general fees.

Eligibility: U.S. citizens or permanent residents from one or more of the most underrepresented groups at the Villanova University.

Anthony Randazzo Endowed Presidential Scholarship: Full tuition, room, board (up to 21 meals per week plan), general fee, and the cost of textbooks for eight consecutive semesters.

Eligibility: Awarded to a first year African American/Black student | Applicant must reside in the city of Philadelphia, Pennsylvania.

Application Deadline: January 2

Application Link:
https://www1.villanova.edu/university/undergraduate-admission/Financial-Assistance-and-scholarship/merit-based-scholarships.html

6 University of Pittsburgh

Location: Pittsburgh, Pennsylvania
Setting: City (146 Acres)
Undergraduate Enrollment: 19,928
Type: Public

Chancellor's Scholarship: Awards Full tuition, mandatory fees, average room and board plan, Guaranteed Pitt Honors housing.

Eligibility: Applicant must be a U.S. Citizen or Permanent resident.

Requirements: Top scholar in applicants pool.

Stamps Scholarship: Awards Full tuition, mandatory fees, room and board plus an allowance for books and supplies, transportation expenses, and personal costs, Access to an enrichment fund of up to $17,400 to be used over four years for the purpose of global experiences, unpaid internships, leadership training, research, and other academic experiences.

Eligibility: ***Pennsylvania residency*** | Applicant must be a U.S. Citizen or Permanent resident.

Application Deadline: December 1

Application Link:
https://financialaid.pitt.edu/types-of-aid/scholarships/

7 Lincoln University

Location: Oxford, Pennsylvania
Setting: Rural (422 Acres)
Undergraduate Enrollment: 1,712
Type: Public

President's Award: Awards Full tuition & General fees.

Eligibility: International Student's | Minimum GPA: 3.30 cumulative | Minimum Test Score: 1020 SAT / 20 ACT (composite)

Application Deadline: February 1

Application Link: https://www.lincoln.edu/admissions/office-undergraduate-admissions/scholarships

9 Albright College

Location: Reading, Pennsylvania
Setting: Suburban (118 Acres)
Undergraduate Enrollment: 1,298
Type: Private

Warren L. Davis Scholarship: Awards Full tuition, room and board.

Requirements: Top applicants.

P.S: Students who are invited to apply must submit a prompted essay as well as a character recommendation

Application Deadline: December 15

Application Link: https://www.albright.edu/admission-aid/scholarships/

8 Waynesburg University

Location: Waynesburg, Pennsylvania
Setting: Rural (30 Acres)
Undergraduate Enrollment: 1,116
Type: Private

Founders Scholarship: A full tuition and fees scholarship for Pennsylvania residents.

Requirements: Resident of the state of Pennsylvania | High school cumulative GPA of a 3.5 or higher | SAT of 1200 or higher on Evidence-Based Reading & Writing and Math or ACT composite score of 26 or higher.

Application Deadline: January 8

Application Link: https://www.waynesburg.edu/admissions/scholarships-and-awards

1 Providence College

Location: Providence, Rhode Island
Setting: City (105 Acres)
Undergraduate Enrollment: 4,279
Type: Private

Roddy Scholarship: Awards Full tuition, fees, room and board.

Requirements: Applicants must aspire to a career in the medical profession | Consideration is based on outstanding academic achievement in high school | Awarded to first-year students who reside in the United States.

Application Deadline: November 1

Application Link: https://financial-aid.providence.edu/types-of-assistance/institutional-merit-based/

2 University of Rhode Island

Location: South Kingstown, Rhode Island
Settting: Rural (1,245 Acres)
Undergraduate Enrollment: 13,927
Type: Public

Thomas M. Ryan Scholars Program: Awards Full tuition, fees, housing, dining, books, and one Global winter travel J term experience with faculty.

Requirements: Top Applicants.

Alfred J. Verrecchia Business Scholars Program: Awards Full tuition, fees, housing, dining, books, and one Global winter travel J term experience with faculty.

Requirements: Awarded to selected students interested in majoring in Business.

Application Deadline: June 26

Application Link: https://web.uri.edu/admission/scholarships/

1 Allen University

Location: Columbia, South Carolina
Setting: City (150 Acres)
Undergraduate Enrollment: 656
Type: Private

Presidential Scholarship: Awards full tuition, room, board, and fees.

Requirements: A minimum GPA of 3.40 | A minimum 1200 SAT or 25 ACT score.

Application Deadline: June 15

Application Link:
https://allenuniversity.edu/grants-and-scholarships

2 Limestone University

Location: Gaffney, South Carolina
Setting: Suburban (125 Acres)
Undergraduate Enrollment: 1,602
Type: Private

Presidential Palmetto Scholarship: Award covers Full tuition, fees, room & board.

Requirements: Applicant must be a SC Palmetto Fellows recipient.

Application Deadline: November 15

Application Link:
https://www.limestone.edu/financial-aid/scholarships-and-grants

3 Francis Marion University

Location: Florence, South Carolina
Setting: Rural (832 Acres)
Undergraduate Enrollment: 3,635
Type: Public

Robert E. McNair Scholarship: Awards Full tuition, housing, and a meal plan. It also offers funding for a study abroad experience.

Requirements: Top scholars in applicants' pool.

Application Deadline: December 1

Application Link:
https://www.fmarion.edu/financialassistance/scholarships/

4 South Carolina State University

Location: Orangeburg, South Carolina
Setting: City (160 Acres)
Undergraduate Enrollment: 2,374
Type: Public

Presidential Scholarship: Award covers full tuition, room & board.

Requirements: A minimum GPA of 3.50 | Achieve at least 1200 (CR+M) on the SAT 1 test or 27 on the ACT test.

Application Deadline: This scholarship is awarded based on availability of funds.

Application Link:
https://www.scstategives.com/scholarships-and-funds/

5 Clemson University

Location: Clemson, South Carolina
Setting: Rural (17,000 Acres)
Undergraduate Enrollment: 22,566
Type: Public

National Scholars Program: Full tuition, fees, room & board, and other expenses.

Criteria: Selection is based on a review of top applications to the Clemson University Honors College and a rigorous interview process.

Application Deadline: December 15

Application Link:
https://www.clemson.edu/financial-aid/types-of-aid/clemson-scholarships/index.html

6 University of South Carolina

Location: Columbia, South Carolina
Setting: City (444 Acres)
Undergraduate Enrollment: 27,343
Type: Public

Gamecock Guarantee: Award covers full cost of tuition and technology fees.

Eligibility: Applicant must be a South Carolina resident and come from a **low-income** family.

Application Deadline: December 1

Application Link:
https://www.sc.edu/about/offices_and_divisions/undergraduate_admissions/tuition_scholarships/guarantee/index.php

7 College of Charleston

Location: Charleston, South Carolina
Setting: Urban (95 Acres)
Undergraduate Enrollment: 9,972
Type: Public

There are lot's of scholarship opportunities available for undergraduate study at the College of Charleston,

P.S: The value for most of the scholarships weren't attached.

Application Link:
https://admissions.cofc.edu/applyingtothecollege/international-students/tuition.php

8 Erskine College

Location: Due West, South Carolina
Setting: Rural (90 Acres)
Undergraduate Enrollment: 817
Type: Private

Presidential Scholarship: Awards Full tuition, required fees, room and board.

Requirements: Top applicants.

Application Deadline: October 15

Application Link:
https://www.erskine.edu/admissions-aid/financial-aid/scholarships/

9 North Greenville University

Location: Tigerville, South Carolina
Setting: Rural (330 Acres)
Undergraduate Enrollment: 1,839
Type: Private

The Lifeshape Scholarship: Award covers Full tuition, room & board, books/materials (through Slingshot), and required fees.

Requirements: A minimum 3.75 unweighted GPA | 1320 SAT or 28 ACT or 88 CLT

NGU Fellows Scholarship: Awards Full tuition, room & board (*to South Carolina residents)*

Eligibility: South Carolina residents who meet the requirements for the Palmetto Fellows Scholarship will be considered for the NGU Fellows Scholarship.

Application Deadline: October 15

Application Link: https://ngu.edu/admissions/financial-aid/undergraduate/

10 Wofford College

Location: Spartanburg, South Carolina
Setting: Urban (170 Acres)
Undergraduate Enrollment: 1,823
Type: Private

Richardson Family Scholarship: Award covers Full tuition, fees, room & board, a monthly stipend for books and miscellaneous expenses, A laptop computer for entering first-year students, Summer internships, with one involving opportunity for overseas travel, A January travel experience.

Criteria for selection: Applicants must be nominated as a Wofford Scholar by their high school guidance counsellors | Moral force of character | Strong family commitment | Instincts to lead | Scholarly accomplishments and lots more.

Bonner Scholars Program: Bonner Scholars receive substantial grant and scholarship assistance to meet their ***financial need in full***.

Requirements: Top Applicants

Check the website for more details...

Army ROTC Scholarship: Awards full tuition and fees. In addition to the awarded scholarship, each winner receives a flat rate of $1,200 annually for books and supplies, as well as a tax-free monthly stipend.

Requirements: Top applicants | Applicant must be a U.S citizen.

Application Deadline: November 15

Application Link: https://www.wofford.edu/admission/scholarships

11 Presbyterian College

Location: Clinton, South Carolina
Setting: Rural (240 Acres)
Undergraduate Enrollment: 955
Type: Private

Griffith Scholarship: Awards Full tuition, fees, room and board for four years.

Requirements: Top students in applicants pool.

ROTC Scholarships

U.S Army ROTC: Awards Full tuition and fees, $1,200 annually for books, and a monthly stipend for contracted cadets. Presbyterian College may pay room and board for these scholarship recipients.

Requirements: Applicant must be a U.S. citizen | Be between the ages of 17 and 26 | Have a high school GPA of at least 2.50 | Have a high school diploma or equivalent | Score a minimum of 920 on the SAT (math/verbal) or 19 on the ACT (excluding the required writing test scores)

P.S: Applicants must meet physical standards.

Check the website for more details...

Application Deadline: December 1

Application Link:
https://www.presby.edu/admissions/tuition-aid/scholarships/

12 The Citadel – Military College of South Carolina

Location: Charleston, South Carolina
Setting: Urban (300 Acres)
Undergraduate Enrollment: 2,695
Type: Military

Full Academic Scholarships: Award covers full tuition, room & board plus quartermaster charges.

Requirements: Top Applicants

ROTC Scholarships are also available, check site for more details...

Application Deadline: October 1

Application Link:
https://www.citadel.edu/financial-aid/scholarships/cadet-scholarships/

13 Furman University

Location: Greenville, South Carolina
Setting: Suburban (800 Acres)
Undergraduate Enrollment: 2,283
Type: Private

James B. Duke Scholarships: Award covers full tuition, room & board and all fees for four years.

Requirements: Top scholars in applicants' pool.

James A. Vaughn Scholarships: Award covers full tuition, room & board and all fees for four years.

Eligibility: Scholarships will be awarded to ***new incoming Black or African-American students*** who currently reside in the state of South Carolina and have demonstrated outstanding academic achievement and a strong commitment to their communities.

ROTC Scholarships: Awards up to full tuition and fees, plus a monthly stipend during the academic year.

Requirements: Top Applicants

Application Deadline: April 15

Application Link:
https://www.furman.edu/financial-aid/aid-types/merit-based-scholarships/

14 Claflin University

Location: Orangeburg, South Carolina
Setting: City (46 Acres)
Undergraduate Enrollment: 1,749
Type: Private

Claflin Presidential Scholars Program: Awards Full tuition, room, board, textbooks and a monthly stipend.

Requirements: A minimum SAT score of 1200 or ACT equivalent score of 27.

Claflin Honors College Scholarship: Award value ranges from $2,000 to the full cost of tuition, room and board.

Requirements: A minimum SAT score of 1100 or ACT equivalent score of 24.

Application Deadline: July 31

Application Link:
https://www.claflin.edu/admissions-aid/financial-aid/scholarships-and-grants

1

University of South Dakota

Location: Vermillion, South Dakota
Setting: Rural (274 Acres)
Undergraduate Enrollment: 7,132
Type: Public

Academic Achievement Scholarships:

Mickelson Scholarships: Award covers full tuition, general fees, double occupancy room and board.

Requirements: Scholarship recipients must be residents of South Dakota | A minimum ACT score of 28 (1320 SAT)

George S. Mickelson Scholarship: Awards Full tuition, general fees, double occupancy room (funded by a Housing Scholarship) and standard board charges for four years.

Requirements: Scholarship recipients must be residents of South Dakota | A minimum ACT score of 28 (1320 SAT)

Field of Study Scholarships:

Dorothy C. Schieffer Political Science Scholarship: Awards full tuition, fees, books, room and board. At least one international travel or study abroad experience and a working internship or service opportunity may be included after consultation with faculty advisor and non-faculty mentor.

Criteria: Awarded to full-time students who major or minor in political science.

Nolop Institute Scholarship for Medical Biology: Awards in-state tuition, fees, room, board and books for up to four years of full-time study.

Eligibility: This scholarship is awarded to a talented and ambitious student majoring in medical biology who wishes to participate in meaningful research with plans to attend medical school.

Reserve Officers Training Corp (ROTC): Awards full tuition, money for books and a non-taxed monthly stipend.

Application Deadline: November 15

Application Link:
https://www.usd.edu/Admissions-and-Aid/Financial-Aid/Types-of-Aid/Scholarships

1 Vanderbilt University

Location: Nashville, Tennessee
Setting: Urban (333 Acres)
Undergraduate Enrollment: 7,151
Type: Private

Chancellor's Scholars: Full tuition, plus a one-time summer stipend for an immersive experience following the sophomore or junior year.

Cornelius Vanderbilt Scholarship: Full tuition, plus a one-time summer stipend for an immersive experience following the sophomore or junior year.

Ingram Scholars Program: Full tuition, plus a stipend for a special summer service project.

Requirements: Top students from applicants pool.

Application Deadline: December 1

Application Link: https://www.vanderbilt.edu/scholarships/

2 Union University

Location: Jackson, Tennessee
Setting: Suburban (360 Acres)
Undergraduate Enrollment: 1,899
Type: Private

Founders Scholarship: Awards full tuition, room & board, meals and student services fees for credit hours taken during Fall and Spring terms for a maximum of eight undergraduate semesters.

Scholars of Excellence Awards: All applicants who meet the requirements for Scholars of Excellence and participate in the on-campus competition weekend will be awarded a Scholars of Excellence Award that may be combined with all other institutional aid.

P.S: No student will be awarded beyond the cost of attendance through a combination of institutional and non-institutional source.

Requirements: 29 ACT minimum score or a minimum SAT score of 1330 | 3.5 minimum high school GPA.

ROTC Programs

Army ROTC scholarship: Awards full tuition, $1,200 annually for books, supplies and equipment, as well as $420/month tax-free stipend.

Requirements: U.S. citizen | GPA of 2.5 or better.

Application Deadline: January 5

Application Link: https://www.uu.edu/financialaid/scholarships/

3 Bryan College

Location: Dayton, Tennessee
Setting: Rural (128 Acres)
Undergraduate Enrollment: 1,376
Type: Private

Bryan Opportunity Scholarship Program: Award covers Full tuition, room & board.

Requirements: A minimum cumulative high school GPA of 3.75 and ACT 29 or SAT 1330.

Application Deadline: December 15

Application Link:
https://www.bryan.edu/scholarship/bryan-opportunity-scholarship-program/

4 The University of the South

Location: Sewanee, Tennessee
Setting: Rural (13,000 Acres)
Undergraduate Enrollment: 1,613
Type: Private

Vice-Chancellor's Scholarship: Awards Full tuition, fees, room and board annually.

Benedict Scholarship: Awards Full tuition, fees, room and board annually.

Requirements: Top scholars from applicants pool.

Application Deadline: January 15

Application Link:
https://new.sewanee.edu/admission-aid/cost-financial-aid/scholarships/

5 Belmont University

Location: Nashville, Tennessee
Setting: City (93 Acres)
Undergraduate Enrollment: 7,376
Type: Private

Archer Presidential Scholarship: Awards Full tuition, fees, books, room & board for four academic years.

Requirements: Top Applicants.

William Randolph Hearst Endowed Scholarship: Awards Full tuition, fees, books, room & board.

Eligibility: A freshman student from a diverse background.

Requirements: Top Applicants.

Application Deadline: December 1

Application Link:
https://www.belmont.edu/sfs/scholarships/

6 Middle Tennessee State University

Location: Murfreesboro, Tennessee
Setting: City (550 Acres)
Undergraduate Enrollment: 17,438
Type: Public

The ROTC Opportunity: Awards Full tuition, fees, $1200 per year for books, monthly stipend for every month school is in session up to $5,000 per year, Eligibility for room and board scholarship for up to $4,000 dollars a year.

Eligibility: Applicant must be a U.S. citizen | Be between the ages of 17 and 26.

Requirements: A minimum high school GPA of 2.50 | Have a high school diploma or equivalent | Meet physical standards and be medically qualified.

Application Deadline: October 1

Application Link:
https://www.mtsu.edu/arotc1/scholarships/index.php

1 Baylor University

Location: Waco, Texas
Setting: City (1,000 Acres)
Undergraduate Enrollment: 15,213
Type: Private

Getterman Scholars Program: Awards Full tuition, fees, room & board, along with support for study abroad, research and mission/service experiences.

Requirements: Top students from applicants pool.

Application Deadline: November 1

Application Link:
https://admissions.web.baylor.edu/costs-aid/freshman-scholarship-programs

2 University of Texas at Austin

Location: Austin, Texas
Setting: Urban (431 Acres)
Undergraduate Enrollment: 41,309
Type: Public

Forty Acres Scholars Program: A full ride scholarship that covers the total cost of attendance.

Requirements: Applicant must be a U.S citizen or permanent U.S. resident at the time of application.

Application Deadline: November 1

Application Link:
https://www.texasexes.org/scholarships

3 University of Texas at Arlington

Location: Arlington, Texas
Setting: Urban (420 Acres)
Undergraduate Enrollment: 30,791
Type: Public

National Merit: Award covers Full tuition, fees, on-campus housing, and includes a stipend for books, supplies, and other educational expenses for fall and spring semesters.

Requirements: National Merit recipient.

Application Deadline: February 14

Application Link:
https://www.uta.edu/administration/fao/scholarships

4 Southern Methodist University

Location: Dallas, Texas
Setting: Urban (234 Acres)
Undergraduate Enrollment: 7,056
Type: Private

President's Scholars Program: Awards full tuition and fees plus study abroad stipend. Students who live on campus also receive a scholarship for room and board.

Requirements: Top applicants.

Application Deadline: November 1

Application Link:
https://www.smu.edu/EnrollmentServices/financialaid/TypesOfAid/Scholarships

5 University of Houston

Location: Houston, Texas
Setting: Urban (895 Acres)
Undergraduate Enrollment: 37,943
Type: Public

Tier One Scholars: Award covers full tuition and mandatory fees, on-campus housing and meal plan for the first two years, $1,000 stipend to support undergraduate research, $2,000 stipend to support learning abroad and lot's more.

Requirements: Top applicants.

National Merit Scholarship Finalist: Full tuition and required fees, plus a one-time $1,000 undergraduate research stipend and a one-time $2,000 study abroad stipend.

Eligibility: Awarded to National Merit Scholarship finalists who select the University of Houston as their first-choice institution.

Terry Foundation Scholarship: Awards up to a Full-ride scholarship to ***Texas high school seniors.***

Eligibility: Applicants must demonstrate financial need, a record of leadership, and strong academic abilities.

Learn more: https://terryfoundation.org/

Application Deadline: November 8

Application Link:
https://uh.edu/financial/undergraduate/types-aid/scholarships/

6 University of Texas in Dallas

Location: Richardson, Texas
Setting: Suburban (500 Acres)
Undergraduate Enrollment: 21,617
Type: Public

Academic Excellence Scholarship Program: Full ride scholarship.

Eugene McDermott Scholars Program: Awards full scholarship plus a stipend package.

Terry Foundation Scholarship: A full ride scholarship that covers the total cost of undergraduate studies.

Requirements: Top applicants.

Application Deadline: December 1

National Merit Scholars Program: Award covers full tuition and mandatory fees, $4,000 per semester cash stipend to defray the costs of books, supplies and other expenses, $1,500 per semester on-campus housing stipend, one-time study abroad stipend up to $6,000 to support an international education experience.

Requirements: Applicant must be named a National Merit Finalist by the National Merit scholarship Corporation | List UT Dallas as their first-choice school through the National Merit Scholarship Corporation online portal.

Application Deadline: July 31

Application Link:
https://finaid.utdallas.edu/scholarships/

7 Prairie View A&M University

Location: Prairie View, Texas
Setting: Rural (1,502 Acres)
Undergraduate Enrollment: 8,372
Type: Public

TieRegent's Student Merit Scholarship: The Regent's scholarship covers up to $10,000 per academic year for tuition and mandatory fees. Each Regent Scholar will receive additional Scholarship funding to meet the cost for up to 18 credit hours, on campus housing, meals and books ($600 per semester).

Requirements: Applicant must have graduated from a high school within 12 months of enrolling at Prairie View A&M University | A minimum 3.50 cumulative high school GPA | A minimum SAT score of 1260 or ACT composite score of 26.

Application Deadline: December 1

Application Link:
https://www.pvamu.edu/oss/types-of-scholarships/

8 Texas Woman's University

Location: Denton, Texas
Setting: City (270 Acres)
Undergraduate Enrollment: 10,150
Type: Public

Terry Foundation Scholarship: Full tuition, fees, room and board on campus, books, and supplies.

Requirements: Applicant must be a U.S. Citizen or permanent resident and demonstrate financial need | 3.0 minimum high school GPA | Will graduate from a Texas high school or home-school program in Texas.

Chancellor's Endowed Scholarship: Full tuition, mandatory fees, and a book stipend for up to four years.

Requirements: Top scholars from applicants pool.

TWU Presidential Scholarship: Full tuition and mandatory fees for up to four years.

Eligibility: Awarded to freshmen who are Valedictorian or Salutatorian of an accredited high school class.

Application Deadline: March 15

Application Link:
https://catalog.twu.edu/undergraduate/financial-aid/scholarships/

9 Texas State University

Location: San Marcos, Texas
Setting: Suburban (507 Acres)
Undergraduate Enrollment: 33,834
Type: Public

Terry Foundation Scholarship: Awards Full academic scholarship up to the total cost of attendance.

Requirements: Top applicants | Applicant must be a U.S. Citizen or permanent resident and demonstrate financial need | Will graduate from a Texas high school or home-school program in Texas.

Application Deadline: December 15

Application Link:
https://www.finaid.txst.edu/scholarships/freshman.html

10 University of Texas at Tyler

Location: Tyler, Texas
Setting: City (320 Acres)
Undergraduate Enrollment: 6,971
Type: Public

Patriot Promise: Full tuition and mandatory fees.

Criteria: Applicant must be a Texas resident with a household adjusted gross income of not more than $80,000 | Graduate from a Texas high school and enroll at The University of Texas at Tyler within seven months of graduation, or transfer directly from another college.

Valedictorian Scholarship: Full tuition, fees, books, room & board.

Criteria: Applicant must be Valedictorian from high school residing in Smith County, or the cities of Palestine or Longview.

Salutatorian Scholarship: Full tuition & fees.

Criteria: Applicant must be Salutatorian from high school residing in Smith County, or the cities of Palestine or Longview.

Need Based Scholarship: Full tuition and Mandatory fees.

Criteria: Applicant must be a dependent member of a household whose parent's adjusted gross income is $80,000 or lower.

Application Deadline: May 1

Application Link:
https://www.uttyler.edu/scholarships/freshman-23-24/

11

Texas Christian University

Location: Fort Worth, Texas
Setting: Suburban (307 Acres)
Undergraduate Enrollment: 10,523
Type: Private

Chancellor's Scholarship: Full tuition & fees.

Requirements: Top students from applicants pool.

NAACP Scholarship: Full tuition and fees for up to four years.

Eligibility: Applicant must be planning to pursue a degree in education and make a 3 year commitment to teach in the FWISD.

John V. Roach Family Endowement: Provides full room, board and books for top students in the class who have been offered full tuition from another academic scholarship.

Trustee Scholarship: Combines with other academic awards to provide a full scholarship covering room, board and books.

Check the website for more details and a list of other scholarship awards.

Application Deadline: Applicant's are highly encouraged to apply Early Action.

Application Link: https://admissions.tcu.edu/afford/scholarship-aid/index.php

1

University of Utah

Location: Salt Lake City, Utah
Setting: Urban (1,534 Acres)
Undergraduate Enrollment: 26,355
Type: Public

FOR UTAH Scholarship Program: Awards Full tuition and fees to Utah residents who are eligible for the Pell Grant.

Eligibility: Utah residents | High school average GPA of at least 3.2

Application Deadline: February 1

Application Link: https://financialaid.utah.edu/types-of-aid/scholarships/freshman/index.php

1

University of Vermont

Location: Burlington, Vermont
Setting: Suburban (460 Acres)
Undergraduate Enrollment: 11,898
Type: Public

Army ROTC Scholarships: Award covers full tuition and fees.

Air Force ROTC Scholarships: Award covers full tuition and fees.

Eligibility: Applicant must be a U.S. citizen | Eligibility determined by ROTC.

Application Deadline: January 10

Application Link:
https://www.uvm.edu/studentfinancialservices/prospective_undergraduate_student_scholarships_requiring_separate

1 Virginia Military Institute

Location: Lexington City, Virginia
Setting: City (200 Acres)
Undergraduate Enrollment: 1,512
Type: Military

Peay Merit Scholarships: Awards full tuition, fees, room and board.

Requirements: A minimum High school GPA of 3.75

Application Deadline: February 1

Application Link:
https://www.vmi.edu/about/offices-a-z/financial-aid/types-of-aid/

3 Virginia Commonwealth University

Location: Richmond, Virginia
Setting: Urban (198 Acres)
Undergraduate Enrollment: 20,958
Type: Public

Presidential Scholarship: Award covers Full tuition, fees, room and board.

Requirements: An average GPA of 4.59 | Average SAT score of 1513.

Application Deadline: November 1

Application Link:
https://admissions.vcu.edu/cost-aid/scholarships-funding/

2 Washington and Lee University

Location: Lexington City, Virginia
Setting: City (430 Acres)
Undergraduate Enrollment: 1,867
Type: Private

The Johnson Scholarship: Award covers Full tuition, room & board. Johnson Scholars receive funding up to $7,000 to support summer experiences during their time at W&L.

P.S: Students with financial need higher than this amount will have any additional need met by the scholarship.

Requirements: Top applicants.

Regional Scholarships

Darnall W. Boyd Jr. Memorial Honor Scholarship: Awards Full tuition, room and board.

P.S: This scholarship was established for entering first-year students from *South Carolina*, with a preference for students from the *Columbia area*.

Requirements: Top applicants.

Application Deadline: December 1

Application Link:
https://www.wlu.edu/admissions/financial-aid/

4 Hampden-Sydney College

Location: Hampden Sydney, Virginia
Setting: Rural (1,343 Acres)
Undergraduate Enrollment: 835
Type: Private

Madison Scholarship: Award covers Full tuition, fees, room (double occupancy) & board for four years. Plus a stipend for books and a tablet, and funding for either a summer internship, or a study abroad opportunity.

Requirements: A minimum high school GPA of 4.0 | Reading and Mathematics SAT score of 1450+, or an ACT composite score of 32+ | Class rank in the top 5% (if reported)

Application Deadline: January 15

Application Link: https://www.hsc.edu/admission-and-financial-aid/financial-aid/types-of-aid/academic-and-leadership-awards

5 Hollins University

Location: Roanoke, Virginia
Setting: Suburban (475 Acres)
Undergraduate Enrollment: 691
Type: Private

Artemis Scholarship for Women in STEM: Award covers Full tuition, room and board, and other additional benefits.

Requirements: Top applicants.

Eligibility: Applicants must be full-time students who intends to major in biology, chemistry, environmental science, or mathematics | Be a United States citizen, permanent resident, national, or lawfully admitted refugee | Demonstrate financial need through the FAFSA application | Demonstrate academic motivation and a strong interest in STEM through the Artemis application.

Application Deadline: January 1

Application Link: https://www.hollins.edu/admission-aid/undergraduate-financial-aid-scholarships/

6 Virginia Technology University

Location: Blacksburg, Virginia
Setting: Rural (2,600 Acres)
Undergraduate Enrollment: 30,434
Type: Public

Presidential Scholarship Program: Award covers Full tuition, fees, room and board, a structured, well established academic support and enrichment, plus a lot of other benefits.

Eligibility: Applicant must be a ***Virginia resident*** | Graduate from a ***Virginia high school*** | Be Pell grant eligible with significant financial need | Demonstrate potential for stellar academic performance | Show evidence of leadership potential.

Learn more: https://finaid.vt.edu/undergraduate/typesofaid/scholarships/presidential-scholarship-programs.htmlRequirements: Top Students.

Stamps Scholars: Award covers Full tuition, fees, room and board.

Eligibility: Stamps Scholars.

Military Scholarships

Army ROTC: Award covers Full tuition, mandatory fees, $1,200 per year for textbooks, supplies and equipment; and a monthly stipend of $420 per month depending on the student's academic year.

Eligibility: Applicant must be a U.S. citizen, and both medically and physically qualified to be eligible.

Air Force (AFROTC) and Naval ROTC scholarships are also available.

Application Deadline: January 15

Application Link: https://finaid.vt.edu/undergraduate/typesofaid/scholarships/military-scholarships.html

7 Virginia State University

Location: Petersburg, Virginia
Setting: Suburban (231 Acres)
Undergraduate Enrollment: 4,242
Type: Public

The Four-Year Army ROTC Scholarship Program: Award covers full tuition and fees or Housing and Living Allowance, a $1,200 yearly book allowance, ROTC stipends of $420 a month.

Criteria: Applicant must be 17 years before scholarship is effective | A minimum 1,000 SAT score or ACT composite score of 19 | A minimum high school GPA of 2.5 or higher.

Requirements: Top applicants.

Application Deadline: December 15

Application Link: https://www.vsu.edu/sola/departments/military-science/benefits.php

8 College of William & Mary

Location: Williamsburg, Virginia
Setting: Suburban (1,200 Acres)
Undergraduate Enrollment: 6,797
Type: Public

1693 Scholars Program: Award covers the cost of in-state tuition, general fees, room and board plus a $5,000 stipend to support independent projects.

Requirements: Applicant must rank in the top 1% of their graduating high school class | 33+ ACT or 1500+ SAT (Test Optional).

William & Mary Scholars: Awards are worth the amount of in-state tuition and fees.

Application Deadline: April 1

Application Link: https://www.wm.edu/admission/undergraduateadmission/costs-aid/scholarship/

9 University of Richmond

Location: Richmond, Virginia
Setting: Suburban (350 Acres)
Undergraduate Enrollment: 3,145
Type: Private

Richmond Scholars Program: Full tuition, room and board (in addition to other program benefits)

Requirements: Top applicants.

Richmond's Promise to Virginia: Awards full tuition, room, and the Spider Unlimited meal plan for **Virginia resident's.**

Eligibility: U.S. citizens or U.S. permanent residents | Qualify for need-based financial aid.

Application Deadline: December 1

Army ROTC scholarships are also available for interested applicants.

Application Link: https://financialaid.richmond.edu/types-of-aid/merit-based/scholarships.html

10 University of Virginia

Location: Charlottesville, Virginia
Setting: Suburban (1,682 Acres)
Undergraduate Enrollment: 17,496
Type: Public

Jefferson Scholarship: Awards full tuition, room and board plus a funding for research, summer experiences, study abroad, etc. There are also extensive enrichment and programming opportunities for Jefferson Scholars.

Criteria: The Jefferson Scholarship is awarded through the Jefferson Scholars Foundation | Top applicants.

UVA Questbridge Scholarship: A full ride scholarship.

Requirements: Applicant must demonstrate financial need and have satisfactory academic performance.

Application Deadline: November 1

Application Link:
https://www.jeffersonscholars.org/

11 Hampton University

Location: Hampton, Virginia
Setting: Urban (314 Acres)
Undergraduate Enrollment: 2,794
Type: Private

Reserve Officer's Training Corps (ROTC):

Army ROTC Scholarship: Awards full tuition and mandatory fees plus a monthly stipend. Also Cadets receive $1,200 annually for textbooks.

Navy ROTC Scholarship: Awards full tuition and mandatory fees. Also Navy cadets will receive a $400 monthly stipend as well as funding for textbooks.

Hampton University awards merit based scholarships that range from $5,000 - $25,000 per academic year. These generous award amounts are designed to provide many awards to a vast number of students, as opposed to awarding a few large amounts to a smaller population. Hence, the University no longer has scholarships that are named Trustee, Presidential, Legacy, etc.

Application Deadline: November 1

Application Link:
https://home.hamptonu.edu/admissions/

1 Pacific Lutheran University

Location: Tacoma, Washington
Setting: Suburban (156 Acres)
Undergraduate Enrollment: 2,301
Type: Private

Army ROTC Scholarship: Awards full tuition, on campus room/meals.

Requirements: Top scholars.

P.S: Applicants must file FAFSA for on-campus living costs to be covered.

Application Deadline: October 15

Application Link:
https://www.plu.edu/student-financial-services/types-of-aid/scholarships-and-grants/

3 University of Puget Sound

Location: Tacoma, Washington
Setting: City (97 Acres)
Undergraduate Enrollment: 1,712
Type: Private

Matelich Scholarship: Awards Full tuition and fees, (standard double room, standard medium meal plan, and student government fee) for up to four years.

Requirements: Top scholars in applicants' pool.

Application Deadline: December 1

Application Link:
https://www.pugetsound.edu/admission/cost-aid/types-aid/scholarships-grants

2 George Washington University

Location: Washington, D.C
Setting: Urban (43 Acres)
Undergraduate Enrollment: 11,482
Type: Private

District Scholars: This scholarship makes it possible for the University to meet full demonstrated need for qualifying residents of the District of Columbia.

Eligibility: Applicant must be a resident of the District and qualify for the D.C. Tuition Assistance Grant | Have an annual family income as determined by George Washington that does not exceed $75,000.

Stephen Joel Trachtenberg Scholarship: Awards Full tuition, room and board, books and fees.

Eligibility: Applicant must be a *District of Columbia* resident | Attend a regionally accredited secondary school in the District of Columbia.

P.S: Students must apply to GW by January 5 and be nominated by their high school counsellor by January 11

Scholars are selected based on academic record, including GPA, course of study, teacher recommendations, leadership qualities, community service, and other extracurricular activities and achievements.

Application Deadline: January 5

Application Link:
https://undergraduate.admissions.gwu.edu/merit-scholarships

4 The Catholic University of America

Location: Washington, D.C
Setting: Urban (176 Acres)
Undergraduate Enrollment: 3,011
Type: Private

ROTC Scholarships: Students who earn Full tuition *ROTC Scholarships* from the Army, Navy, or Air Force will automatically be eligible for the ROTC Room and Board Matching Scholarship.

Requirements: Top Applicants

Application Deadline: March 30

Application Link:
https://www.catholic.edu/admission/undergraduate/first-year-students/scholarships/index.html

6 Gonzaga University

Location: Spokane, Washington
Setting: Urban (152 Acres)
Undergraduate Enrollment: 5,084
Type: Private

Army ROTC Scholarship: Awards Fully paid Dorm room, Fully paid Boarding (Meal Plan), $600 a semester for books, a $420 per month Monthly stipend (non-taxed), a $40 waiver of the university application fee, plus other benefits.

Requirements: Top students in applicants pool.

Application Deadline: December 15

Application Link:
https://www.gonzaga.edu/academics/undergraduate/military-science/scholarships

5 Seattle University

Location: Seattle, Washington
Setting: Urban (50 Acres)
Undergraduate Enrollment: 4,099
Type: Private

Sullivan Leadership Award: Awards Full tuition, room and board for four years.

Requirements: A minimum high school GPA of 3.7 | U.S. residents.

P.S: Consideration is reserved for first-year students living in and attending school in the United States.

Fostering Scholars: Award covers Full tuition, books, and other education related expenses, Waiver of all enrollment related fees, Student health insurance (if needed), Assistance finding on-campus employment opportunities, Assistance finding on-campus employment opportunities, plus other benefits.

Eligibility: Applicant must be a ***Washington State*** resident.

Requirements: Top applicants.

Application Deadline: March 1

Application Link:
https://www.seattleu.edu/undergraduate-admissions/finances/scholarships/firstyear/

7 American University

Location: Washington, D.C
Setting: Urban (90 Acres)
Undergraduate Enrollment: 7,917
Type: Private

American University District Scholars Award: Covers full tuition, room and board.

Requirements: Applicant must be a DC resident attending a DC Public or Public Charter High School | Top Applicants.

Frederick Douglass Distinguished Scholars Program: Full tuition, room and board, meal plan, books, mandatory fees and public transportation (U-Pass)

Requirements: A minimum 3.8 GPA (unweighted) or 4.0 GPA (weighted)

P.S: Submission of ACT or SAT scores are optional.

Application Deadline: December 15

Application Link:
https://www.american.edu/financialaid/freshman-scholarships.cfm

8 Howard University

Location: Washington, D.C
Setting: Urban (257 Acres)
Undergraduate Enrollment: 9,809
Type: Public

Howard University Freshman Scholarship: HU Presidential Scholarship | HU Founders Scholarship | HU Capstone Scholarship | HU Leadership Scholarship | HU Opportunity Grant

These scholarships can cover the cost of up to full tuition, fees, room, board and book voucher, etc.

Requirements: Top scholars in applicants' pool.

Application Deadline: March 27

Application Link:
https://admission.howard.edu/financialsupport

1 West Liberty University

Location: West Liberty, West Virginia
Setting: Rural (290 Acres)
Undergraduate Enrollment: 2,125
Type: Public

Full Ride Elbin Scholarship: Full tuition, mandatory fees, base room and board.

Requirements: Minimum high school GPA of 4.0 | 30 ACT or 1400 SAT.

Bessie Anderson College of Education Honors Scholarship: Covers the cost of tuition, fees, room and board.

Eligibility: West Virginia residents | Minimum high school GPA of 3.5

Application Deadline: April 15

Application Link:
https://westliberty.edu/financial-aid/west-liberty-university-scholarships/

2 Fairmont State University

Location: Fairmont, West Virginia
Setting: City (120 Acres)
Undergraduate Enrollment: 2,790
Type: Public

Charles J. McClain Presidential Scholarship: Awards Full tuition, fees, room and board for on-campus students, and a $500/per semester book scholarship for the on-campus Bound for Success Bookstore.

Eligibility: Applicant must be a ***West Virginia*** Student.

Requirements: A minimum cumulative high school GPA of 3.5 | Have ACT composite score of 26+ or 1190+ SAT (combined Critical Reading and Math scores) or 1260+ SAT total score.

Application Deadline: February 1

Application Link:
https://www.fairmontstate.edu/financial-aid/scholarships/charles-j-mcclain-presidential.aspx

3 West Virginia State University

Location: Institute, West Virginia
Setting: Suburban (100 Acres)
Undergraduate Enrollment: 3,634
Type: Public

Presidential Scholarship: Awards Full tuition, fees, room and board for four years.

Eligibility: Enrollment in an academic degree program in a Science, Technology, Engineering or Mathematics (STEM) or Healthcare Field.

Requirements: A minimum high school GPA of 3.5 (4.0 scale)

Application Deadline: March 31

Application Link:
https://www.wvstateu.edu/admissions/scholarships.aspx

4 University of Charleston

Location: Charleston, West Virginia
Setting: City
Undergraduate Enrollment: 2,115
Type: Private

Presidential Scholarship: Awards Full tuition, mandatory fees, room and board for four years. In addition to incredible financial support, the Presidential Scholarship also provides you with the opportunity to meet regularly with UC President Roth for mentoring and leadership skill development.

Requirements: A minimum high school GPA of 3.75 | A demonstrated record of leadership and citizenship | A desire to become a campus leader while serving the UC & Charleston communities.

Application Deadline: December 15

Application Link:
https://www.ucwv.edu/admissions/financial-aid/types-of-aid/scholarships/

1 St. Norbert College

Location: De Pere, Wisconsin
Setting: Suburban (116 Acres)
Undergraduate Enrollment: 1,814
Type: Private

Army ROTC Scholarship: Awards Full tuition, room and board plus additional allowances for books and fees.

Requirements: Top applicants.

Application Deadline: January 20

Application Link: https://www.snc.edu/affordability/apply-for-aid/incoming-students/scholarship-calculator.html

2 Mount Mary University

Location: Milwaukee, Wisconsin
Setting: Urban (80 Acres)
Undergraduate Enrollment: 716
Type: Private

Caroline Scholars Program: Awards Full tuition, room and board for four years.

Requirements: A minimum cumulative, unweighted High school GPA of 3.5

Check the website for more details...

Application Deadline: January 1

Application Link: https://mtmary.edu/costs-aid/scholarships/index.html

3 Milwaukee School of Engineering

Location: Milwaukee, Wisconsin
Setting: Urban (23 Acres)
Undergraduate Enrollment: 2,575
Type: Private

MSOE Presidential Scholarship: Awards Full tuition, room and board for four years.

Requirements: A minimum unweighted High school GPA of 3.5 on a (4.0 scale)

P.S: Currently, International Students are *not* eligible to receive the Presidential scholarship.

Application Deadline: October 25

Application Link: https://www.msoe.edu/admissions-aid/financial-aid-scholarships/scholarships-and-grants/

4 Carthage College

Location: Kenosha, Wisconsin
Setting: Suburban (80 Acres)
Undergraduate Enrollment: 2,559
Type: Private

There are competitive scholarships available for undergraduate studies at the Carthage College.

Applicant's can win scholarships ranging from 75 percent of tuition to full tuition, room, and board through a variety of scholarship competitions.

Requirements: Top applicants.

Application Deadline: December 3

Application Link: https://www.carthage.edu/admissions/undergraduate-students/undergraduate-scholarships/

5 University of Wisconsin, Milwaukee

Location: Milwaukee, Wisconsin
Setting: Urban (277 Acres)
Undergraduate Enrollment: 18,751
Type: Public

Anu and Satya Nadella Scholarship: Award covers Full tuition, fees, room and board for up to five years.

Eligibility: Applicant must be a graduate from a public or private high school in the city of Milwaukee | Admitted to UWM as a freshman in one of the following majors: BS Applied Mathematics and Computer Science, BS Computer Engineering, BA or BS Computer Science, BS Data science, BS Information Science & Technology, BBA Information Technology Management.

Demonstrated Academic merit or potential

Demonstrated Financial need.

Requirements: Top applicants.

Application Deadline: August 15

Application Link:
https://uwm.edu/undergrad-admission/scholarships-aid/

6 Edgewood College

Location: Madison, Wisconsin
Setting: City (55 Acres)
Undergraduate Enrollment: 1,377
Type: Private

Community Scholars Award: Awards Full tuition + 1st & 2nd Year room and board.

Eligibility: Underrepresented, BIPOC, or 1st generation students graduating from a Dane County high school are encouraged to apply.

P.S: You must be a resident of Dane County to apply.

Requirements: Top applicants.

Application Deadline: December 1

Application Link:
https://www.edgewood.edu/admissions/tuition-and-financial-aid/freshman-scholarships

7 University of Wisconsin

Location: Madison, Wisconsin
Setting: City (936 Acres)
Undergraduate Enrollment: 37,230
Type: Public

International Scholarships

King-Morgridge Scholars Program: Awards full tuition and fees, on-campus room and board, health insurance, airfare, and a stipend for miscellaneous expenses.

Eligibility: King-Morgridge Scholars will hail from countries in Africa, the Caribbean, Latin America, South and Southeast Asia.

There are lot's of scholarship opportunities available for undergraduate study at the University of Wisconsin.

Application Deadline: February 8

Application Link: https://admissions.wisc.edu/international-scholarships/

8 University of Wisconsin, Platteville

Location: Platteville, Wisconsin
Setting: Rural (820 Acres)
Undergraduate Enrollment: 6,266
Type: Public

Capstan Scholarship: Awards Full tuition, room and board.

Requirements: A cumulative GPA of 2.0-3.25.

Eligibility: Applicant must be a U.S. Citizen | Applicant must be pursuing a bachelor's degree in a STEM field, Accounting, or Finance | Applicant's hometown must be in the heart of the Midwestern United States, this includes the following states: Wisconsin, Iowa, Illinois, Minnesota, or Michigan | Applicant must show need based on the FAFSA.

Application Deadline: April 1

Application Link: https://www.uwplatt.edu/department/financial-aid-scholarships/scholarships

9

Marquette University

Location: Milwaukee, Wisconsin
Setting: Urban (107 Acres)
Undergraduate Enrollment: 7,528
Type: Private

Ann Kenny Carr Cristo Rey Scholarship: Awards Full tuition, room and board for four years.

Eligibility: Awarded to graduates of Cristo Rey Pilsen High School.

Requirements: Top students in applicant pool.

Do Great Things Full Tuition Scholarship: Awards Full tuition and 2 years of room (on-campus, standard double occupancy) and board.

Eligibility: Applicant must attend Green Bay West High School | Demonstrated financial need as determined by the Free Applicatio for Federal Student Aid or Net Price Calculator.

Requirements: Top Applicants.

The Donald J. and Frances I. Herdrich Endowed Scholarship for Engineering: Awards Full tuition, fees, on-campus housing and meals to students with financial need who are admitted to the ***Opus College of Engineering.***

Requirements: Top applicants

P.S: Priority will be given to first-generation students (i.e. neither parent graduated from college)

Application Deadline: December 1

Application Link: https://www.marquette.edu/explore/scholarships.php

1

University of Wyoming

Location: Laramie, Wyoming
Setting: Suburban (1,993 Acres)
Undergraduate Enrollment: 8,518
Type: Public

Trustees Scholars Award: Awards full tuition, mandatory fees, university room and board.

Eligibility: Wyoming Residents | Applicants must demonstrate or have a track record of excellence.

Application Deadline: January 5

Application Link: https://www.uwyo.edu/sfa/scholarships/index.html

CHAPTER 2

FULL RIDE EXTERNAL $CHOLARSHIP$

Morehead-Cain Scholarship

OVERVIEW

Morehead-Cain Scholarship Program – A fully-funded educational experience without peers. This scholarship is awarded annually, covering the student's *tuition, room and board* expenses for four years of undergraduate study. It offers (and funds) life-changing summer enrichment and extracurricular learning experiences. It provides immersion in a dynamic student body at a world-class university. And, it promises a lifetime connection to an extraordinary community of Morehead-Cain's scattered throughout the world.

It is the first merit scholarship program established in the United States. Founded at the first public university in the United States. It provides a four-year, fully funded educational experience for exceptional student leaders at the University of North Carolina at Chapel Hill.

International students are eligible to apply for this scholarship. It is open to both in-state, out-of-state, and international applicants.

SPECIAL NOTE: Morehead-Cain is an equal opportunity organization. It is the policy of the Morehead-Cain Foundation not to discriminate against any nominee or applicant based on race, color, national origin, ancestry, gender, sexual orientation, age, religion, creed, disability, marital status, veteran status, political affiliation, or any other factor protected by law.

Selection Criteria

Primary Criterion: Academic Excellence

Secondary Criteria:

Applicants should posses good LEADERSHIP qualities.

CHARACTER – Courage, humility, Intergrity, maturity, perseverance, self-awareness, generosity, and Empathy – These are the core values of the Morehead-Cain Community.

PHYSICAL VIGOR – You value what is gained – collaboration, sportsmanship, discipline, stamina, and persistence – by preparing for and engaging in competitions and performances.

P.S: Due consideration is given to nominees with physical limitations.

The deadline for this scholarship is October 1st.

P.S: For more details or information on the Morehead-Cain Scholarship, please visit the Scholarship Site.

Application Link: https://moreheadcain.org/

2

Richmond Scholars Program

OVERVIEW

Richmond Scholars Program – The most prestigious academic merit award, given by the University of Richmond. This scholarship awards full tuition, room and board plus other program benefits. Scholars are defined by academic achievement, engaged leadership, strong sense of purpose, and investment in a diverse and inclusive campus community.

All applicants for first-year admission are automatically considered for this scholarship, provided that they submit a complete admission application by December 1st.

The final test dates accepted for Richmond Scholars' consideration are the October ACT and November SAT administrations.

The Richmond Scholars awards are funded by the University with the support of several endowments, including the Brockenbrough Family Scholarship, Elizabeth Ramos Dunkum Scholarship, Richard A. Mateer Scholarship, Oldham Scholars, Mildred Crowder Pickels Scholars Program, E. Claiborne Robins, Sr. Science Honors Scholarship, Guy A. Ross Scholarship, Minnie Roth Weinstein Memorial Scholars Program, and D. Chris Withers Merit Scholarship.

The goals of the Richmond Scholars program are to bring engaged, high-achieving students to campus and to retain those students through strong mentorship and programming.

Selection Criteria

Richmond Scholars will demonstrate a commitment to four main criteria, broadly defined:

Academic Achievement

Engaged Leadership

Strong Sense of Purpose

Interest in Diverse and Inclusive Community.

The deadline for this scholarship is December 1st.

P.S: For more details or information on the Richmond Scholars Program, please visit the Scholarship Site.

Application Link: https://scholars.richmond.edu/

3

Jefferson Scholars Foundation

OVERVIEW

The mission of the **Jefferson Scholars Foundation** is to benefit the University of Virginia by identifying, attracting, and nurturing individuals of extraordinary intellectual range and depth who possess the highest qualities of leadership, scholarship, and citizenship.

The award for the Jefferson Scholarship is intended to cover the entire cost of attendance for four years at the University of Virginia, plus coverage of supplemental enrichment experiences.

The total value of the Jefferson Scholarship exceeds $333,000 for non-Virginian students and $177,000 for Virginian students. The stipends will exceed $72,000 for non-Virginian students and $36,000 for Virginian students.

The stipend includes tuition, fees, books, supplies, room, board, and personal expenses.

Jefferson Scholarship is awarded to individuals who have undergone a rigorous selection process and who possess an exceptional record of accomplishment both inside and outside the classroom.

P.S: No one may apply for the Jefferson Scholarship directly. Candidates must be nominated by their high schools (*Eligible High Schools*) based on their demonstrated excellence and exceptional potential in the areas of leadership, scholarship, and citizenship. Once nominated, students are placed into regional competitions and may be invited to participate in one or more rounds of interviews. These interviews will determine the regional finalist(s) who will be invited to participate in the final stage of the Jefferson Scholarship competition.

All counselors and Jefferson scholar nominees must submit a completed nomination form by December 1. Schools in the At-Large region have a separate deadline of November 15.

Application Link: **https://www.jeffersonscholars.org/**

4

Stamps Scholars Program

OVERVIEW

The Stamps Scholars Program, with its partner schools, seeks students who demonstrate academic merit, strong leadership potential, and exceptional character.

The Stamps Scholars Program welcomes and supports students from all backgrounds and areas of study. Financial need is not a consideration. At some of the partner schools, international students are eligible for the Stamps Scholarship. Students should check directly with the program that they are interested in to view eligibility requirements.

If you are interested in being considered for a Stamps Scholarship, please contact one (or more) of the partner schools directly. Scholarships are awarded by the partner schools. Scholarship terms vary, so please check with the schools in which you are interested in for more details on how to apply and what the benefits of the award are at that college or university.

There are 37 Stamps Scholar partner schools across the US and into the UK.

Through partnerships with institutions across the U.S. (and into the U.K.), Scholars receive annual awards that range from $5,400 to $75,000 (four-year awards total an average of $21,600-$300,000) with additional funds for enrichment activities such as study abroad, academic conferences, and leadership training. The Stamps Scholars Program and partner schools evenly share the costs of the awards.

Selection Criteria:

Applying for a Stamps Scholarship is easy. A student must apply directly to one or more of the partner schools to be considered for the Stamps Scholarship. If you qualify, you'll automatically be considered for a Stamps award.

In some cases, however, some partner schools may request a separate application for consideration of the Stamps Scholarship.

At certain schools, the Stamps Scholarship Program is part of an umbrella program for scholars, such as the Foundation Fellows at the University of Georgia or the Carolina Scholars at the University of South Carolina.

Generally Top Applicants are selected!

Stamps scholarship application deadline varies from one partner school to another. Please check with the schools you are interested in for more details on how to apply.

P.S: For more details or information on the Stamps Scholars Program, please visit the Scholarship Site.

Application Link: https://www.stampsscholars.org/

5

Ingram Scholars Program

OVERVIEW

The Ingram Scholars Program challenges students to create and implement substantial service projects in the community. The program supports students who demonstrate a willingness and ability to combine a successful business or professional career with a lifelong commitment to finding solutions to critical problems facing modern society. Ingram Scholars are expected to devote approximately twenty hours each month during the academic year and at least one of their undergraduate summers to relevant community outreach and service projects.

Ingram Scholars receive full-tuition support each year plus a stipend for a special summer service project. Vanderbilt will provide additional need-based financial aid to those Ingram Scholarship recipients whose demonstrated financial need exceeds the amount of full tuition.

Ingram Scholars are selected on the basis of commitment to civic-minded service, an entrepreneurial spirit, strength of personal character, and leadership potential. In evaluating candidates, the selection committee reviews the Ingram Scholars Program application along with the entire application for first-year admission. Ingram Scholar Finalists are also required to interview with the selection committee.

The Ingram Scholars Program is a unique and innovative example of how a university can prepare students for responsible careers and a lifetime of useful contributions to the well-being of others. If you are committed to generating positive social change, and if you possess the qualities of maturity, leadership, and initiative, you should consider this challenging and rewarding program.

Selection Criteria

The Ingram Scholars Program application is strongly encouraged; preference is given to those who apply. Applicants apply via MyAppVU after submitting an admission application.

Ingram Scholars are selected on the basis of commitment to civic-minded service, an entrepreneurial spirit, strength of personal character, and leadership potential.

Generally Top Applicants are selected!

Ingram Scholars Program applications for prospective freshmen must be submitted electronically via your MyAppVU account by December 1.

Application Link: https://www.vanderbilt.edu/scholarships/ingram.php

6

Evans Scholars Foundation

OVERVIEW

The Evans Scholarship is a full tuition and housing college scholarship for high-achieving caddies with limited financial means.

To qualify, caddies must meet the requirements of having a strong caddie record, excellent academics, demonstrated financial need and outstanding character.

Scholarship applications are accepted at the beginning of an applicant's senior year of high school, as well as from college freshmen.

This is the largest scholarship program **for caddies in the United States.**

The program has helped thousands of hardworking young men and women get into college since 1930. The Evans Scholars Program addresses the barriers to college graduation faced by students and prepares them for a lifetime of success.

The Western Golf Association conducts championships for professional and amateur golfers, promotes the use of caddies and supports the Evans Scholars Foundation's efforts to award full tuition and housing college scholarships to hardworking caddies with limited financial means.

Selection Criteria

All applicants must possess the following requirements:

- **Strong Caddie Record:** Applicants must have caddied, regularly and successfully, for a minimum of two years and are expected to caddie at their sponsoring club the year they apply for the Scholarship.
- **Excellent Academics:** Applicants must have completed their junior year of high school with above a B average in college preparatory courses. SAT and ACT test scores are also required.
- **Demonstrated Financial Need.**
- **An Outstanding Character.**

The entire application – including supporting documents like evaluations, recommendation letters, transcripts, test scores, a CSS profile and FAFSA information – is expected to be completed by October 30. The Scholarship Committee will begin its review when the application is complete.

P.S: For more details or information on the Evans Scholarship, please visit the Scholarship Site.

Application Link: https://wgaesf.org/

Park Scholarship Program

OVERVIEW

The Park Scholarship Program provides a four-year, full ride scholarship to North Carolina State University. Awarded on the basis of outstanding accomplishments and potential in scholarship, leadership, service, and character.

The mission of the Park Scholarships program is to bring exceptional students to NC State, based on outstanding accomplishments and potential in scholarship, leadership, service, and character.

Park Scholars are intellectually curious students who think critically and seek learning experiences outside the classroom. They listen well, lead by example, take risks, and champion original ideas. Park Scholars dedicate themselves to making a positive difference in their communities while demonstrating integrity, honesty, and conscientiousness.

In addition to academic and professional pursuits, the Park Scholars engage in several team and class endeavors during their four years at NC State. They are creative, smart, motivated, service-oriented, and participate in a wide array of extracurricular activities, including student government, varsity and intramural athletics, fraternities and sororities, academic and cause-related clubs, entrepreneurial ventures, and arts organizations.

Selection Criteria

To be eligible for the Park Scholarships program, candidates **must** be United States citizens, permanent residents of the U.S., or graduating from a high school located in the U.S. (regardless of citizenship status)

Top applicants to the North Carolina State University are duly considered for this scholarship.

The Park Scholarships application asks that you provide:

- Names and email addresses of two recommenders,
- Information about advanced coursework completed and two essays.

The Park Scholarships program is named for the late Roy H. Park an NC State alumnus who created the charitable Park Foundation, dedicated to education, media, and the environment.

Applicants should submit a complete Park Scholarships application by November 1.

P.S: For more details or information on the Park Scholarship Program, please visit the Scholarship Site.

Application Link: **https://park.ncsu.edu/**

8 JP Morgan Chase & Co.: Thomas G. Labrecque Smart Start Program

OVERVIEW

Thomas G. Labrecque Smart Start Program is designed for ambitious, analytical New York City high school students who are willing to get a head start on a career in financial services.

If you're an ambitious, analytical **New York City high school student** who is ready to get a head start on a career in financial services, then Smart Start is the program for you. You'll gain real-world experience working in industry-leading businesses while attending university on a full four-year scholarship.

Applicants will learn the skills needed for a successful career in financial services while working part-time during the school year and full-time during the summer. Each year, you'll rotate to another area of the firm as you expand your knowledge, learn about the variety of roles in financial services, and build the foundation for your future career.

The thrilling part is you'll do all of this on a full four-year scholarship to an approved college or university.

Applicant must be a graduating senior from a New York City high school who is a New York City resident that has been accepted to one of the following colleges: Barnard College, Baruch College, Brooklyn College, City College, Columbia University, Fordham University (Lincoln Center campus, Rosehill campus), Long Island University (Brooklyn campus), New York University, Pace University (Manhattan campus), Polytechnic Institute of New York University, St. Francis College, or St. John's University.

Three essays and recommendations required. Financial need and community involvement must be demonstrated.

Selection Criteria

Applicants must rank in the top 90 percent of their class and have SAT/ACT scores (minimum 1000 combined for verbal and math, and 21 for ACT.)

Applicant must have an interest in ***financial services*** as well as the discipline to simultaneously pursue their education and work in a fast-paced environment. You should be flexible, adaptable, detail oriented, have good judgment and the ability to manage multiple responsibilities.

P.S: Life science or fine art majors are not eligible for this scholarship.

The deadline for this scholarship is January 17.

Application Link:

https://careers.jpmorgan.com/us/en/students/programs/smart-start

9 Bruce Fishkin Scholarship Fund

OVERVIEW

The Bruce Fishkin Scholarship fund awards up to the entire cost of a college education to outstanding students believed to deserve an investment of the time and money.

Awards are not based upon need, but rather on ability, individuality, and potential. If you have always known deep inside that given the chance, you'd achieve greatness, well, here is that chance.

The scholarship fund is in search of high school students in their senior year who seek to challenge themselves to succeed and accomplish what most people never imagined. Selection is based upon application essays, followed by personal interviews.

Selection Criteria

Applicant must be a resident or attend high school in any one of the following areas: Chicago, Illinois or the counties of Cook, DuPage, Kane, Lake, McHenry or Will, Illinois – Las Vegas, Nevada and suburbs of the area – Fairfield, Greens Farms, Redding or Westport, Connecticut.

A minimum high school GPA of 3.0 on a 4.0 scale, or the equivalent thereof in cases where the applicable high school does not employ a traditional 4.0 system.

A minimum ACT score of 22 OR a minimum SAT score of 1100.

Plan on attending an accredited college or university for a Bachelor's degree or four-year program in the United States.

P.S: Only students from the United States are eligible to apply for this scholarship. You can also be eligible for this scholarship if you are a US Permanent Resident residing in the catchment area of the scholarship.

Applications for this scholarship may be submitted beginning Sept 1st at 12:00 PM, and will be accepted until October 17th at 11:59 AM.

P.S: For more details or information on the Bruce Fishkin Scholarship, please visit the Scholarship website.

Application Link: **https://brucefishkinscholarshipfund.com/**

10 National Merit Scholarship Program

OVERVIEW

The National Merit Scholarship Program is an academic competition for recognition and scholarships that began in 1955. Approximately 1.5 million high school students enter the program each year. It is one of the largest scholarship programs in the United States.

Since its founding, the National Merit Scholarship Program has recognized over 3.4 million students and provided some 451,000 scholarships worth over $1.8 billion. The honors awarded by NMSC to exceptionally able students are viewed as definitive marks of excellence.

Merit Scholarship awards are of three types:

- National Merit $2500 Scholarships – Every finalist competes for these single-payment scholarships, which are awarded on a state-representational basis. Winners are selected by a committee of college admission officers and high school counselors without consideration of family financial circumstances, college choice, or major and career plans.
- Corporate-sponsored Merit Scholarship Awards – Corporate sponsors designate their awards for children of their employees or members, for residents of a community where a company has operations, or for Finalists with career plans the sponsor wishes to encourage.
- College-sponsored Merit Scholarship Awards – Officials of each sponsor college select winners of their awards from Finalists who have been accepted for admission and have informed NMSC by the published deadlines that the sponsor college or university is their first choice. These awards are renewable for up to four years of undergraduate study.

Student Entry Requirements

Candidates should take the PSAT/NMSQT in the specified year of the high school program and no later than the third year in grades 9 through 12.

Attend high school in the United States, the District of Columbia, or U.S. commonwealth and territory; or meet the citizenship requirements for students attending high school outside the United States (check site for more details).

Typically, all interested candidates that meet the student entry requirements are eligible to participate in the competition.

Please refer back to the Full ride section and check out for schools (i.e. *College-sponsored Merit Scholarship awards*) that offer Full ride scholarships to National Merit Finalists.

Application Link: https://www.nationalmerit.org/s/1758/start.aspx?gid=2&pgid=61

Johnson Scholarship

OVERVIEW

Washington and Lee University offers the **Johnson Scholarship Program** which selects students on the basis of academic achievement, demonstrated leadership and their potential to contribute to the intellectual and civic life of the W&L campus and of the world at large in years to come.

The Johnson Scholarship recipients receive awards of at least tuition, room and board to attend Washington and Lee University. Students with financial needs higher than this amount will have any additional needs met by the scholarship. In addition, Johnson Scholars receive funding up to $7,000 to support summer experiences during their time at W&L.

Finalists for Johnson Scholarships participate in an on-campus competition and are notified in late March of their status. All costs associated with attending the competition will be paid by Washington and Lee University, including travel expenses (airfare or mileage costs), meals and lodging for the duration of the competition.

Students who wish to be considered for a Johnson Scholarship must submit a complete Common App, including the additional Johnson Scholarship application essay, no later than December 1.

Selection Criteria

A complete application consists of:

- A complete Common App, including the Johnson Scholarship Application essay.
- An official copy of your high school transcript.
- Self-reported or official scores from the SAT or ACT
- Two teacher recommendations.
- One school counsellor recommendation and secondary school form.

Applicants should demonstrate potential for stellar academic performance. Top applicants to Washington and Lee University are duly considered for this scholarship.

P.S: All Johnson Scholarship application instructions are included in W&L's section of the Common App.

For more details or information on the Johnson Scholarship Program, please visit the Scholarship Site.

Application Link: https://my.wlu.edu/the-johnson-program

12

Alfond Scholars Program

OVERVIEW

The Alfond Scholars Programs annually awards full ride scholarships – including tuition, double room, and unlimited board – to entering first-year students in the College of Liberal Arts at Rollins College with the desire and commitment to pursue additional prestigious recognition such as Rhodes, Goldwater, or Truman scholarships during their undergraduate years.

Scholarship totals include federal and state awards for which a student might already be eligible. Alfond Scholarships are renewable for three additional years, bringing the value of each scholarship to more than $280,000 over four years.

Scholarship recipients will be identified from the fall applicant pool on the basis of strength of selection criteria. A select number of qualified applicants will be invited to the Scholars Weekend interview competition which will introduce students to the extraordinary benefits of being a scholar at Rollins. The academic competition portion of the weekend will consist of a mock classroom experience and individual and group interviews with Rollins faculty, staff, and students.

Selection Criteria

Scholarship finalists are selected from the College of Liberal Arts applicant pool.

Qualifying applicants typically have SATs higher than 1450 (Evidence Based Reading and Math) or ACTs higher than 32 (Composite) and GPAs higher than 3.8. Test-optional students are considered as well.

Strength of high school curriculum and extracurricular involvement are also important factors.

Scholarship finalists are selected from the College of Liberal Arts applicant pool. All admission applicants who submit all application materials by the Priority Scholarship Deadline (Nov. 15) are considered for Alfond Scholarships on the basis of their overall academic record.

P.S: For more details or information on the Alfond Scholars Program, please visit the Scholarship website.

Application Link:

https://www.rollins.edu/scholarships-aid/scholarships/alfond-scholars-program/

13

Cunniffe Presidential Scholarship

OVERVIEW

The Maurice J. and Carolyn Dursi Cunniffe Presidential Scholarship is awarded to entering traditional first-year students who generally rank in the top 1 to 2 percent in their high school class.

The award covers tuition, room, board, and fees and is renewable for four years. Recipients are also eligible for a maximum of $20,000 over four years to use for academic enrichment experiences.

This scholarship is awarded by Fordham University. The scholarship is awarded on the basis of excellent academic achievement in high school, test scores and personal characteristics.

Fordham University is devoted to the transmission of learning, through research and through undergraduate, graduate, and professional education of the highest quality. It encourages the growth of a life of faith consonant with moral and intellectual development.

The Cunniffe Presidential Scholars are generally ranked in the top 1-2% of their high school class and represent the most talented students as demonstrated by their outstanding academic performance, personal characteristics, as well as their commitment, leadership, and service.

Selection Criteria

The Cunniffe Presidential Scholarship is awarded to entering traditional first-year students who generally rank in the top 1 to 2 percent in their high school class.

Top applicants to Fordham University are duly considered for this scholarship.

The deadline is typically in March. Award recipients will be selected by mid-April.

P.S: For more details or information on the Cunniffe Presidential Scholarship, please visit the Scholarship website.

Application Link:

https://www.fordham.edu/undergraduate-admission/apply/scholarships-and-grants/

Belk Scholarship

OVERVIEW

The John M. Belk Scholarship provides comprehensive funding (tuition, fees, room and board) plus special study stipends that allow you greater flexibility in the on-and off-campus opportunities you choose to explore. Those experiences, paired with the academic programs, deepen your intellect, maturity, and global understanding.

Nomination & Selection Process:

Applicants are required to be nominated by their high school Guidance counsellors, heads of school, or principals. One or two candidates may be nominated from each school.

The admission staff may also nominate students based on the strength of their application for admission.

The John M. Belk Scholarship is awarded at Davidson College in Davidson, North Carolina.

The Program is built around a belief that, as a Belk Scholar, you possess unique talents that should be recognized and nurtured.

Selection Criteria

This is a nomination Scholarship.

Guidance counselors, heads of school, or principals may nominate one or two candidates from each school. The admission staff may also nominate students based on the strength of their application for admission.

Typically, candidates with high grades are nominated for this scholarship.

A candidate's record and recommendations must demonstrate academic excellence and purposeful engagement in the classroom, in student and civic organizations, on the athletic field, or in the arts. While academic achievement is paramount, Belk Scholars also exhibit intellectual curiosity and a commitment to both their local and global communities.

Nominations must be made by December 1 by completing the online nomination form and submitting the required documentation (recommendation letter and transcript) to Admission and Financial Aid.

Application Link:

https://www.davidson.edu/admission-and-financial-aid/financial-aid/scholarships

15

Wells Scholars Program

OVERVIEW

The Wells Scholar Program created in honour of Herman B Wells, 11th President of the University of Indiana, is one of the most competitive and prestigious awards offered by an American University. The Wells Scholars Program guarantees the full cost of attendance for four years of undergraduate study on IU's Bloomington campus.

The Wells Scholars Program uses a nomination rather than an application process for the selection of scholars.

Each year, selected incoming freshmen to the University of Indiana receive the award, based solely on merit. In addition, one to two current IUB students are selected to join the junior or senior class of Scholars.

Wells Scholars are also members of the Hutton Honors College, where they can apply for grants in support of research, internships, creative activity, conference travel, and honors thesis work.

The ideals of the Wells Scholar Program are not interested in students who see a brilliant career as their primary goal, they are interested in scholars who want to contribute and make an impact on their community, the nation, and the world at large.

Selection Criteria

There is no strict model of an award recipient: however, past successful nominees have typically;

- Shown exceptional qualities of character and leadership
- Been significantly involved in extracurricular activities
- Demonstrated a concern for their community
- Excelled in terms of class rank, GPA, and/or (optional) standardized test scores
- Expressed interest in joining a community of scholarly individuals with diverse interests beyond a pre-professional track.

In addition to a pattern of serious commitment to one or more activities outside of class, past successful nominees generally place in the top 5% by class rank, have a GPA of at least 3.9 out of 4.0, and (optionally) a 1430+ SAT score and/or 32+ ACT score.

The deadline for receipt of fully completed electronic nominations and supplementary materials, including letters of recommendation and student essays is by November 1. Complete nominations that include all required items must be submitted through the online portal.

Application Link: https://wellsscholars.indiana.edu/

16

The Coolidge Scholarship

OVERVIEW

The Collidge Scholarship is awarded annually, it covers the student's tuition, room, board, and expenses for four years of undergraduate study.

It may be used at any accredited college or university in the United States.

Scholars from any background, pursuing any academic discipline of study may apply to this unbiased and need-blind program.

Requirements: Good academic achievement, extracurricular record and excellence in character.

Students apply for the Coolidge Scholarship during their junior year of high school. Finalists are flown in for a finalist weekend at the Coolidge Historic Site in Plymouth Notch, Vermont where they interview with the Coolidge Scholars Finalist Jury.

This Scholarship is in honor of Calvin Coolidge, the 30th President of the United States of America. He served from August 2, 1923 to March 4, 1929.

Calvin Coolidge worked hard in academics; the young New Englander's only sport was public speaking, often on public policy. The main criterion that distinguishes Coolidge Scholars therefore is academic excellence. Secondary criteria include: demonstrated interest in public policy; an appreciation for the values Coolidge championed; as well as humility and service.

Selection Criteria

Primary Criterion: Academic Excellence.

Secondary Criteria:

- Interest in Public Policy and Appreciation of Coolidge Values
- Humility and Service.

The Coolidge Scholarship is non-partisan and is awarded on merit regardless of race, gender, or background.

The deadline for this scholarship is usually around January 26th Annually.

Application Link: https://coolidgescholars.org/

17 USDA 1890 National Scholars Program

OVERVIEW

The USDA/1890 National Scholars Program was established in 1992 as part of the partnership between the U.S. Department of Agriculture and the 1890 Land-Grant Universities.

The goal is to increase the the number of minorities studying agriculture, food, natural resource sciences, and the related disciplines.

Furthermore, the USDA/1890 National Scholars Program will provide full tuition, employment, employee benefits, fees, books, and room and board for up to 4 years to selected students. It is available for only bachelor's degree.

The scholarships are awarded annually and must be used at one of the 1890 Historically Black Land-Grant Universities. Also, the scholarship may be renewed each year, contingent upon satisfactory academic performance and normal progress toward the bachelor's degree.

General Eligibility Requirements

Interested candidates must meet the following requirements:

- ✓ Be a U.S. Citizen.
- ✓ Have a cumulative GPA of 3.0 or better (on a 4.0 scale)
- ✓ Have been accepted for admission or currently attending on of the nineteen 1890 Historically Black Land-Grant Universities
- ✓ Study agriculture, food, natural resouces sciences, or other related academic disciplines.
- ✓ Demonstrate leadership and community service
- ✓ Submit an official transcript with the school seal and an authorized official's signature
- ✓ Submit a signed application (original signature only)
- ✓ 21 ACT, 1080 SAT scores.

The deadline for this scholarship is usually around January 15th Annually.

P.S: For more details or information on the USDA/1890 National Scholars Program, please visit the Scholarship website.

Application Link: https://www.usda.gov/partnerships/1890NationalScholars

18

Cameron Impact Scholarship

OVERVIEW

The Cameron Impact Scholarship is a four-year, full-tuition (plus fees, and books) impact-driven undergraduate scholarship awarded annually. It may be used at any accredited college or university in the United States.

The scholarship is targetted at exceptional high school student who have demonstrated excellence in leadership, community service, extracurricular activities and academics.

As a merit-based program, the Cameron Impact Scholarship is open to all applicants who meet the GPA and citizenship requirements, regardless of race, socioeconomic status, religion, sexual orientation or any other background factors.

The Bryan Cameron Education Foundation is a private family foundation established in 2015 on the principle of making a difference by investing in young people's education. Their specific intent is to identify a select group of outstanding rising college students each year who we expect to positively impact the lives of their family, friends, colleagues, and fellow citizens.

Founder Bryan Cameron has enjoyed a long and successful career in asset management. His recognition and appreciation of his own blessings has inspired his extensive philanthropic initiatives over the years.

The Bryan Cameron Education Foundation core values are: Impact | Choice | Diversity | Higher Education | Merit | Service | and Accountability.

General Eligibility:

US Citizens who have an unweighted GPA of 3.7 or higher are eligible to apply. The foundation is specifically looking for candidates who have displayed strong evidence of leadership, involvement in extracurriculars and community service, and who want to make a positive impact on the world around them.

The deadline for this scholarship is usually around May 20th (Early) & September 9th (Regular) -- Both Annually.

Application Link: https://www.bryancameroneducationfoundation.org/

19

The Gates Scholarship (TGS)

OVERVIEW

The Gates Scholarship (TGS) is a highly selective, last-dollar scholarship for outstanding, minority, high school seniors from low-income households. Each year, the scholarship is awarded to exceptional student leaders, with the intent of helping them realize their maximum potential.

It may be used at any US accredited, four-year, not-for-profit, private or public college or university. The institution must be based in the US or United States territory.

Scholars will receive funding for the full cost of attendance that is not already covered by other financial aid and the expected family contribution, as determined by the Free Application for Federal Student Aid (FAFSA), or the methodology used by a Scholar's college or university.

Cost of Attendance = tuition, fees, room, board, books, and transportation, and may include other personal costs.

The Gates Scholarship Program was launched in 2017. The Bill & Melinda Gates Foundation continues its long-standing commitment to helping outstanding minority students who come from low-income backgrounds realize their maximum potential.

Who is eligible to apply for The Gates Scholarship?

To apply, students must be:

- A high school senior
- From at least one of the following ethnicities: African American, American Indian/Alaska Native, Asian & Pacific Islander American, and/or Hispanic American
- Pell-eligible
- A US citizen, national, or permanent resident
- In good academic standing with a minimum cumulative weighted GPA of 3.3 on a 4.0 scale (or equivalent)

Additionally, a student must plan to enroll full-time, in a four-year degree program, at a US accredited, not-for-profit, private or public college or university.

For American Indian/Alaska Native, proof of tribal enrollment will be required.

This prestigious scholarship program is based on evidence that by eliminating the financial barriers to college, a last-dollar scholarship can enable high-potential, low-income minority students to excel in their course work, graduate college, and continue to be leaders throughout their lives.

The deadline for this scholarship is usually around January 15th Annually

P.S: For more details or information on the Gates Scholarship (TGS), please visit the Scholarship website.

Application Link: https://www.thegatesscholarship.org

20 Questbridge National College Match with Full Ride Scholarships

OVERVIEW

The QuestBridge National College Match is targeted at low-income high school seniors who have excelled academically, but are financial disadvantaged.

These students will be matched with top colleges and considered for early admisssion and full four-year scholarships. Questbridge partners with over 30 colleges and universities that will offer full ride scholarships to these students.

The full scholarship covers tuition, fees, room & board, other expenses. It may be used at any of the 30+ questbridge college(s) or universities.

Over 10,500 students have been admitted with full four-year scholarships. Students who attend the partner colleges are supported in their college years and beyond through on-campus chapters and nationwide opportunities offered through the QuestBridge Scholars Network and QuestBridge Alumni Association.

QuestBridge grew from a few simple ideas and a lot of help along the way. With roots extending to 1987.

P.S: Most of the students who are selected as Finalists come from households earning less than $65,000 per year for a typical family of four with minimal significant assets. However, there are no absolute cut-offs. If a student comes from a household earning more than this amount but feels that they have faced economic hardship and fit the QuestBridge criteria of high-achieving, low-income students, we would encourage that student to apply. There is room on the application to explain the family's situation.

The Quest Scholars Program officially started in 1994 as a five-week residential summer enrichment program for high school juniors on Stanford University's campus. After the summer session, Quest provided five years of academic and personal support to our students. Ten years later in 2004, Quest launched QuestBridge in an effort to expand the number of high school students it reached.

The deadline for this scholarship is usually around September 27th Annually.

Application Link: https://www.questbridge.org/high-school-students

21 The Cooke College Scholarship Program

OVERVIEW

The Cooke College Scholarship program is awarded annually, it covers a student's tuition, living expenses, books and required fees throughout years of undergraduate study.

Also, recipients have access to one-on-one advising about selecting a college, navigating financial aid, transitioning to college, and maximizing the college experience; And may be eligible to apply for the Cooke Graduate Scholarship.

It is available to high-achieving high school seniors with financial need who seek to attend and graduate from the nation's best four-year colleges and universities. Scholars are allowed to study a field of their choice.

The Jack Kent Cooke Foundation is dedicated to advancing the education of exceptionally promising students who have financial need. Since 2000, the Foundation has awarded over $230 million in scholarships to more than 2,930 students from 8th grade through graduate school, along with comprehensive educational advising and other support services. The Foundation has also provided $119.5 million in grants to organizations that serve such students.

Selection Criteria

Cooke College Scholarship recipients are selected from a nationwide applicant pool each year. As minimum criteria, students must:

- Plan to graduate from a U.S. high school in spring of application year.
- Intend to enroll full time in an accredited 4- year college in fall of application year.
- Earn a cumulative unweighted GPA of 3.5 or above in high school.
- Demonstrate financial need. It considers applicants with family income up to $95,000. Last year's cohort of new College Scholarship recipients had a median family income of approximately $35,000

Cooke Scholars come from diverse racial and ethnic backgrounds and from rural, suburban, and urban communities. Many Scholars are the first in their families to pursue higher education.

The deadline for this scholarship is usually around October 30th Annually.

P.S: For more details or information on the Cooke College Scholarship program, please visit the Scholarship Site.

Application Link:

https://www.jkcf.org/our-scholarships/college-scholarship-program/

22 The Flinn Foundation Scholarship

OVERVIEW

The Flinn Foundation Scholarship is awarded annually, it covers a student's tuition, fees, housing, and meals throughout the student's undergraduate years of study.

Applicants must study at one of Arizona's three public universities, and the scholarship includes a study abroad package as well.

The student must be a U.S. citizen or lawful permanent resident (Green Card holder) by the time of application. Also, student(s) must be an Arizona resident.

As a general rule, Flinn Scholarship applicants should also:

Attain at least a 3.5 grade-point average (unweighted);

Rank in the top 5 percent of their graduating class (if the school reports class rank); and

Participate and demonstrate leadership in a variety of extracurricular activities.

The Flinn Foundation is a privately endowed, philanthropic grant-making organization established in 1965 by Dr. Robert S. and Irene P. Flinn.

It's mission is to improve the quality of life in Arizona to benefit future generations.

Flinn Scholarship Application Requirement

To be awarded the Flinn Scholarship, an applicant must:

- Be a U.S. citizen or lawful permanent resident (Green Card holder) by time of application;
- Be an Arizona resident for two full years immediately preceding entry to the university.

As a general rule, Flinn Scholarship applicants should also:

- Attain at least a 3.5 grade-point average (unweighted);
- Rank in the top 5 percent of their graduating class (if the school reports class rank); and
- Participate and demonstrate leadership in a variety of extracurricular activities.

The deadline for this scholarship is usually around Mid-september annually.

P.S: For more details or information on the Flinn Foundation Scholarship, please visit the scholarship website.

Application Link:

https://flinn.org/flinn-scholars/

23

DOD Smart Scholarship

OVERVIEW

The SMART Program, part of the Department of Defense (DoD) science, technology, engineering and mathematics (STEM) portfolio, provides STEM students with the tools needed to pursue higher education and begin a rewarding career with the DoD.

SMART Scholars are provided with the tools required to pursue their STEM education and begin their career in a prestigious civilian position with the Department of Defense (DoD).

Benefits include:

- ✓ Full tuition and education related educational expenses (meal plans, housing, and parking not included)
- ✓ Stipend paid at a rate of $25,000 - $38,000 a year depending on degree level (may be prorated depending on award length)
- ✓ Summer research internships ranging from 8 to 12 weeks
- ✓ Health Insurance allowance of up to $1,200 per academic year
- ✓ Miscellaneous allowance of up to $1,000 per academic year
- ✓ An experienced mentor at one of the Sponsoring Facilities
- ✓ Employment placement at a DoD facility upon degree completion.

Scholarships are awarded for a minimum of 1 year and a maximum of 5 years of funding, depending on degree requirements. SMART is a one-for-one commitment; for every year of degree funding, the scholar commits to working for a year with the DoD as a civilian employee.

The deadline for this scholarship is usually around December 1st Annually.

It usually opens August 1st every year.

P.S: For more details or information on the SMART Program, please visit the scholarship website.

Application Link:

https://www.smartscholarship.org/smart

The program focuses on students pursuing disciplines that are critical to national security functions of the Department of Defense (DoD). The following is a list of SMART's 21 approved STEM disciplines. These disciplines are general umbrella disciplines – specific applicant majors or fields of study may fall under one or more discipline on this list.

Please note, non-technical degrees, including management, arts, or humanities, are not approved or funded by SMART.

Aeronautical and Astronautical Engineering

Biosciences

Biomedical Engineering

Chemical Engineering

Chemistry

Civil Engineering

Cognitive, Neural, and Behavioral Sciences

Computer and Computational Sciences and Computer Engineering

Electrical Engineering

Environmental Sciences

Geosciences

Industrial and Systems Engineering

Information Sciences

Materials Science and Engineering

Mathematics

Mechanical Engineering

Naval Architecture and Ocean Engineering

Nuclear Engineering

Oceanography

Operations Research

Physics

Eligibility Requirements

Who can apply?

The SMART application is open August through December of every year, with awards being granted the following spring. Review the below requirements to ensure you are eligible to apply for this life-changing opportunity.

All applicants must be:

- A citizen of the United States, Australia, Canada, New Zealand, or United Kingdom at time of application,
- 18 years of age or older as of August 1, 2023
- Requesting at least 1 year of degree funding prior to graduation (which starts at the program start date),
- Able to complete at least one summer internship (multi-year scholars only)
- Willing to accept post-graduation employment with the DoD,
- A student in good standing with a minimum cumulative GPA of 3.0 on a 4.0 scale,
- Pursuing a technical undergraduate or graduate degree in one of the 21 STEM disciplines listed below,
- Able to produce a fall 2022 college transcript from a regionally accredited US college or university, OR be pursuing a graduate degree at a regionally accredited US college or university.

24 The Science Ambassador Scholarship

OVERVIEW

The Science Ambassador scholarship is a full tuition scholarship for a woman in science, technology, engineering, or math. Funded by Cards Against Humanity.

It may be used at any accredited college or university in the United States.

The scholarship is open to only undergraduate and high school seniors.

Eligibility:

This scholarship is for only **female** scholars.

You do not need to be a U.S. citizen to apply, but you do need to attend college (or plan to attend college) in the United States or a United States Territory.

N.B: Runner-ups will be awarded between $5,000 to $1,000 towards their tuition cost.

Which fields of study are eligible?

All fields within science, technology, engineering, and math are eligible.

P.S: STEM must be your major field of study (not your minor).

Application Link: https://www.scienceambassadorscholarship.org/

25 The 5 Strong Scholarship

OVERVIEW

5 Strong partners with Historically Black Colleges and Universities (HBCUs) to provide promising student leaders with full-tuition scholarships and ongoing mentorship and support from matriculation to graduation.

The scholarship may only be used only at a 5-Strong HBCU partner College(s)/Universities.

For years, as a teacher and counselor, 5 Strong founder Andrew Ragland watched HBCUs (Historically Black Colleges and Universities) nurture his former students, especially the ones without outstanding scores but plenty of potential. An HBCU graduate himself, Ragland and his team believe these institutions are uniquely positioned to give students who might be overlooked the support they need to shine.

In 2015, Ragland opened 5 Strong, and began linking students waiting to shine with HBCUs that he knew can best help them on their journey to become change makers and leaders. 5 Strong worked with HBCUs to arrange full-tuition scholarships so a lack of money wouldn't stand in the way of young scholars' dreams; And Ragland built an intensive college success program run by an experienced team ready to embrace their students like family. Today, this model has been proven: more and more HBCUs are signing on, and 84% of 5 Strong's scholars are on track to graduate — more than twice the national average.

Most of the HBCU partners still require that 5 Strong applicants submit standardized test scores (ACT/SAT) in order to receive the full tuition scholarships. All applicants must still take either the ACT or SAT before submitting an application or your application will be deleted.

P.S: Check the website for more details.

The deadline for this scholarship is usually around December 31st Annually.

Application Link: https://www.5strongscholars.org/apply

26 The Robertson Scholars Program

OVERVIEW

The Robertson Scholars Leadership Program provides eight semesters of full tuition, room and board, and most mandatory fees for Scholars at Duke and UNC-Chapel Hill. Scholars also have access to generous funding for up to three summer experiences, funding for conferences throughout the academic year, and for two semesters of study abroad.

It may be used either at Duke University or University of North Carolina, Chapel Hill.

Julian H. Robertson, Jr. and his late wife, Josie, are the founders of the Robertson Scholars Leadership Program. In 2000, the Robertson family donated $24 million to create The Robertson Scholars Leadership Program in his native North Carolina, to encourage collaboration between Duke and the University of North Carolina and to promote the development of young leaders.

The first class of Robertson Scholars graduated in 2005. Robertson Scholars continue to make impacts on both campuses and within the Chapel Hill and Durham communities, much like Julian and Josie had envisioned. Collaborations between Duke and UNC Scholars have resulted in start-ups, non-profits, research collaborations, and more.

Mr. Robertson and his sons continue to work alongside the Robertson Program staff to make this a one-of-a-kind Program.

Robertson Scholars participate in mandatory programs, including but not limited to: retreats, the campus switch, cross-campus coursework, community events, and at least two summer enrichment programs (domestic and international, following the Scholar's first and second years, respectively).

The Robertson Scholars Leadership Program expects all Scholars to uphold the academic standards for which they were awarded the scholarship.

The deadline for this scholarship is usually around January 26th Annually.

Application Link: **https://robertsonscholars.org/**

27 Air Force ROTC (AFROTC) Scholarship

OVERVIEW

The US Airforce ROTC scholarship is awarded annually, it covers the scholar's tuition, fees, and monthly living expense and annual book stipend.

It may be used at any of the AFROTC featured 1,100 colleges and universities in the continental United States, Puerto Rico and Hawaii.

The US Airforce ROTC are dedicated to developing leaders of tomorrow who will go on to fulfill the Air Force mission, represent the core values and live up to the rich history of Air Force ROTC.

This program promises more than just education. It offers:

- Leadership opportunities
- Professional Development
- Start as a Manager (Enter the Air Force or Space Force an an officer and leader)
- Salary & Benefits.

Selection Criteria

The AFROTC scholarship program have specific requirement which are categorized as follows:

- Academic Standards
- Fitness Requirements
- Medical Requirements
- Enlisted Requirements

The deadline for this scholarship is usually around December 31th Annually.

Application Link: https://www.afrotc.com/scholarships/

28 Army ROTC Scholarship

OVERVIEW

The US Army ROTC is awarded annually, it can cover the scholar's tuition and fees, or room and board, and each comes with stipends for living and books.

Receive monthly stipends to offset costs of living and books.

- All scholarships include an extra $420 per month for the school year to use toward monthly expenses, like housing,
- All scholarships also allow $1,200 per year to spend toward books.

Your achievements and grades determine if you'll be awarded a scholarship, not your financial need.

It may be used at any of the Army ROTC featured 1,000 colleges and universities in the continental United States, Puerto Rico and Hawaii.

You may choose any major you wish and commission as an Officer into the active-duty Army, Army Reserve, or Army National Guard.

ARMY ROTC allows you become a leader and serve your country, all without sacrificing your college experience. In Army Reserve Officers' Training Corps (ROTC), a career is waiting for you when you graduate.

This program promises more than just education. It offers:

- Leadership opportunities
- Professional Development
- Start as a Manager (Enter the U.S. ARMY as an officer and leader)
- Salary & Benefits

The deadline for this scholarship is usually around February 4th Annually.

Application Link: https://www.goarmy.com/careers-and-jobs/find-your-path/army-officers/rotc/scholarships.html

29 The Minuteman Campaign under the Army ROTC Scholarship

OVERVIEW

The Minuteman is a Guaranteed Reserve Forces Duty (GRFD) scholarship that provides full in-state tuition and fees, or up to $10,000 room and board between 2-4 years for eligible candidates. The Minuteman scholarship guarantees the candidate will commission into the USAR upon graduation with an eight-year service obligation.

If you are a high school senior interested in receiving an Army Reserve Officer Training Corps (ROTC) scholarship and commissioning into the Army Reserve, the GRFD Scholarship Minuteman Campaign provides you an excellent opportunity.

The Minuteman campaign offers two types of 4 year scholarships.

1) 4-year scholarship may only be awarded to incoming college freshmen attending a host ROTC program or a public university at resident rates.
2) 3-year awarded to an incoming college sophomore that pays the last 3 years of benefits provided the applicant successfully meets the requirements to contract.
3) 2-year awarded to an incoming college junior or graduate student that pays the last 2 years of benefits provided the applicant successfully meets the requirements to contract.

Scholarship recipients also receive a monthly stipend of $420, and a yearly book allowance of $1,200. In addition, Minuteman recipients participate in the Simultaneous Membership Program, which gives them experience with an Army Reserve unit while earning additional money for their service.

To get started, high school seniors should contact the Professor of Military Science or Recruiting Operations Officer at the Army ROTC program that serves their college or university. There are 275 host programs that cover nearly 3,000 schools across the United States.

SCHOLARSHIP BENEFITS:

- Receive full tuition and fees (in-state) or room and board ($10,000 per year) at the participating University of attendance
- Receive Cadet stipend monthly ($420 Freshman-Senior)
- Receive a book stipend of $1,200 annually ($600 per semester)

REQUIREMENTS:

- Minimum high school GPA: 2.5
- Minimum test scores: SAT 850 or ACT 19
- Enlisted or Eligible to enlist
- Must be a U.S. Citizen
- Eligible to participate in the Simultaneous Membership Program(SMP), an experience with an Army Reserve unit while earning additional money for service
- Meet physical fitness requirements
- Between the age(s) of 17-28.

Application deadline is usually around August 5th yearly.

Application Link: https://www.usar.army.mil/MinutemanCampaign/

30 Naval ROTC Scholarship

OVERVIEW

The US Navy ROTC is awarded annually, it can cover the scholar's tuition and fees, three(3) summer cruises, stipends for living and books.

Subsistence allowance each academic month: Freshmen - $250/month | Sophomore - $300/month | Junior - $350/month | Senior - $400/month.

The purpose of the Navy ROTC Program is to educate and train qualified young men and women for service as commissioned officers in the Navy's unrestricted line, the Navy Nurse Corps and the Marine Corps. As the largest single source of Navy and Marine Corps officers, the Navy ROTC Scholarship Program plays an important role in preparing mature young men and women for leadership and management positions in an increasingly technical Navy and Marine Corps.

Students may start the process of applying during the second semester of their junior year of high school. Students may apply for only one of the three scholarship program options-Navy, Nurse or Marine Corps.

The Naval Reserve Officers Training Corps (Navy ROTC) Program was established in 1926 to provide a broad base of citizens knowledgeable in the arts and sciences of Naval Warfare. The program provided an opportunity for young men to undertake careers in the naval profession. In the beginning, there were six Navy ROTC units located at the University of California at Berkeley, Georgia Institute of Technology, Northwestern University, University of Washington, and Harvard and Yale Universities. In June of 1930, 126 midshipmen graduated from college, and received commissions in the United States Navy. At least 3 of the graduates went on to obtain flag rank.

P.S: For more details or information on the US Navy ROTC Program, please visit the scholarship website.

The deadline for this scholarship is usually around February 4th Annually.

Application Link: https://www.netc.navy.mil/NSTC/NROTC/

31

Onsi Sawiris Scholarship Program

OVERVIEW

The Onsi Sawiris Scholarship Program is a fully funded scholarship program for undergraduate and graduate students. The scholarship is open for all Egyptian students seeking to pursue their degrees at prestigious universities in the United States with the aim of bolstering Egypt's economic competitiveness.

This program is a precedent in Egypt for private sector involvement in educational programs on a sustainable basis. The aim of which is to facilitate the academic development and character building of young Egyptians giving them the tools to develop their careers hence benefiting their communities in which they live.

The Onsi Sawiris Scholarship Program is only granted to the list of endorsed universities provided in the "Approved Universities" Selection as a nominee for the Onsi Sawiris scholarship Program does not guarantee university acceptance. Applicants will be supported in applying to these universities. If nominated for the scholarship; the Onsi Sawiris Scholarship Program award will be made once university acceptance is obtained.

Approved universities are: Stanford University | Harvard University | University of Chicago | University of Pennsylvania.

Selection Criteria

Applicants should have a minimum GPA of 3.5/90% in Thanaweyya Amma certification (Secondary year) or equivalent certificates.

TOEFL iBT ®: 100 or above (taken within 2 years).

Minimum SAT I Score: 1450 (Taken within 2 years) or Minimum ACT Score: 32 (Taken within 2 years)

Extracurricular Activities: Have been involved or are currently involved in extracurricular activities.

Fields of Study: Engineering, Economics, Political Science, Finance and Management.

Be Egyptian nationals, who are residents of Egypt (preference will not be given to dual nationality applicants).

Be committed to coming back to Egypt for two years directly after the successful completion of their bachelor's degree.

P.S: Preference will be given to candidates who have not lived, worked, or studied abroad for a significant period of time.

The deadline for this scholarship is July 31st .

N.B: For more details or information on the Onsi Sawiris Scholarship Program, please visit the scholarship website.

Application Link: https://www.onsisawirisscholarship.org/

CHAPTER 3

FULL RIDE NEED-BASED $CHOLARSHIP$

1 Princeton University

Location: Princeton, New Jersey
Setting: Suburban (600 Acres)
Undergraduate Enrollment: 4,773
Type: Private
Acceptance Rate: 6%
Early Acceptance Rate: 14.7%

Financial aid Admission at Princeton university is awarded solely based on financial need, there are no merit scholarship awards. Princeton's admissions is need-blind for all applicants, including international students.

The student's need is determined through a careful review of each family's individual financial circumstances. Most importantly, the full need of every admitted student is met through grants.

Application Deadline: Usually around November 9th

View more information using the table below:

Gross Family Income	Percent Qualified	Average Grant	What It Covers
$0 – 65,000	100%	$77,240	Full tuition, room + board
$65,000 – 85,000	100%	$70,520	Full tuition, 80% room + board
$85,000 – 100,000	100%	$68,180	Full tuition, 67% room + board
$100,000 – 120,000	100%	$65,750	Full tuition, 54% room + board
$120,000 – 140,000	100%	$62,780	Full tuition, 37% room + board

Gross Family Income	Percent Qualified	Average Grant	What it Covers
$140,000 – 160,000	100%	$57,550	Full tuition, 8% room + board
$160,000 – 180,000	100%	$53,360	95% tuition
$180,000 – 200,000	98%	$44,440	79% tuition
$200,000 – 250,000	95%	$68,180	66% tuition
$250,000 and above (most who qualify have 2 children in college)	43%	$68,180	51% tuition

Full tuition = $68,180

Room and board = $18,180

P.S: For detailed information about the Princeton scholarship and how to apply for the need based scholarship, please visit the Princeton scholarship website.

Application Link: https://admission.princeton.edu/cost-aid/apply-financial-aid

Harvard University

Location: Cambridge, Massachusetts
Setting: Urban (5,076 Acres)
Undergraduate Enrollment: 5,222
Type: Private
Acceptance Rate: 5%
Early Acceptance Rate: 13.9%

" 55%" of students receive need-based Harvard scholarships. 1 in 5 pays nothing to attend."

Harvard scholarships are orchestrated to cover 100% of a student's demonstrated financial need.

Below is Harvard's Aid Process:

First they determine your award by establishing your parent contribution

Then they factor in student employment and any outside awards the student has received.

Your remaining need will be covered by scholarship funds which are grant-based and never need to be repaid.

US Citizens, permanent residents and international students are eligible for Harvard need-based scholarships.

US Citizens and Permanent Residents

US citizens and permanent residents may be eligible to receive a Federal Pell Grant or a Supplemental Educational Opportunity Grant (SEOG). The scholar's eligibility is determined by the information they provide in their Free Application for Federal Student Aid (FAFSA).

Pell Grants and SEOG are awarded by the federal government and administered by Harvard's office, based on financial need. Roughly 17% of Harvard College students are Pell Grant recipients.

P.S: For detailed information about this scholarship and how to apply for the need based scholarship, please visit the Harvard scholarship website.

Application Link: https://college.harvard.edu/financial-aid/how-aid-works/types-aid

3

Yale University

Location: New Haven, Connecticut
Setting: City (373 Acres)
Undergraduate Enrollment: 4,703
Type: Private
Acceptance Rate: 7%

A ***Yale financial aid*** award meets 100% of a student's demonstrated financial need based on the estimated cost of attendance and a calculated expected family contribution. This is done regardless of citizenship or immigration status—without relying on student loans, for all four years.

Every Yale financial aid award includes two parts: Grant aid and the Student Share. Grant aid may include a need-based Yale Scholarship and/or funds from external sources including entitlement grants (Federal Pell Grant, Supplemental Educational Opportunity Grant/SEOG, and state grants) or merit-based scholarships a student may have earned from outside organizations. Yale does not give out any merit-based scholarships.

The Student Share is a fixed amount students receiving aid should anticipate contributing from term-time and summer job earnings. The grant aid and Student Effort in every Yale financial aid award will meet a student's full demonstrated financial need.

P.S: For detailed information about this scholarship and how to apply for the need based scholarship, please visit the scholarship website.

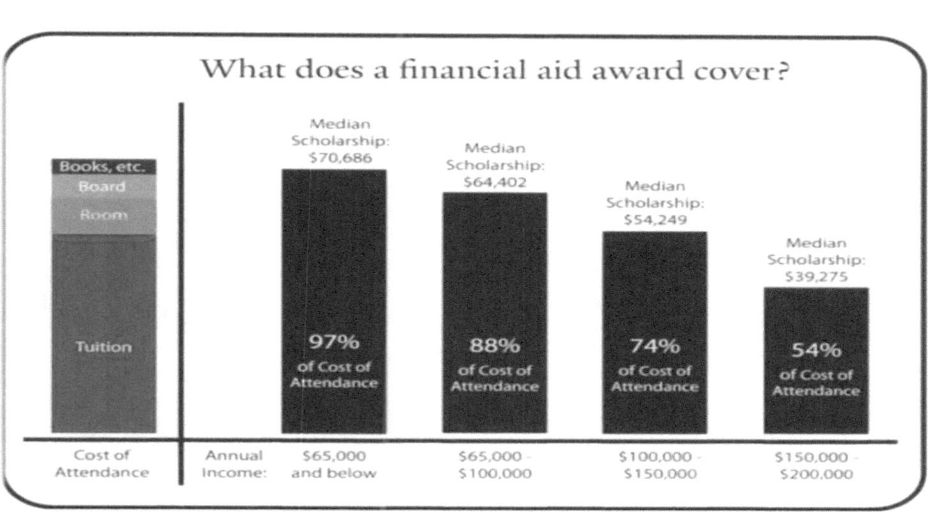

Application Link: https://finaid.yale.edu/costs-affordability/affordability

4 Columbia University

Location: New York, New York
Setting: Urban (36 Acres)
Undergraduate Enrollment: 6,170
Type: Private
Acceptance Rate: 5%
Early Acceptance Rate: 13.9%

Scholarships/Financial aid at Columbia University is totally need based. They evaluate the student's family ability to pay for education costs. In Columbia, there are no academic, athletic or talent-based institutional scholarships.

Columbia evaluates admission applications of US Citizens and Eligible Non-Citizens without regard to your financial need. Admissions for international students are however need aware.

At Columbia University, 100% of the demonstrated financial need for all first-years and transfers pursuing their first degree are met. Up to all four years of study. International students are also highly considered.

About Columbia University Financial Aid Programs:

- No loans – Columbia's need-based aid is in the form of grants and student work only. Loans are not used to meet financial need or included in initial financial aid awards.
- $0 parent contribution - For students coming from families with calculated total incomes of less than $66,000 annually (and typical assets), parents are not expected to contribute to the cost of attendance.
- Free Tuition - Students coming from families with calculated total incomes of less than $150,000 annually (and typical assets) will be able to attend Columbia tuition-free.
- Start-Up Grants
- Broad Aid Eligibility
- Funding Opportunities
- International Aid
- Guidance for All

Application Link: https://cc-seas.financialaid.columbia.edu/how/aid/works

5

Brown University

Location: Providence, Rhode Island
Setting: City (146 Acres)
Undergraduate Enrollment: 6,792
Type: Private
Acceptance Rate: 8%

The Sidney E. Frank Scholarship is awarded to the neediest undergraduate students at Brown University who cannot otherwise afford the full cost of tuition and other costs of receiving an education at Brown.

In September 2004, Sidney E. Frank, a member of the class of 1942, made a gift of $100 million to Brown University — the largest gift in the University's history.

Eligibity & Selection Criteria

Undergraduate students who are U.S. citizens or eligible non-citizens and who enter Brown through the Early Admission and Regular Admission process will be eligible for consideration as Frank Scholars.

There is no separate application required. Students who meet the criteria will automatically be considered assuming that all financial aid application requirements and deadlines are met.

For more Information visit the Sidney E. Frank Scholarship page and/or send an email to the financial aid office.

P.S: For detailed information about this scholarship and how to apply for the need based aid, please visit the scholarship website.

Application Link:

https://finaid.brown.edu/aid-types/grants-scholarships/sidney-e-frank-scholars

Dartmouth College

Location: Hanover, New Hampshire
Setting: Rural (237 Acres)
Undergraduate Enrollment: 4,170
Type: Private
Acceptance Rate: 9%

Dartmouth Scholarships and endowment grants are need-based and are given without expectation of repayment. Amounts range from $1,000 to over $50,000, depending on our determination of your eligibility

Dartmouth can cover 100% of student's cost of attendance based on the student's need.

Cost of Education – Family Contribution = "Need"

There is zero parent contribution for families with income below $65,000

Dartmouth's Tuition Guarantee

Students from families with total incomes of $125,000 or less—and possessing typical assets, will receive scholarship that will at least cover the cost of tuition.

Families with Income Above $125,000

There is no income cut off for scholarship consideration at Dartmouth. We take an individual look at all applications, and families earning over $125,000 per year do receive scholarship assistance.

IMPORTANT DEADLINES

Early Decision	*Regular Decision*	*Transfer Students*
CSS Profile: November 1	CSS Profile: February 1	CSS Profile: March 1
FAFSA: November 1	FAFSA: February 1	FAFSA: March 1
IDOC: November 1	IDOC: February 1	IDOC: March 1

Application Link:

https://financialaid.dartmouth.edu/apply-aid/current-students/types-financial-aid/grants-scholarships

7

Cornell University

Location: Ithaca, New York
Setting: Rural (745 Acres)
Undergraduate Enrollment: 14,743
Type: Private
Acceptance Rate: 11%

Cornell University Grant & Scholarships

Cornell Grants and scholarships are available to students with financial need, as determined by the Office of Financial Aid and Student Employment. The aid comes from several sources - university endowments, alumni gifts, and a general fund. Things to keep in mind:

There is no minimum or maximum amount of grant awarded.

There is no standard "income bracket" or cut-off for grant aid recipients; eligibility is determined on a case-by-case basis.

University grants are awarded after non-university funds, work-study, and loans.

You are automatically considered for these funds when you apply for financial aid; there is no separate application process.

P.S: For detailed information about this scholarship and how to apply for the need based aid, please visit the Cornell University's scholarship website.

Application Link: https://finaid.cornell.edu/types-aid

8 Massachusetts Institute of Technology

Location: Cambridge, Massachusetts
Setting: Urban (168 Acres)
Undergraduate Enrollment: 4,361
Type: Private
Acceptance Rate: 7%
Early Acceptance Rate: 7.4%

MIT is committed to meeting 100% of demonstrated financial need for both domestic students (U.S. citizens and Permanent residents) and international students.

About 60% of MIT undergraduates receive scholarships.

MIT Aid Application Deadlines.

Application deadlines are the same for both domestic and international students.

Early Action applicants: November 30. The application deadline for Early Action is November 30 and awards are released in mid-January.

Regular Action applicants: February 15. The application deadline is February 15, and awards are released in mid-March.

Continuing students: April 15. The financial aid application deadline for the following academic year is April 15. You will receive your award in late May or early June.

Three Steps to Apply for Aid (For Domestic Students)

FAFSA: The form you need to fill out to receive any federal or state student aid

CSS Profile: A tool provided by the College Board that we use to determine if you qualify for a need-based MIT Scholarship.

Parental tax returns or income documentation: Your parents' tax returns or income documentation must be submitted through the College Board's secure IDOC platform.

Two Steps to Apply for Aid (For International Students)

CSS Profile: A tool provided by the College Board that we use to determine if you qualify for a need-based MIT Scholarship.

Parental tax returns or income documentation: your parents' tax returns or income documentation must be submitted through the College Board's secure IDOC platform. If your parents live outside the U.S., please provide the tax return from that country, along with a translation to English if applicable.

Application Link: https://sfs.mit.edu/undergraduate-students/types-of-aid/mit-scholarship/

9

Stanford University

Location: Stanford, California
Setting: Suburban (8,180 Acres)
Undergraduate Enrollment: 6,366
Type: Private
Acceptance Rate: 5%

Almost half of all Stanford undergraduates receive need-based financial aid. Families earning less than $150,000 with assets typical of that income level pay no tuition. Families earning less than $75,000 with assets typical of that income level pay no tuition or room and board.

The need based scholarships are available for both domestic (U.S. Citizens & permanent residents) and international students.

Total (Gross) Family Income	Average Scholarship and Grant	Average Net Cost	% of applicants who qualify for scholarship aid from Stanford
Less than $75,000	82,356	$4,118	99%
$75,000 – $100,000	73,906	$8,180	96%
$100,000 – $125,000	66,256	$14,404	100%
$125,000 – 150,000	59,971	$20,840	100%
$150,000 – $175,000	51,210	$29,558	94%
$175,000 – $200,00	$43,745	$36,913	89%

Total (Gross) Family Income	Average Scholarship and Grant	Average Net Cost	% of applicants who qualify for scholarship aid from Stanford
$200,000 – 225,000	35,663	$44,956	93%
$225,000 – 250,000	34,040	$46,665	90%
$250,000 – 275,000*	23,146	$57,471	63%
$275,000 – 300,000*	21,768	$58,897	56%
Greater than $300,000*	21,768	$58,897	56%

Most who qualify for (*) "Total (Gross) Family Income" have 2 or more children in college.

Factors such as family size, number of family members in college and family asset are also considered.

P.S: You can contact Stanford's admission office for more information.

Application Link: https://admission.stanford.edu/afford/

10 California Institute of Technology

Location: Pasadena, California
Setting: Suburban (124 Acres)
Undergraduate Enrollment: 987
Type: Private
Acceptance Rate: 7%

Caltech will meet 100% of a student's demonstrated financial need through a combination of awards known as a financial aid package. These needs are met through grants, scholarships, and student employment.

Cost of Attendance – Family Contribution = Demonstrated Financial Need.

Learn more about family contribution here:
https://www.finaid.caltech.edu/HowItWorks/familycontribution

The Cost of Attendance is the total cost of attending Caltech for one year. It includes both direct charges from Caltech, like tuition and fees, as well as other expenses, like books and supplies.

The Family Contribution represents the amount of money your family would be expected to pay for one year of school. They calculate the exact amount of your family's contribution with their needs analysis formula.

Caltech Financial Aid Scholarship: https://www.finaid.caltech.edu/Applying

P.S: Learn more about the Caltech Financial aid by contacting their admission office.

University of Chicago

Location: Chicago, Illinois
Setting: Urban (217 Acres)
Undergraduate Enrollment: 7,470
Type: Private
Acceptance Rate: 7%

UChicago meets 100% of demonstrated need in the form of grants (which do not need to be repaid) instead of loans for all families.

Cost of Attendance – Family Contribution = Demonstrated Financial Need

Your family contribution is then subtracted from the total cost of attendance. The cost of attendance represents actual and estimated costs for one year at UChicago, including tuition, housing, a meal plan, and estimates for additional costs like books and personal expenses.

P.S: For detailed information about this scholarship and how to apply for the need based aid, please visit the UChicago scholarship website.

Application Link: https://collegeadmissions.uchicago.edu/financial-support/applying-aid

CHAPTER 4

SCHOLARSHIP APPLICATION TIPS

Dear scholarship award aspirants, we have listed out the various full ride scholarships that are available for undergraduate study at universities and colleges in the United States. These scholarships are available to both U.S. residents and international students (unless otherwise indicated).

Instead of writing wordy sentences, we will go straight to giving the key scholarship tips!

With the aid of this book, aspirants can have a full view of suitable universities/colleges they can apply to and gain financial aid.

Here are Key Guidelines/Tips to Aid Students Win Scholarships

- **Apply By Early Action**: Students are advised to apply early in order to be duly considered for scholarship awards. The scholarship application for some schools goes together with the application for admissions, while other scholarship programs require entirely separate applications for them. Be sure to apply well ahead of the scholarship deadline(s).

N.B: Confirm the deadline of the scholarship and make sure you beat the deadline. Applications submitted after deadlines are usually disregarded.

- **Fill & Submit FAFSA**: Fill out and submit your FAFSA before the deadline. Filing a FAFSA is a requirement for many full ride scholarships. You'll learn more on the key definitions page of this book.
- **Apply For Scholarships You are Most Qualified For:** Scholarships have their requirements, these are put in place to provide the awards to deserving students. Therefore, it is highly advisable that you apply only for scholarships that you meet their requirements. It is also worth noting that meeting the minimum requirements doesn't guarantee that you'll obtain the scholarship. Why? Scholarships are competitive you should present yourself in the best way possible – by exuding excellence – to stand a chance. Scholarship opportunities at less known/less populated schools have shown to be easier to get.
- **Have a Good Test Score & GPA | Unique Talent**: SATs, ACTs, CLTs, and other grading system test scores should have been taken and scores obtained before applying for scholarships. A high test score combined with a superb high school GPA will increase the chances of you getting a scholarship as the majority of full ride scholarships are centred around the academic performance of scholars. Other criteria like leadership abilities, cultural background, unique talent, or life challenges are considered for some scholarships.
- **Craft Your Applications/ Essays to Impress:** Pay close attention to application essay topics and do thorough work in crafting a well-written essay and write to impress the reviewer highlighting your achievements in a very impressive manner. Ensure that your essay is well structured and free of any errors. Write award-winning essays!
- **Get Outstanding Recommendations/Nominations**: For scholarships requiring Nominations please ensure that you're nominated on time. Also, ensure that your recommendation letters show how much of an outstanding student you are.

- **Apply for as Many Scholarships as Possible:** Do not limit yourself to one scholarship. In as much as you meet the requirements for scholarships, give it your best shot. Several students have received multiple full ride scholarship offers from which they chose the best – that can be your story too.
- **Prepare Properly for Scholarship Interviews:** If the scholarship you apply for requires you to go through an interview process, prepare properly for it. Take your interview session with confidence.
- **DO NOT FALL Victim for Scholarship Scams:** Apply directly to the University/College of your interest or on the ***official website*** of the external scholarship(s) you wish to apply for. Do not enrich fraudsters using unauthorized means in applying for scholarships.

A Typical Scholarship Award Process

Find Scholarship(s) → Start Application → Submit Documents →

Submit Application → Attend Interview (Not applicable in all cases) →

Receive Scholarship($)/Get Feedback.

CHAPTER 1

FULL TUITION INSTITUTIONAL $CHOLARSHIP$

1 University of Alabama

Location: Tuscaloosa, Alabama
Setting: Suburban (1,143 Acres)
Undergraduate Enrollment: 32,458
Type: Public

Presidential Scholarship: Awards Full tuition scholarship to **in-state students**.

Requirements: A minimum ACT Score of 30 or SAT score of 1360 | High school GPA of 3.50+

Application Deadline: October 31 (Application deadline for the first round)

Application Link: https://afford.ua.edu/scholarships/in-state-freshman/

3 University of Alabama in Huntsville

Location: Huntsville, Alabama
Setting: City (432 Acres)
Undergraduate Enrollment: 7,169
Type: Public

Merit Tuition Scholarship: Awards Full tuition to incoming freshmen.

Requirements: A minimum ACT Score of 30 or SAT score of 1390 | High school GPA of 3.50

Application Deadline: December 15

Application Link: https://www.uah.edu/admissions/undergraduate/financial-aid/scholarships/freshmen

2 University of Alabama at Birmingham

Location: Birmingham, Alabama
Setting: Urban (437 Acres)
Undergraduate Enrollment: 13,032
Type: Public

Presidential Recognition: Awards Full tuition and fees to **in-state students**.

Requirements: A minimum ACT Score of 30 or SAT equivalent | High school GPA of 3.50 or higher.

Presidential Scholarship for National Scholars: Awards Full tuition and fees, one year on campus housing allotment, one time $2,500 experiential learning stipend and one-year $1,000 Provost First year Scholarship.

Eligibility: National Merit Finalists and National Hispanic Recognition Program Scholars.

Application Deadline: April 1 for the June intake. May 1 for the August intake. November 1 for the January intake.

Application Link: https://www.uab.edu/admissions/cost/scholarships

4 Tuskegee University

Location: Tuskegee, Alabama
Setting: Rural (5,000 Acres)
Undergraduate Enrollment: 2,100
Type: Private

University Merit Scholarship: Awards Full tuition and an $800 book stipend.

Requirements: A High School GPA of 3.5 | SAT score of 1200-1290 or ACT composite score of 25-27

Application Deadline: May 1

Application Link: https://www.tuskegee.edu/programs-courses/scholarships/freshman-scholarships

5 University of Alabama in Tuscaloosa

Location: Tuscaloosa, Alabama
Setting: Suburban (1,143 Acres)
Undergraduate Enrollment: 32,458
Type: Public

Presidential Scholarship: Awards Full tuition to ***in-state freshmen***.

Requirements: An ACT score of 30-36 or 1360-1600 SAT | High school GPA of 3.50+

P.S: The Presidential Elite Scholarship covers the Full cost of tuition plus other benefits. It is available to both in-state, out-of-state and international students.

Application Deadline: December 15

Application Link: https://afford.ua.edu/scholarships/

6 Alabama A&M University

Location: Montgomery, Alabama
Setting: Urban (1,173 Acres)
Undergraduate Enrollment: 5,206
Type: Public

The AAMU Merit Scholarship: Award covers the cost of tuition.

Requirements: A minimum ACT Score of 23 or SAT score of 1130 | High school GPA of 3.25+

Application Deadline: February 28

Application link:
https://www.aamu.edu/admissions-aid/financial-aid/scholarships/index.html

8 University of South Alabama

Location: Mobile, Alabama
Setting: Suburban (1,224 Acres)
Undergraduate Enrollment: 8,491
Type: Public

USA Freshman Admission Scholarship: Awards Full tuition.

Eligibility: Applicant must be a U.S. citizen, applied for/obtained Permanent residency, or a student attending a U.S. High school with a qualified visa status.

Requirements: A minimum ACT Score of 32 or SAT score of 1420 | High school GPA of 3.50.

Application Deadline: December 1

Application link:
https://www.southalabama.edu/departments/financialaffairs/scholarships/freshscholarships/

7 Alabama State University

Location: Huntsville, Alabama
Setting: City (172 Acres)
Undergraduate Enrollment: 3,296
Type: Public

Academic Incentive Scholarship: Awards Full tuition and a $500 book award.

Requirements: A minimum ACT Score of 20 or a comparable SAT score of 1020 (EBR/W and math) | High school GPA of 3.0 or higher.

Black and Gold Scholarship: Awards Full tuition, required fees, and/or on campus room and board as follows:

The Black and Gold Scholarship pays $4,000 a year for a maximum of eight semesters for freshmen and a maximum of six semesters for college transfer students.

Requirements: A minimum ACT Score of 18 or a comparable SAT score of 940 (EBR/W and math) | High school GPA of 2.75 or higher.

Application Deadline: February 15

Application Link:
https://www.alasu.edu/admissions/undergrad-admissions/asu-academic-scholarships

1 John Brown University

Location: Siloam Springs, Arkansas
Setting: City (200 Acres)
Undergraduate Enrollment: 1,659
Type: Private

Presidential Scholarship: Awards $27,500. This covers the total cost of tuition.

Requirements: A minimum 3.6 cumulative high school GPA | ACT score of 32+ or SAT score of 1420+ (Applicant's can make up for a low GPA with high test scores and vice versa)

Application Deadline: November 5 (Fall) | March 4 (Spring)

Application link: https://www.jbu.edu/financial-aid/on-campus-undergraduate/scholarships-and-aid/scholarships/

2 Hendrix College

Location: Conway, Arkansas
Setting: Subruban (175 Acres)
Undergraduate Enrollment: 1,130
Type: Private

Provost Scholarship: Awards Full tuition.

Requirements: ACT Score of 32 or SAT score of 1430 | High school GPA of 3.6

President's & Madison Murphy Leadership Scholarship: Full tuition, board, half the room.

Requirements: ACT Score of 32 or SAT score of 1430 | High school GPA of 3.6

Application Deadline: November 15

Application Link: https://www.hendrix.edu/financialaid/scholarships/

3 Harding University

Location: Searcy, Arkansas
Setting: City (350 Acres)
Undergraduate Enrollment: 3,523
Type: Private

Trustee Scholar Award: Award covers Full tuition.

Requirements: 31+ ACT composite score, 1390+ SAT combined critical reading and math score | A minimum 3.5 high school GPA.

Application Deadline: March 15

Application link: https://www.harding.edu/admissions/scholarships

4 University of the Ozarks

Location: Clarksville, Arkansas
Setting: Rural (45 Acres)
Undergraduate Enrollment: 784
Type: Private

Full Need Tuition Scholarship: Awards need-based full tuition scholarship to Arkansas students from Johnson, Logan, Franklin, Madison, and Newton counties.

Requirements: Top Applicants.

Application Deadline: Check website for application procedure.

Application link: https://ozarks.edu/admissions-aid/costs-and-aid/grants-and-scholarships/

5 Williams Baptist College

Location: Walnut Ridge, Arkansas
Setting: Rural (250 Acres)
Undergraduate Enrollment: 562
Type: Private

President's Scholarship: Awards $10,000 per year. (This covers the total cost of tuition)

Requirements: ACT 22-26 / SAT equivalent.

Founders Scholarship: Awards $12,000 per year. (This covers the total cost of tuition)

Requirements: ACT 27+ / SAT equivalent.

Application Deadline: June 1

Application Link:
https://williamsbu.edu/financial-aid/scholarships/

6 Ouachita Baptist University

Location: Arkadelphia, Arkansas
Setting: Rural (200 Acres)
Undergraduate Enrollment: 1,730
Type: Private

President's Scholarship: Awards $18,500/year (This covers the total cost of tuition)

Requirements: High school GPA of 4.0 or higher.

Founder's Scholarship: Awards $15,000/year (This covers the total cost of tuition)

Requirements: High school GPA of 3.85-3.99.

Application Deadline: January 15

Application Link:
https://obu.edu/finaid/obu.php

7 Lyon College

Location: Batesville, Arkansas
Setting: City (136 Acres)
Undergraduate Enrollment: 495
Type: Private

Honors Fellows Program: A Fellow receives an annual stipend up to the cost of tuition.

Trustee Scholarship: Awards up to Full tuition.

Requirements: Top Applicants.

Application Deadline: Check the website for more details.

Application link:
https://www.lyon.edu/scholarships-aid-programs

8 Philander Smith College

Location: Little Rock, Arkansas
Setting: Urban (9 Acres)
Undergraduate Enrollment: 769
Type: Private

Thomas Mason Scholarship: Full tuition and Fees.

Requirements: A minimum 3.2 high school GPA | ACT composite score of 21 | SAT composite score of 1060.

Application link:
https://www.philander.edu/admissions/paying-for-college/scholarships

1 University of Arizona

Location: Tucson, Arizona
Setting: City (392 Acres)
Undergraduate Enrollment: 40,407
Type: Public

All-Arizona Academic Team Award: Awards full tuition scholarship to ***Arizona residents***.

Eligibility: Applicant must be a U.S. citizen or permanent resident or demonstrate lawful immigration status | Top applicants.

Arizona Academy Scholars Tuition Award: Provides $8,000 - $12,500 per academic year.

(This covers the total cost of tuition)

The Arizona Academy is UArizona's premier opportunity for international high school students to earn university credit while still enrolled in secondary school.

Requirements: Students must successfully complete the Arizona Academy program | Top applicants.

Arizona Tuition Award: Awards $1,000 - $35,000 per academic year. (This covers the total cost of tuition)

Eligibility: Applicant must be a U.S. citizen or permanent resident or demonstrate lawful immigration status | Be classified as a ***non-Arizona*** resident | Top applicants.

The **Foster Care tuition** award covers the full amount of Arizona resident undergraduate base tuition,mandatory fees and course fees.

Application Deadline: May 3

Application link: https://financialaid.arizona.edu/types-of-aid/scholarships/incoming-first-year-transfer

2 Northern Arizona University

Location: Flagstaff, Arizona
Setting: City (882 Acres)
Undergraduate Enrollment: 23,207
Type: Public

Lumberjack Scholars Award: Awards full tuition scholarship to ***Arizona residents***.

Requirements: A minimum 3.5 unweighted core high school GPA | Top applicants.

Application Deadline: August 1 (Fall) | December 1 (Spring)

Application link: https://nau.edu/office-of-scholarships-and-financial-aid/freshman-merit-based-tuition-scholarships/

3 Grand Canyon

Location: Phoenix, Arizona
Setting: Urban (100 Acres)
Undergraduate Enrollment: 65,870
Type: Private

Barnabas Pastoral Program Scholarship: Award covers Full tuition and other benefits.

P.S: This scholarship is designed for students to complete their Bachelors degree and Master of Divinity in as little as five years.

Requirements: Check the website for more details.

Colangelo Scholarship: Awards full tuition.

Requirements: A 3.75+ cumulative, unweighted GPA

Application Deadline: December 31

Application Link: https://www.gcu.edu/financial-aid/scholarships-grants/additional

1 University of Southern California

Location: Los Angeles, Carlifornia
Setting: Urban (226 Acres)
Undergraduate Enrollment: 20,699
Type: Private

Mork Family Scholarship: Awards Full tuition plus $5000/year additional housing stipend.

Trustee Scholarship: Awards Full tuition.

Requirements: Application is open to incoming freshmen through the USC Office of Admission. Candidates are selected from an extremely competitive pool.

Application Deadline: December 1

Application Link:
https://financialaid.usc.edu/undergraduate-financial-aid/admitted-and-continuing-students/scholarships/

2 California Lutheran University

Location: Thousand Oaks, California
Setting: Suburban (290 Acres)
Undergraduate Enrollment: 2,513
Type: Private

Presidential Scholarship: Awards $25,000 up to Full tuition.

Requirements: This scholarship is awarded to graduating high school seniors in the top tier of the application pool.

Steven Dorfman Scholarship: 75% up to full tuition.

Requirements: Top Applicants.

Application Deadline: November 15

Application Link:
https://www.callutheran.edu/financial-aid/scholarships-grants/undergraduate.html

3 Loyola Marymount University

Location: Los Angeles, California
Setting: Suburban (142 Acres)
Undergraduate Enrollment: 7,299
Type: Private

Arrupe Scholarships: Awards up to full tuition for all four (4) years.

Requirements: Recipients are selected from among the best applicants.

Application Deadline: Contact Admission Office.

Application Link:
https://financialaid.lmu.edu/prospectivestudents/scholarships/lmuacademicscholarshipsforfirst-yearstudents/

4 Harvey Mudd College

Location: Claremont, Carlifornia
Setting: Suburban (33 Acres)
Undergraduate Enrollment: 906
Type: Private

President's Scholars Program: Full tuition scholarship which is renewable for four (4) years.

Requirements: Applicant(s) must be a U.S. citizen or permanent resident | Have a proven record of academic success with excellent grades | Show leadership capabilities.

Application Deadline: January 20

Application Link:
https://www.hmc.edu/admission/afford/scholarships-and-grants/merit-based-scholarships/presidents-scholars-program/

5 University of California - Davis

Location: Davis, California
Setting: City (5,300 Acres)
Undergraduate Enrollment: 31,532
Type: Public

UC Davis' Scholarships: The scholarships can range from $100 to $14,000 per academic year. (This covers the base tuition for california residents)

UC Blue and Gold Opportunity Plan: The Blue and Gold Opportunity Plan ensures that eligible California undergraduates with an annual family income of less than $80,000 will have their systemwide – or base – tuition and fees covered by gift aid.

Requirements: A minimum 3.25 GPA.

Application Deadline: November 30

Application Link: https://financialaid.ucdavis.edu/scholarships/campus

6 Saint Mary's College of California

Location: Moraga, Carlifornia
Setting: Suburban (420 Acres)
Undergraduate Enrollment: 2,003
Type: Private

The East Bay Performing Arts Scholarship for Black Students or Students of African Descent: Awards Full tuition.

Requirements: The recipient must agree to major or minor in the program awarding the scholarship.

Mentored Access to Programs in Science (MAPS): Awards Full tuition.

Eligibility: This scholarship is awarded to high achieving students with financial need interested in studying Biology, Mathematics, Physics, Chemistry, or Biochemistry.

Application Deadline: January 15

Application Link: https://www.stmarys-ca.edu/financial-aid/scholarships/first-year-students

7 Claremont McKenna College

Location: Claremont, Carlifornia
Setting: Suburban (69 Acres)
Undergraduate Enrollment: 1,386
Type: Private

Seaver Scholars Program: Scholarship awards full tuition for all four (4) years.

Requirements: Students who demonstarte exceptional leadership promise along with a commitment to making a positive impact in the world.

Interdisciplinary Science Scholars: Scholarship awards full Science tuition scholars for all four (4) years + plus summer fellowships, internships, or research experiences.

Requirements: Students with a passion for Science and Leadership.

Application Deadline: Contact Admission Office.

Application Link: https://www.cmc.edu/admission/scholarships

1 Regis University

Location: Denver, Colorado
Setting: Suburban (90 Acres)
Undergraduate Enrollment: 2,398
Type: Private

Presidential Catholic Schools Scholarship: Awards Full tuition scholarship to residential students.

Eligibility: High achieving graduating seniors from parochial high schools within the United States and Puerto Rico are eligible for this scholarship.

Requirements: Graduating seniors must be nominated by their high school principals or secondary school counselors.

Connors Scholarship: Awards Full tuition. ***Eligibility***: Applicant must have an affiliation with a Boston area services organization | Have a cumulative recalculated high school GPA of at least 3.5

Massachusetts Nursing Association COVID-19 Scholarship: Awards Full tuition. ***Eligibility***: Applicant must be the dependent of a member of the Massachusetts Nursing Associate who has been working on the front lines during the COVID-19 pandemic | Plan to major in nursing or a health related field | A recalculated high school GPA of at least 3.5

Regis College Puerto Dear Neighbor Scholarship: Awards Full tuition scholarship to residential students who demonstrate the values of the Sisters of Saint Joseph of Boston.

These values include:

- ✓ Gracious hospitality
- ✓ Love and service of the Dear Neighbor without distinction
- ✓ Peaceful resolution of conflict
- ✓ Care for all God's creation.

Sloane Scholarship: Awards Full tuition.

Requirements: Applicant must plan to major in a program within the Sloane School of Business and Communication | A recalculated high school GPA of at least 3.5

Application Deadline: January 1

Application Link:
https://www.regiscollege.edu/admission-and-aid/undergraduate-admission/cost-and-financial-aid/scholarships

2 Colorado College

Location: Colorado Springs, Colorado
Setting: City (100 Acres)
Undergraduate Enrollment: 2,241
Type: Private

Otis A. and Margaret T. Barnes: Awards Full tuition. Otis A. and Margaret T. Barnes established two trusts that provide full tuition scholarships to Colorado College. The first is to be used for awards in Chemistry and Biochemistry, and the second for awards in Biology, Environmental Sciences, Geology, Mathematics, Physics, and Psychology (including Neuroscience).

Requirements: Top Applicants.

Application Deadline: November 1

Application Link:
https://www.coloradocollege.edu/admission/financialaid/scholarships.html

3 Colorado Christian University

Location: Lakewood, Colorado
Setting: Suburban (53 Acres)
Undergraduate Enrollment: 7,966
Type: Private

World Changers Scholarship: Awards Full tuition.

Requirements: A minimum ACT score of 28 or SAT composite score of 1320 | 3.8 high school GPA.

P.S: This is an invitation only scholarship.

Application Deadline: December 20

Application Link:
https://www.ccu.edu/undergrad/financial-aid/scholarships/ccu-scholarships/

5 Colorado Mesa University

Location: Grand Junction, Colorado
Setting: City (86 Acres)
Undergraduate Enrollment: 8,681
Type: Public

Distinguished Scholar (*Colorado Resident*): Awards Full tuition.

Requirements: A minimum 3.75 high school GPA (weighted) | ACT composite score of 29 | SAT combined score of 1340 | Top 5% of their Class.

CMU and Donor Scholarships: These scholarships range from a cash stipend to full tuition and fees. Housing Scholarships are available for prospective students.

Application Deadline: December 31

Application Link:
https://www.coloradomesa.edu/financial-aid/scholarships/freshmen.html

4 University of Colorado, Colorado Springs

Location: Colorado Springs, Colorado
Setting: City (550 Acres)
Undergraduate Enrollment: 9,540
Type: Public

UCCS Chancellor's Award: This $10,000 scholarship covers the total cost of Tuition, Books and Supplies and other Fees for **in-state students**.

Peak Scholarship: This $25,000 scholarship covers the total cost of Tuition, Books and Supplies and other Fees for **out-of-state students**.

Requirements: Top Applicants.

Application Deadline: Admitted students can apply between Dec 1 – May 1 for the upcoming aid year.

Application Link:
https://www.uccs.edu/degreesandprograms/scholarships-uccs

1 University of Connecticut

Location: Storrs, Connecticut
Setting: Rural (4,076 Acres)
Undergraduate Enrollment: 18,983
Type: Public

Presidential Scholars Award: Covers the Full cost of tuition plus a one-time $2,500 enrichment award. *(Available only to Connecticut students)*

Requirements: Applicant must be a Valedictorian/Salutatorian to be considered for this award | A Connecticut resident graduating from a Connecticut high school.

Leadership Scholarship: Awards Full tuition to ***in-state students*** and half tuition for ***out-of-state students.***

Requirements: Top Applicants.

Application Deadline: December 1

Application Link:
https://admissions.uconn.edu/cost-aid/scholarship/

2 Western Connecticut State University

Location: Danbury, Connecticut
Setting: Urban (398 Acres)
Undergraduate Enrollment: 3,165
Type: Public

President-to-President Scholarship: In-state tuition and fees for 2 years.

Requirements: Awarded to an outstanding graduating Naugatuck Valley Community College student who has been accepted to WSCU | A minimum 3.3 GPA.

Application Deadline: March 1

Application Link:
https://www.wcsu.edu/admissions/merit-scholarships/

1

University of Delaware

Location: Newark, Delaware
Setting: Suburban (1,996 Acres)
Undergraduate Enrollment: 18,883
Type: Private-Public

ROTC Scholarships

U.S. Air Force ROTC: There are three different types of scholarships under this category.

This award covers full tuition and authorized fees, plus a monthly living expense stipend and an annual book stipend.

Requirements: U.S. citizens | SAT composite score of 1240 or ACT composite score of 26 | A minimum cumulative unweighted GPA of 3.0 | Applicant must be physically fit.

Application Deadline: January 14

Application Link: https://www.udel.edu/students/student-financial-services/undergraduate/

1 Florida International University

Location: Miami, Florida
Setting: Urban (344 Acres)
Undergraduate Enrollment: 45,442
Type: Public

FIU College Board Recognition Program Scholarship: Awards Full tuition and fees, a book stipend plus a $1,000 meal plan stipend per semester.

Requirements: Applicant must be a U.S citizen, a U.S. lawful permanent resident or an international student with intention of receiving the F-1 visa to study in the United States | Awarded one of the recognition awards below from the College Board:

- ✓ African American Recognition
- ✓ Hispanic Recognition
- ✓ Indigenous Recognition
- ✓ Rural and Small Town Recognition

Presidential Merit Scholarship: Awards Full tuition and fees, plus a book stipend.

Requirements: 4.0 GPA | A minimum SAT score of 1370 or ACT score of 30 or Top 5% of a Florida High School Graduating Class | Applicant must be a U.S citizen, a U.S. lawful permanent resident or an international student with intention of receiving the F-1 visa to study in the United States.

Application Deadline: January 31

Application Link:
https://scholarships.fiu.edu/browse-scholarships/merit-scholarships/index.html

2 Stetson University

Location: DeLand, Florida
Setting: Suburban (185 Acres)
Undergraduate Enrollment: 2,561
Type: Private

Global Citizen Scholarship: Awards Full tuition scholarship to students who display characteristics of a global citizen.

Requirements: A minimum GPA of 3.5 | Applicant must write a 500 word or less Essay on - How will your education prepare you to be a global citizen?

Students eligible to apply must be from one of the following regions:

- Americas – Andes, Southern Cone
- Middle East, North Africa and Central Asia
- Sub-Saharan Africa – East and Southern.

Application Deadline: March 1

Application Link:
https://www.stetson.edu/administration/financial-aid/scholarships/

3 Florida Institute of Technology

Location: Melbourne, Florida
Setting: Suburban (174 Acres)
Undergraduate Enrollment: 3,374
Type: Private

Panther Distinguished Scholar Award *(Available only to Florida Residents)*: This is a combination of scholarships and grants that covers full tuition plus the facilities and activities fees to attend Florida Tech.

Eligibility: High school students who qualify for the Bright Futures Florida Academic Scholars (FAS) award are eligible to be considered for this scholarship.

Application Deadline: February 1

Application Link:
https://www.fit.edu/admission/scholarships--aid/

4 Full Sail University

Location: Winter Park, Florida
Setting: Urban (200 Acres)
Undergraduate Enrollment: 19,171
Type: Private

Emerging Technology Scholarship: This is a full scholarship that covers full tuition and provides a laptop.

Eligibility: A cummulative high school GPA of 3.8 or higher, 1133 in SAT or higher (25 ACT or higher) | Meet admissions requirements for an eligible Bachelor of Science degree.

Women in Technology Scholarship: This is a full scholarship that covers full tuition and provides a laptop.

Eligibility: Identify as a female | A cummulative high school GPA of 3.8 or higher, 1133 in SAT or higher (25 ACT or higher) | Meet admissions requirements for an eligible Bachelor of Science degree

Application Deadline: June 26

Application Link:
https://www.fullsail.edu/admissions/scholarships

5 University of Miami

Location: Coral Gables, Florida
Setting: Suburban (239 Acres)
Undergraduate Enrollment: 12,504
Type: Private

Isaac Bashevis Singer Scholarship: Awards full tuition.

Requirements: Top Applicants.

Ronald A. Hammond Scholarship: Awards full tuition.

P.S: This scholarship is open only to U.S. citizens and U.S. permanent residents.

Marta S. and L. Austin Weeks Endowed Scholarship: Awards full tuition.

Eligibility: This scholarship is open only to U.S. citizens and U.S. permanent residents.

Requirements: Top Applicants.

Application Deadline: November 1

Application link:
https://admissions.miami.edu/undergraduate/financial-aid/scholarships/freshman/index.html

6 Lynn University

Location: Boca Raton, Florida
Setting: Suburban (123 Acres)
Undergraduate Enrollment: 2,792
Type: Private

Top Achiever Scholarship: Awards full tuition.

Eligibility: Candidates must be a National Merit Finalist, A New undergraduate, day, freshman, Sophomore, junior and senior students.

Application link:
https://www.lynn.edu/admission/tuition-aid/financial-aid/top-achiever-scholarship

7 Barry University

Location: Miami Shores, Florida
Setting: Urban (124 Acres)
Undergraduate Enrollment: 3,122
Type: Private

Founders' Scholarship: Award covers Full tuition for four years.

Eligibility: Open to a graduating senior from an archdiocesan Catholic high school in South Florida. The student ***does not*** have to be Catholic.

Requirements: A 3.5+ weighted High school GPA.

Application Deadline: March 15

Application Link:
https://www.barry.edu/en/financial-aid/money-for-college/

1 Piedmont College

Location: Demorest, Georgia
Setting: Rural (370 Acres)
Undergraduate Enrollment: 1,245
Type: Private

Piedmont Premier Scholarship: This scholarship may provide **up to the cost of tuition** and will be reduced by any state and institutional aid a student receives.

Requirements: Applicant must be a Valedictorian of a HOPE eligible high school from the state of Georgia.

Application Deadline: February 15

Application Link:
https://www.piedmont.edu/admission-aid/financial-aid/scholarships/

2 Emory University

Location: Atlanta, Georgia
Setting: City (631 Acres)
Undergraduate Enrollment: 7,101
Type: Private

Courtesy Tuition Benefit: Awards Full tuition Scholarship to dependent children of eligible Emory Faculty and Staff based on employee hire date and years of service.

Requirements: Top applicants.

Application Deadline: November 15

Application Link:
https://studentaid.emory.edu/undergraduate/types/grants-scholarships/index.html

3 Brenau University

Location: Gainesville, Georgia
Setting: City (57 Acres)
Undergraduate Enrollment: 1,367
Type: Private

Women's College Academic Scholarships

The Brenau Scholars Program: Awards Full tuition scholarship to residential students.

Requirements: A minimum ACT Score of 27 or SAT score of 1270 | High school GPA of 3.50+

Application Deadline: February 1

Application Link:
https://www.brenau.edu/admissions/freshman/

4 Georgia Southern University

Location: Statesboro, Georgia
Setting: Rural (900 Acres)
Undergraduate Enrollment: 22,003
Type: Public

HOPE/Zell Miller Scholarship *(Available only to Georgia Residents)*: Awards Full tuition.

Requirements: A minimum High school GPA of 3.7 | A minimum ACT composite score of 26 or a comparable SAT score of 1,200 (Reading and Math)

Application Deadline: February 1

Application Link:
https://em.georgiasouthern.edu/finaid/hope-scholarship/

5 Spelman College

Location: Atlanta, Georgia
Setting: Urban (39 Acres)
Undergraduate Enrollment: 2,374
Type: Private

Dewitt Dean's Scholarship: Award covers full tuition for four years.

Requirements: A minimum SAT score of 1330 or 31 ACT | A minimum High school GPA of 3.8 (weighted)

Application Deadline: February 1

Application Link:
https://www.spelman.edu/admissions/financial-aid/scholarships

7 Savannah State University

Location: Savannah, Georgia
Setting: City (201 Acres)
Undergraduate Enrollment: 3,148
Type: Public

Zell Miller Scholarship *(Available only to Georgia Residents)*: Awards Full tuition.

Requirements: Applicant must be a Valedictorian or Salutatorian for their graduating class; or received a score of at least 1,200 combined critical reading score and math score on a single administration of the SAT or an ACT composite scale score of at least 26 | A minimum High school GPA of 3.7

Application Deadline: Check the website for more details.

Application Link:
https://www.savannahstate.edu/financial-aid/types-of-aid/ssu-scholarships.shtml

6 LaGrange College

Location: LaGrange, Georgia
Setting: Rural (120 Acres)
Undergraduate Enrollment: 607
Type: Private

The National History Day Georgia Fellows Scholarship: Awards Full tuition.

Requirements: Applicants for this scholarship must be graduating seniors from a Georgia high school or home school program | Qualified to participate at the NHD Georgia State Contest | A minimum high school GPA of 3.5 or its equivqlent.

Application Deadline: April 10

Application Link:
https://www.lagrange.edu/academics/undergraduate/majors/history/national-history-day/nhd-fellows.html

The Presidential Learning Scholarship: Awards Full tuition.

Requirements: Top applicants.

Application Deadline: January 1

Application Link:
https://www.lagrange.edu/ADMISSIONS/COST%20AND%20AID/Scholarships.html

8 Oglethorpe University

Location: Atlanta, Georgia
Setting: Suburban (100 Acres)
Undergraduate Enrollment: 1,491
Type: Private

James Edward Oglethorpe: Awards Full tuition + Stipend for a junior year study abroad experience.

Civic Engagement: Awards Full tuition and an internship with a non-profit organization.

Oglethorpe Theatre: Awards Full tuition and an internship with a professional theatre company.

Hammack Business: Awards Full tuition plus Stipend for study abroad or internship experience.

P.S: Full tuition awards are determined by performance at Oglethorpe's Scholarship Weekend. Scholarship Weekend is by invitation only.

Application Deadline: November 1

Application Link: https://oglethorpe.edu/admission/undergraduate-admission/scholarships-and-aid/

9 Georgia Institute of Technology

Location: Atlanta, Georgia
Setting: Urban (400 Acres)
Undergraduate Enrollment: 18,415
Type: Public

Neilsen Foundation Scholarship: This scholarship provides Full tuition for in-state students and 125% of in-state tuition cost for out-of-state students.

Eligibility: Applicant must be in good academic standing | Undergraduate or Graduate students (enrolled online or on campus) who have experienced **neurological and functional impairment** due to a traumatic **spinal cord injury**, a **degenerative disease primary to the spinal cord**, or **damage to the spinal cord due to tumors or surgery.**

CyberCorps Scholarship for Service: Awards Full tuition and stipend to students in exchange for commitments to serve the U.S. Government in a cybersecurity role after graduation.

Requirements: Applicantion is open to students who are enrolled in the Computer Science, the Electrical and Computer Engineering, the Public Policy or International Affairs departments at Georgia Tech | Applicant must demonstrate strong interest in the field of cybersecurity.

Application Deadline: March 24

Application Link: https://finaid.gatech.edu/undergraduate-types-aid/scholarships/

10

Wesleyan College

Location: Macon, Georgia
Setting: Suburban (200 Acres)
Undergraduate Enrollment: 695
Type: Private

Lane Scholars Program: Awards Full tuition.

Requirements: Applicant must intend to major in the area of Fine Arts | A minimum High school GPA of 3.0 | Top Applicants.

Findlay Scholars Program: Awards Full tuition.

Requirements: Applicant must intend to major in either the Humanities or Social Sciences | A minimum High school GPA of 3.49 | Top Applicants.

Munroe Scholars Program: Awards Full tuition plus a research stipend of up to $1,000.

Requirements: Applicant must intend to major in the Sciences, Mathematics, or dual-degree Engineering | A minimum High school GPA of 3.5 | Top Applicants.

Mary Knox Mcneill Scholars Program: Awards Full tuition scholarship to students who demonstrate a commitment to faith and community service.

Requirements: A minimum High school GPA of 3.25 | Check site for more details.

Margaret Pitts Scholarship: Awards Full tuition scholarship to students who are active members of the United Methodist Church.

Requirements: A minimum High school GPA of 3.0 | Top Applicants.

Application Deadline: February 15

Application Link: https://www.wesleyancollege.edu/admission/invitation-scholarships.cfm

Mercer University

Location: Macon, Georgia
Setting: City (150 Acres)
Undergraduate Enrollment: 4,859
Type: Private

Five Star Scholarship: Awards Full tuition and fees.

Eligibility: High school seniors who reside in one of the following central Georgia counties: Baldwin, Bibb, Butts, Crawford, Houston, Jasper, Jones, Lamar, Peach, Twiggs, Upson, or Wilkinson.

Macon Impact Scholarship: Awards Full tuition and fees.

Eligibility: Awarded to High school seniors with demonstrated financial need who live in the Bibb County school district and have been enrolled in an accredited Bibb County Public School since the ninth grade.

Media Changemaker Scholarship: Awards Full tuition.

Eligibility: Awarded to High school seniors accepted to Mercer University and pursuing a major in journalism or media studies.

Presidential Scholars Weekend: Awards range up to Full tuition.

Heritage Scholars Weekend: Awards range up to Full tuition.

Eligibility: Awarded to High school seniors who submit a completed application for admission by the Early Action I deadline on November 1

Tuition Exchange Scholars Program: Awards Full tuition and fees.

Eligibility: Awarded to High school seniors whose parents are employed at a Tuition Exchange partner institution.

P.S: ROTC Room and Board Scholarships are also available.

Application Deadline: November 15 (Early -Action) | February 1 (Priority Scholarship)

Application Link: https://undergrad.mercer.edu/mercer-scholarships/#module-standard-content-scholarship

1

University of Hawaii

Location: Honolulu, Hawaii
Setting: Urban (320 Acres)
Undergraduate Enrollment: 14,198
Type: Public

The Reagents and Presidential Scholarships covers the cost of tuition, and includes a $4000 stipend per year.

Eligibility: Reagents Scholarships are awarded to outstanding freshmen who has a minimum SAT total score of at least 1340 or ACT combined score of at least 29 | A minimum High school GPA of 3.5

Application Deadline: January 15

Application Link: https://www.hawaii.edu/offices/student-affairs/regents-and-presidential-scholars-program/

1

University of Idaho

Location: Moscow, Idaho
Setting: Rural (810 Acres)
Undergraduate Enrollment: 8,809
Type: Public

National Merit Scholarship: This award covers basic registration fees/tuition and the university defined cost for room and board as long as you live in a U of I residence hall.

Requirements: Achieve Finalist standing with the National Merit Scholarship Corporation.

Application Deadline: May 31

ROTC Military Scholarships

United States Army ROTC: This program offers 3.5 year, 3 year, 2.5 year and 2 year on campus scholarships that will pay for in/out state tuition and fees, pay $510 for books annually, and give at least $250 per month as a stipend while in school.

Call: University of Idaho Army ROTC for application at 208-885-6528

United States Air Force ROTC: This program offers scholarships to students who have at least two years remaining towards their bachelor degree when the scholarship starts. Awards full tuition, books, fees, and a monthly stipend during the academic year.

Call: University of Idaho Unit Admissions Officer, AFROTC Detachment 905, at 208-885-6129 or 800-622-5088.

United States Navy/Marine ROTC: This program offers scholarships to students selected through national competition. It covers college tuition, lab fees, books, uniforms, and includes a monthly stipend.

Call: University of Idaho, Commanding Officer, Naval Science Department at 208-885-6333.

Application Link: https://www.uidaho.edu/financial-aid/scholarships/undergraduate

1 Lewis University

Location: Romeoville, Illinois
Setting: Suburban (410 Acres)
Undergraduate Enrollment: 3,933
Type: Private

St. John Baptist DeLaSalle Scholarship: Awards full tuition.

Requirements: Top Applicants.

Application Deadline: January 15

Application Link:
https://www.lewisu.edu/admissions/finaid/scholarships.htm

2 Quincy University

Location: Quincy, Illinois
Setting: City (70 Acres)
Undergraduate Enrollment: 1,146
Type: Private

Quincy University Presidential Scholarship: Awards Full tuition.

Requirements: A minimum ACT Score of 26 or SAT score of 1230 | A minimum high school GPA of 3.4 (on a 4.0 scale)

Application Deadline: January 10

Application Link:
https://www.quincy.edu/admissions/financial-aid-and-tuition/scholarships/

3 Illinois State University

Location: Normal, Illinois
Setting: Urban (1,180 Acres)
Undergraduate Enrollment: 18,055
Type: Public

McLean County Full Tuition Scholarship: Awards Full tuition.

Eligibility: This scholarship is awarded to new freshmen from McLean County for demonstrating leadership, service, and commitment to their community | Top applicants.

Application Deadline: February 1

Application Link:
https://illinoisstate.edu/admissions/scholarships/

4 University of Illinois

Location: Urbana-Champaign, Illinois
Setting: City (1,783 Acres)
Undergraduate Enrollment: 35,120
Type: Public

James Hunter Anthony & Gerald E. Blackshear Endowment: Awards up to full tuition and fees for an academic year.

Requirements: Illinois Resident who have graduated from an Illinois high school | Top applicants.

Provost Scholarship: Awards full tuition.

Requirements: Top Applicants.

Application Deadline: December 1

Application Link:
https://www.admissions.illinois.edu/invest/scholarships-all

5 Illinois Wesleyan University

Location: Bloomington, Illinois
Setting: Suburban (82 Acres)
Undergraduate Enrollment: 1,527
Type: Private

President's Scholarships: Awards Full tuition (*to highly qualified international students*)

Requirements: Top Applicants.

Application Deadline: February 15

Application Link:
https://www.iwu.edu/international/scholarships.html

6 Rockford University

Location: Rockford, Illinois
Setting: City (130 Acres)
Undergraduate Enrollment: 951
Type: Private

Charles & Dianna Colman Scholarship: Awards Full tuition.

Requirements: A minimum cumulative high school GPA of 3.75

Application Deadline: February 1

Application Link:
https://www.rockford.edu/admission/financialaid/programs/

7 Olivet Nazarene University

Location: Bourbonnais, Illinois
Setting: Suburban (275 Acres)
Undergraduate Enrollment: 2,519
Type: Private

Army ROTC: Award covers full tuition and mandatory fees plus a $300 - $500 monthly stipend and an annual allowance of $1,200 for books and miscellaneous fees.

P.S: Check the website for more details.

Requirements: Top Applicants.

Application Link:
https://www.olivet.edu/admissions/financial-aid-new-student-tuition/scholarships/

8 Loyola University Chicago

Location: Chicago, Illinois
Setting: Urban (105 Acres)
Undergraduate Enrollment: 11,703
Type: Private

Ignatian Scholarship: Awards full tuition.

Requirements: Top Applicants.

P.S: The Ignatian scholarship is an invite-only full tuition scholarship.

A full tuition scholarship is also available to National Merit/National Achievement finalists by the National Merit Corporation.

Application Deadline: December 1

Application Link:
https://www.luc.edu/finaid/scholarships/undergraduate/

9 University of Illinois at Chicago

Location: Chicago, Illinois
Setting: Urban (244 Acres)
Undergraduate Enrollment: 21,807
Type: Public

Lake County, Indiana Tuition Award: The value of this award varies. It can cover up to full in-sate tuition.

P.S: This four-year award program, administered to new incoming first-year and transfer students who are residents of Lake County, Indiana gives recipients the opportunity to study at UIC for the equivalent of in-state tuition.

Requirements: Applicant must be graduating from a high school in Lake County, Indiana | Top applicants.

Tribal Nation Tuition Award: The value of this award varies. It can cover up to full in-sate tuition.

P.S: This four-year grant program, administered to new incoming first-year and transfer students who are members of any of the 573 tribal nations recognized by the Bureau of Indian Affairs, gives recipients the opportunity to study at UIC for the equivalent of in-state tuition.

Requirements: Top Applicants.

Application Deadline: December 1

Application Link:
https://admissions.uic.edu/undergraduate/requirements-deadlines/deadlines/priority-scholarship-date

10 Millikin University

Location: Decatur, Illinois
Setting: City (75 Acres)
Undergraduate Enrollment: 1,812
Type: Private

Presidential Scholarship: Awards Full tuition.

P.S: This award is for the best of the best.

Requirements: 3.5+ GPA (on a 4.0 scale)

Foley music Business Scholarship: Awards Full tuition.

P.S: This scholarship is awarded to students with demonstrated financial need who is majoring in music business.

Requirements: Top applicants.

The Amati String Scholarship: Awards Full tuition.

P.S: This scholarship is awarded to exceptionally talented string students in the School of Music.

Application Deadline: January 15

Application Link:
https://millikin.edu/admission/tuition-fees/scholarships-aid

11 Loyola University, Chicago

Location: Chicago, Illinois
Setting: Urban (105 Acres)
Undergraduate Enrollment: 11,703
Type: Private

Ignatian Scholarship: Awards Full tuition.

P.S: The Ignatian Scholarship is an invite-only full tuition scholarship.

Requirements: Top applicants.

Cristo Rey Scholars Program: Awards Full tuition.

Requirements: Top applicants.

Eligibility: This scholarship is awarded to students attending Cristo Rey Network schools in the United States.

National Merit/National Achievement Finalists: Awards Full tuition.

Eligibility: This scholarship is awarded to students who have been named National Merit/National Achievement finalists by the National Merit Corporation.

P.S: Check the website for more details.

Application Deadline: December 1

Application Link:
https://www.luc.edu/finaid/scholarships/undergraduate/

12 Illinois Institute of Technology

Location: Chicago, Illinois
Setting: Urban (120 Acres)
Undergraduate Enrollment: 3,125
Type: Private

Camras Scholars Program: This scholarship program awards full tuition for four (4)/five (5) years.

Requirements: Satisfy very high selection standards and demonstrate outstanding academics, involvement in extracurricular activities, and dedication to leadership.

Be a United States Citizen or permanent resident.

M.A. and Lila Self Leadership Scholarship:

Academy Scholarship: This scholarship program awards full tuition for four(4)/five(5) years.

Requirements: View scholarship page for detailed information.

Application Deadline: February 15

Crown Scholarship: This scholarship program awards full tuition for five (5) years (College of Architecture Only)

Requirements:

- ✓ Outstanding academic achievement
- ✓ Excelent artistic skills in frehand drawing
- ✓ Be a United States Citizen or permanent resident.

Application Deadline: November 15

Application Link:
https://www.iit.edu/admissions-aid/tuition-and-aid/scholarships

13 Eureka College

Location: Eureka, Illinois
Setting: Rural (65 Acres)
Undergraduate Enrollment: 559
Type: Private

Ronald W. Reagan Leadership Program: Awards Full tuition, two on-site mentorships with prominent leaders plus stipends to cover the program's travel and mentoring opportunities.

Requirements: A minimum cumulative high school GPA of 3.0 (on a 4.0 scale) | Complete the two required essay prompts | Submit a resume along with two references.

Steven W. Rigazio Scholarship: Awards Full tuition.

P.S: This scholarship is awarded to a student who completes his/her second year at Illinois Valley Community College and transfers to Eureka College to pursue their baccalaureate degree.

Requirements: Top applicants.

The Uniquely Eureka Promise: This promise scholarship is designed to cover the remaining tuition charge for in-state students who graduated from specific Illinois high schools.

P.S: Out of state students are also considered for this award.

Requirements: A minimum 3.0 cumulative high school GPA.

Application Deadline: January 25

Application Link:
https://www.eureka.edu/admissions-and-financial-aid/scholarships-awards-and-veteran-benefits/scholarships-and-awards

14 Monmouth College

Location: Monmouth, Illinois
Setting: Rural (112 Acres)
Undergraduate Enrollment: 753
Type: Private

William J. and Beverly Goldsborough scholarship: Awards Full tuition.

Requirements: A minimum 3.6 cumulative high school GPA.

Admiral's Scholarship: Awards Full tuition plus $5,000 educational enrichment fund.

P.S: Recipients are required to participate in the James and Sybil Stockdale Fellows Program.

Requirements: A minimum 3.6 cumulative high school GPA.

Trustees' Scholarship: Awards Full tuition.

Requirements: A minimum 3.6 cumulative high school GPA.

Application Deadline: November 1

Application Link:
https://www.monmouthcollege.edu/offices/student-financial-planning/types-of-aid/scholarships/

1 University of Indiana

Location: Bloomington, Indiana
Setting: City (1,953 Acres)
Undergraduate Enrollment: 35,660
Type: Public

Adam W. Herbert Presidential Scholars Program: Awards a scholarship, a technology stipend, and a study abroad stipend.

Requirements: Check the website for more details.

Application Deadline: November 1

Application Link: https://scholarships.indiana.edu/future-scholars/index.html

2 University of Notre Dame

Location: Notre Dame, Indiana
Setting: Suburban (1,265 Acres)
Undergraduate Enrollment: 8,971
Type: Private

Notre Dame Stamps Scholars: Full tuition and fees for up to four years, books, personal expenses and transportation. Plus enrichment funds.

Requirements: Top Applicants.

Application Deadline: November 1

Application Link: https://scholars.nd.edu/awards/list-of-awards/

3 Trine University

Location: Angola, Indiana
Setting: Rural (400 Acres)
Undergraduate Enrollment: 3,794
Type: Private

Bateman Kolb Scholarship: Awards Full tuition.

Requirements: 3.9 (on a 4.0 scale) High school GPA | SAT 1310 (R+M) / ACT 26

Air Force ROTC Scholarship Program: Awards range from 18,000/year up to full tuition.

Application Deadline: March 5

Application Link: https://www.trine.edu/admission-aid/tuition-aid/types-of-aid/competitive-scholarships.aspx

4 Earlham College

Location: Richmond, Indiana
Setting: City (800 Acres)
Undergraduate Enrollment: 612
Type: Private

Davis UWC Scholars Program: Awards range from partial scholarships to 50% tuition, as well as a $20,000-$25,000 Davis Grant which sums up to the full cost of tuition. In addition, a select number of students qualify for full awards which cover the costs of tuition, fees, room and board.

Requirements: Applicants should be graduates of the United World College.

Application Deadline: December 1

Application Link: https://earlham.edu/cost-affordability/types-of-aid/scholarships/

5 Hanover College

Location: Hanover, Indiana
Setting: Rural (640 Acres)
Undergraduate Enrollment: 951
Type: Private

Pell Promise Award: Awards Full tuition. P.S: This Award covers full tuition for all admitted Indiana students who file the FAFSA by April 15.

Lilly Scholars Promise: Awards Full tuition, required fees and book stipend for 4 years.Eligibility: ***Indiana Resident's.***

Requirements: Top applicants.

Application Deadline: February 15

Application Link: https://www.hanover.edu/admission/financialaid/

6 Ball State University

Location: Muncie, Indiana
Setting: Suburban (1,282 Acres)
Undergraduate Enrollment: 14,416
Type: Public

Dr. T.M. Anderson Scholarship: Awards Full in-state tuition and required fees to a new Honors College student pursuing a major in history or a teaching major with a primary concentration in U.S. history.

P.S: Recipients do not need to be residents of Indiana.

Requirements: Top Applicants.

Deborah S. Wehman Scholarship: Awards Full tuition.

O. L. Strong Memorial Scholarship: Awards Full in-sate tuition.

Requirements: Top Applicants.

Application Deadline: January 6

Application Link: https://www.bsu.edu/academics/collegesanddepartments/honorscollege/admissions-and-financial-aid/scholarships

7 Franklin College

Location: Franklin, Indiana
Setting: Suburban (207 Acres)
Undergraduate Enrollment: 894
Type: Private

Ben Franklin Scholars Program: Awards up full tuition.

Requirements: A minimum 3.9 cumulative high school GPA (on a 4.0 scale) | 1320+ SAT/ 28+ ACT

National Pulliam Journalism Scholarship: Awards full tuition.

P.S: Applicant must be interested in studying journalism | Students must submit a completed application and essay on or before November 15.

Application Deadline: December 1

Application Link: https://franklincollege.edu/admissions/financial-aid/types-financial-aid/scholarships-overview/

8 Marian University

Location: Indianapolis, Indiana
Setting: City (120 Acres)
Undergraduate Enrollment: 2,860
Type: Private

Browning Family Scholarship: Awards full tuition.

Requirements: Top applicants.

Saint Mary Academic Scholarship: Awards full tuition.

Requirements: 3.90+ High school GPA.

21st Century Scholars Tuition Scholarship:

Awards full tuition and fees.

Eligibility: ***Indiana Resident's***

Requirements: Top applicants.

Athletic Award: Amount ranges from partial to full tuition.

P.S: Students selected for athletic scholarships are evaluated based on their athletic abilities and their potential to make a positive team contribution.

Requirements: Top applicants.

Application Deadline: November 15

Application Link:
https://www.marian.edu/admissions/financial-aid-at-marian-university/first-year-scholarships

9 Grace College

Location: Winona Lake, Indiana
Setting: Rural (150 Acres)
Undergraduate Enrollment: 2,069
Type: Private

President's Scholarships: Awards Full tuition.

Requirements: A minimum 3.75 cumulative high school GPA | Top 20% class rank | Score 1260 SAT or 27 ACT

Indiana Low Income Plan: Awards Full tuition.

Eligibility: Applicant must be an ***Indiana Resident*** | Must complete the FAFSA by the Indiana state deadline of April 15 | Expected Family Contribution (EFC) of 0 to $1500 as calculated by the FASFA. Generally, parental income below $60,000 qualifies.

21st Century Scholars Tuition Scholarship: Awards Full tuition.

Eligibility: Applicant must be a 21st Century Scholar.

Application Deadline: October 1

Application Link:
https://www.grace.edu/admissions/undergraduate/financial-aid-scholarships/scholarships-and-grants/

10 Purdue University

Location: West Lafayette, Indiana
Setting: City (2,468 Acres)
Undergraduate Enrollment: 37,949
Type: Private

Lilly Scholars at Purdue Program: Awards full tuition.

Requirements: Top applicants.

The Lilly Scholars program encourages students who are from under-resourced urban and rural populations, who have overcome socioeconomic or educational disadvantages, or who are among the first generation in their family to attend college to apply.

P.S: Those with a shared commitment to reducing barriers to education are also encouraged to apply. Students applying to majors that relate to the ***pharmaceutical manufacturing industry*** will be considered for these awards.

Application Deadline: November 1

Application Link:
https://www.admissions.purdue.edu/costsandfinaid/freshman.php

11 University of Southern Indiana

Location: Evansville, Indiana
Setting: Suburban (330 Acres)
Undergraduate Enrollment: 5,539
Type: Public

Baccalaureate/Doctor of Medicine Scholarship (B/MD): Awards Full tuition and other benefits.

Requirements: A minimum 3.5/4.0 cumulative high school GPA | A combined SAT score of 1280 (Evidence-Based Reading/Writing + Math) or an ACT composite score of 27.

P.S: Check the website for more details.

Application Deadline: November 17

Application Link:
https://www.usi.edu/admissions/scholarships/indiana-freshman-scholarships

12 Goshen College

Location: Goshen, Indiana
Setting: City (135 Acres)
Undergraduate Enrollment: 717
Type: Private

President's Leadership Award: Awards Full tuition.

P.S: This scholarship requires an application, a personal experience portfolio (essay questions), and a video.

Requirements: A minimum high school cumulative GPA of 3.85 (on a 4.0 scale) | Score at least 1340 on the SAT **or** at least 29 on the ACT.

Dream Award: Awards Full tuition.

P.S: This scholarship requires an application, a personal experience portfolio (essay questions), and a video.

Requirements: A minimum high school cumulative GPA of 3.0 (on a 4.0 scale) | Score at least 970 on the SAT **or** at least 18 on the ACT.

Application Deadline: November 15

Application Link:
https://www.goshen.edu/financial-aid/scholarships/achievement/

13 Saint Mary of the Woods College

Location: Saint Mary-of-the-Woods, Indiana
Setting: Rural (227 Acres)
Undergraduate Enrollment: 815
Type: Private

Saint Mother Theodore Guerin Scholarship: Awards up to Full tuition and each winner will receive an iPad.

Requirements: Top applicants.

Center for Leadership Development (CLD): Awards Full tuition.

Eligibility: Applicants must complete the following CLD programs: Self-Discovery/Career-Exploration Project, Emerging Scholars Program, and College Prep Summer Program.

Post-9/11 GI Bill/Yellow Ribbon Program: Award covers the total cost of tuition and fees.

P.S: Qualifications determined by the Department of Veteran Affairs as determined by the Post 9/11 GI Bill and Yellow Ribbon Program requirements.

SMWC Musician of Promise Scholarship: Awards up to full tuition.

Application Deadline: January 22

Application Link:
https://www.smwc.edu/offices-resources/offices/financial-aid/scholarships-and-grants-22-23/2023-24-campus-scholarships/

University of Indianapolis

Location: Indianapolis, Indiana
Setting: Urban (65 Acres)
Undergraduate Enrollment: 3,613
Type: Private

Presidential Scholarship: Awards up to full tuition.

Requirements: Top applicants.

R.B. Annis Engineering Scholarship: Awards Full tuition.

Eligibility: Top Dean Scholars Majoring in Engineering invited to on-campus competition.

P.S: Applicants must apply for admission by December 15

School of Education Scholarship: Awards range from $100 – Full tuition.

Requirements: Top applicants.

UIndy Diversity in Education Teaching Scholarship: Awards up to full tuition and $250 per semester ($500 total) book stipend.

P.S: Award based on demonstrated financial need | Students from underrepresented populations are encouraged to apply | Submit the Scholarship application by February 15 for priority consideration.

University of Indianapolis Freedom Award: Awards up to full tuition.

Eligibility: Applicant must be eligible for full Post 9/11 Veterans benefits and the Yellow Ribbon Program.

Discovery Award: Awards up to full tuition.

Eligibility: Applicant must be designated as a 21st Century Scholar through the State Commission as documented by the high school guidance counselor.

Promise Award: Awards up to full tuition.

Eligibility: ***Indiana students*** who are eligible for the Frank O'Bannon Award and who have maximum need may receive the award | Applicant must be designated as a Frank O'Bannon Award recipient by the Indiana Commission for Higher Education.

Application Deadline: February 15

Application Link: https://www.uindy.edu/financial-aid/scholarships

1 Grand View University

Location: Des Moines, Iowa
Setting: Urban (25 Acres)
Undergraduate Enrollment: 1,694
Type: Private

Presidential Scholarship: Awards full tuition and an additional $5,000 award. P.S: This scholarship is only available to Presidential Scholarship recipients.

Requirements: Top applicants.

Application Deadline: December 1

Application Link:
https://www.grandview.edu/admissions/financial-aid/scholarships-grants

2 Central College

Location: Pella, Iowa
Setting: Rural (200 Acres)
Undergraduate Enrollment: 1,169
Type: Private

Kuyper Scholarships & Rolscreen Scholarships: Awards Full tuition.

Requirements: Top applicants.

P.S: These scholarship is the most prestigious award granted at Central College. Recipients will be chosen after all the Scholar Days are completed.

Application Deadline: January 15

Application Link:
https://central.edu/financial-aid/scholarships-awards/

3 Saint Ambrose University

Location: Davenport, Iowa
Setting: City (113 Acres)
Undergraduate Enrollment: 2,120
Type: Private

Ambrose Advantage: Awards Full tuition.

P.S: Applicant must be an Iowa resident | Federal Pell Grant eligible.

Requirements: A minimum 2.8 high school GPA (unweighted)

Application Deadline: Check the website for more details.

Application Link:
https://www.sau.edu/admissions-and-aid/first-year

4 Briar Cliff University

Location: Sioux City, Iowa
Setting: City (70 Acres)
Undergraduate Enrollment: 709
Type: Private

Presidential Scholarship: Awards Full tuition.

Requirements: A minimum high school GPA of 3.75 | Applicants must provide two letter(s) of recommendation that describe strengths, weaknesses and characteristics that would judge the applicant's ability to succeed, be involved, and become a leader at Briar Cliff University. P.S: Applicants must apply by the first week of December in the year prior.

Application Deadline: January 28

Application Link:
https://www.briarcliff.edu/future-chargers/tuition-and-aid/scholarships

5 Drake University

Location: Des Moines, Iowa
Setting: City (150 Acres)
Undergraduate Enrollment: 2,835
Type: Private

Physics Scholarship: Awards full tuition.

P.S: Summer tuition and fall/spring tuition overload charges (for enrollment exceeding 18 credits) are not covered.

Eligibility: This scholarship is offered annually to an incoming first-time college student majoring in Physics | Top applicants.

Drake Opportunity Scholarship: Awards full tuition (***to Syrian students***)

P.S: Summer tuition and fall/spring tuition overload charges (for enrollment exceeding 18 credits) are not covered.

Eligibility: Top applicants.

Application Deadline: March 1

Application Link:
https://www.drake.edu/finaid/scholarships/

6 Graceland University

Location: Lamoni, Iowa
Setting: Rural (170 Acres)
Undergraduate Enrollment: 890
Type: Private

Prestigious Honors Scholarship: Awards Full tuition.

Requirements: A minimum high school cumulative GPA of 3.75 | Minimum SAT composite score of 1280 **or** at least 27 on the ACT.

Founders Scholarship: The Founders Scholarship will supplement other gift aid until the student's percentage of need, as calculated, has been met.

Eligibility: Applicant must demonstrate financial need.

Application Deadline: January 1

Application Link:
https://www.graceland.edu/admissions-aid/tuition-financial-aid/scholarships-financial-aid/scholarships/

7 Mount Mercy University

Location: Cedar Rapids, Iowa
Setting: City (45 Acres)
Undergraduate Enrollment: 1,271
Type: Private

Sister Mary Iidephonse Holland Scholarship: Awards Full tuition.

P.S: Scholarship is awarded from participation in Scholarship Day.

Requirements: A minimum 26 ACT (SAT 1230) composite score and a 3.7 cumulative GPA.

Catherine McAuley Scholarship: Awards Full tuition

P.S: This is a Need-based free tuition award. Applicant must be Iowa resident and graduate from an Iowa high school.

Requirements: Top applicants.

Application Deadline: March 1

Application Link: https://www.mtmercy.edu/tuition-aid/scholarships/index

8 University of Iowa

Location: Iowa City, Iowa
Setting: City (2,122 Acres)
Undergraduate Enrollment: 21,973
Type: Public

Presidential Scholarship: The value of the award covers full tuition and fees (***Iowa Resident's***)

Requirements: A minimum 3.80 cumulative high school GPA (weighted or unweighted) | 33+ ACT or an equivalent SAT score.

Mark Shapiro Sports Journalism Scholarship: Awards $35,000 (This covers the cost of tuition and fees for out-of-state students)

P.S: This scholarship is awarded to an incoming freshman in the University of Iowa School of Journalism and Mass Communication (SJMC) who is interested in pursuing a career in sports journalism/communication. The incoming freshman student should be a graduate of a high school outside of Iowa.

Requirements: Top applicants.

Application Deadline: March 1

Application Link: https://tippie.uiowa.edu/undergraduate/tuition-aid

9 Wartburg College

Location: Waverly, Iowa
Setting: Rural (170 Acres)
Undergraduate Enrollment: 1,416
Type: Private

McElroy/Slife Scholarship: Awards Full tuition.

P.S: Preference to students from the Waterloo/Cedar Falls, Iowa, area.

Requirements: Applicant is required to write a 250-500 word essay on "How you would benefit from a Wartburg education" | Top applicants.

Tuition Exchange Program for Imports: Awards up to Full tuition.

P.S: Dependents of employees at other higher education institutions may qualify for the tuition exchange program.

Application Deadline: March 15

Application Link: https://www.wartburg.edu/scholarships/

10 Simpson College

Location: Indianola, Iowa
Setting: Suburban (85 Acres)
Undergraduate Enrollment: 1,127
Type: Private

Cowles Fellowship: Award range from $29,000 to full tuition plus a travel stipend to be used for international/domestic travel or internship study to enhance the student's educational experience.

P.S: Candidates must possess extraordinary academic ability and potential as evidenced by high school performance, including standardized test scores.

Trustee Scholarship: Award range from ½ to full tuition.

Requirements: Top applicants.

Application Deadline: February 1

Application Link: https://simpson.edu/admission-aid/tuition-aid/scholarships-grants-awards/first-year-scholarships-and-awards

11 Iowa State University

Location: Ames, Iowa
Setting: City (1,813 Acres)
Undergraduate Enrollment: 25,241
Type: Public

George Washington Carver Program: Awards Full tuition.

Requirements: Applicants must fulfill one of these requirements to be eligible for this scholarship – Have a 3.70 cumulative high school GPA | A minimum SAT score of 1160

(Reading and Writing + Math) OR A minimum ACT composite score of 24.

Application Deadline: January 10

Iowa Resident National Merit Full tuition Scholarship:

Awards Full tuition to National Merit Scholars.

Application Link: https://www.iastate.edu/admission-and-aid/affording-college/scholarships

Coe College

Location: Cedar Rapids, Iowa
Setting: Urban (65 Acres)
Undergraduate Enrollment: 1,264
Type: Private

Distinguished Trustee Scholarship: Awards Full tuition.

Requirements: Top applicants.

Diversity Leadership Scholarship: Awards Full tuition.

Eligibility: Open to prospective students who are U.S. citizens, permanent residents or undocumented residents, from broadly diverse backgrounds.

Requirements: Top applicants.

Sustainability Scholarship: Awards Full tuition.

Eligibility: Open to prospective students who have a passion for the environment, creating sustainable practices and reducing our carbon footprint on the world.

P.S: No ACT/SAT score required to apply.

Requirements: Top applicants.

Marshall Music Scholarship: Awards Full tuition.

Eligibility: Open to prospective students who have the motivation and background necessary to pursue the Bachelor of Music degree.

P.S: No ACT/SAT score required to apply.

Requirements: Top applicants.

National Merit & Achievement: Awards up to full tuition.

Eligibility: This scholarship is awarded to National Merit and National Achievement Finalists.

Global Leadership Scholarship: Awards Full tuition **(to international students)**

Eligibility: Applicant must be a non-U.S. citizen attending high school outside of the U.S.

P.S: Application deadline is February 1

Requirements: Top applicants.

Application Deadline: January 4

Application Link: https://www.coe.edu/admission/first-year-students/scholarships-awards

1 Newman University

Location: Wichita, Kansas
Setting: Urban (61 Acres)
Undergraduate Enrollment: 1,577
Type: Private

St. John Henry Newman Scholarship: Awards Full tuition.

Requirements: Cumulative 3.9+ high school GPA | Super scored 29+ ACT OR Super scored 1330+ SAT.

Check the website for more details.

Application Deadline: December 1

Application Link: https://newmanu.edu/scholarships/fts

2 Southwestern College

Location: Winfield, Kansas
Setting: Rural (85 Acres)
Undergraduate Enrollment: 1,067
Type: Private

Pillars Academic Scholarship: Awards Full tuition.

Requirements: Top Applicants

Moundbuilder Spirit Scholarship: Awards Full tuition. Requirements: Top Applicants.

Application Deadline: January 5

Application Link: https://www.sckans.edu/admissions/scholarships--grants/

3 Barclay College

Location: Haviland, Kansas
Setting: Rural (13 Acres)
Undergraduate Enrollment: 199
Type: Private

Full-Tuition Jubilee Scholarship: Awards Full tuition for four (4) years.

Requirement: Must be a full-time on-campus student with satisfactory academic performance.

Application Deadline: Contact Admission Office.

Application Link: https://www.barclaycollege.edu/admissions/campus/financial-assistance/

4 University of Saint Mary

Location: Leavenworth, Kansas
Setting: Rural (200 Acres)
Undergraduate Enrollment: 903
Type: Private

Full-Tuition Jubilee Scholarship: Awards Full tuition.

Requirements: A minimum 3.7 cumulative high school GPA or be ranked in the top 10 Percent of your graduating high school class | A minimum ACT score of 26 or SAT equivalent.

Application Deadline: December 1

Application Link: https://www.stmary.edu/scholarships/index

5 Ottawa University

Location: Ottawa, Kansas
Setting: Suburban (64 Acres)
Undergraduate Enrollment: 853
Type: Private

Presidential Scholarship: Award covers up to full tuition.

Requirements: Top applicants.

High Achiever Scholarship: Award covers up to full tuition.

P.S: This scholarship is awarded to select senior students who are residents or attending a high school in **Surprise, Arizona**, and who excel academically and show engagement in extracurricular activities.

Requirements: A minimum cumulative high school GPA (unweighted) of 3.50 (4.0 scale) | A minimum ACT composite score of 25 or A minimum SAT composite score of 1200.

Franklin County High Achiever Scholarship:

Award covers up to the full cost of tuition.

P.S: This scholarship is awarded to select graduates from a Franklin County (KS) High School who demonstrates academic achievement and community service.

Requirements: Top applicants.

Application Deadline: August 1

Application Link:
https://www.ottawa.edu/ouks/admissions/scholarships

6 Benedictine College

Location: Atchison, Kansas
Setting: Rural (120 Acres)
Undergraduate Enrollment: 2,261
Type: Private

National Merit Finalist Scholarships: Awards Full tuition (*to National Merit Finalists and National Hispanic Merit Finalists.*)

Requirements: Top applicants.

Presidential Scholarships: Awards Full tuition.

Requirements: A minimum 27 ACT/1260 SAT | A non-weighted 3.5 cumulative high school GPA.

Check the website for more details.

U.S. Army/Air Force ROTC Scholarships are also available.

Application Deadline: January 15

Application Link:
https://www.benedictine.edu/admission/financial-aid/scholarships/index

7 Fort Hays State University

Location: Hays, Kansas
Setting: Rural (200 Acres)
Undergraduate Enrollment: 11,402
Type: Public

RGK Scholarship: Awards $10,000. This covers the value for in-state tuition.

P.S: The application should be accompanied by a letter of introduction from the applicant explaining his/her education and career goals, as well as a letter of recommendation.

Requirements: Top applicants.

Jack and Peggy McCullick Scholarship: Awards $5,450. This covers the value for in-state tuition.

P.S: This scholarship is open to all **College of Business and Entrepreneurship majors** in CIS, accounting and finance who will be classified as juniors or seniors by fall semester.

Requirements: A minimum 3.5 cumulative high school GPA | Top applicants.

Earl O and Winona M Field Athletic Scholarship:

Awards $8,000. This covers the value for in-state tuition.

Ed and Donna Stehno Endowed Scholarship: Awards $7,500. This covers the value for in-state tuition.

P.S: The recipient of this scholarship(s) must be a student athlete at Fort Hays State University.

Application Deadline: February 15

Application Link: https://www.fhsu.edu/admissions/scholarships/freshmen

8 University of Kansas

Location: Lawrence, Kansas
Setting: City (1,000 Acres)
Undergraduate Enrollment: 19,241
Type: Public

International Excellence Award: Award covers up to full tuition.

P.S: This scholarship is awarded to ***international student's.***

Requirements: A minimum 3.5 cumulative high school GPA | Top applicants.

KU Pell Advantage: Award covers up to full tuition.

Eligibility: Applicant must be a ***Kansas Resident*** | Must file the FAFSA by Feb. 1 each year and be Pell Grant eligible.

Requirements: A minimum 3.25 cumulative high school GPA | 22 ACT or 1100 SAT

Check the website for more details.

Application Deadline: March 1

Application Link: https://admissions.ku.edu/afford/scholarships

1 Transylvania University

Location: Lexington, Kentucky
Setting: Urban (46 Acres)
Undergraduate Enrollment: 981
Type: Private

William T. Young: Awards Full tuition and fees.

Eligibility: Students eligible for these Premier Scholarship awards will be selected based on application materials, academics, essays and an interview.

Application Deadline: December 1

Application Link:
https://www.transy.edu/financial-aid/scholarships-grants-aid/

2 Union College

Location: Barbourville, Kentucky
Setting: Rural (100 Acres)
Undergraduate Enrollment: 945
Type: Private

Merit Scholarships: Awards range from $15,000 up to the full cost of tuition.

Requirements: A minimum high school GPA of 2.0 | A minimum ACT composite score of 24.

U|GRAD Program: This program provides all first-time freshmen the opportunity to earn a full-tuition scholarship for the last semester of their senior year.

Application Link:
https://www.unionky.edu/admissions-aid/undergraduate/union-distinction

3 Thomas More University

Location: Crestview Hills, Kentucky
Setting: Suburban (103 Acres)
Undergraduate Enrollment: 1,829
Type: Private

James Graham Brown Honors Program: Top 2 Candidates receive full tuition when combined with other institutional scholarships.

Requirements: 29+ ACT (OR 1130+ SAT OR 90 CLT), and 4.00 GPA | Application Deadline: December 15

Information Systems Workship Program: Full Tuition Guarantee.

Requirements: Test optional 3.5 GPA (OR 3.0 GPA with required test scores (1130+ SAT | 23+ | 74 CLT)

National Merit Finalists: Full Tuition Guarantee.

Application Deadline: March 1

Application Link:
https://www.thomasmore.edu/admissions/scholarships-financial-aid/scholarships/

4 Kentucky Wesleyan College

Location: Owensboro, Kentucky
Setting: Suburban (67 Acres)
Undergraduate Enrollment: 780
Type: Private

Wesleyan Scholars Scholarship Program

James Graham Brown Scholarship: Awards Full tuition.

Requirements: A minimum 3.5 cumulative high school GPA.

Application Deadline: March 1

Application Link:
https://kwc.edu/admissions/financial-aid/scholarships/

5 Bellarmine University

Location: Louisville, Kentucky
Setting: City (145 Acres)
Undergraduate Enrollment: 2,343
Type: Private

Bellarmine Fellow Award: Awards Full tuition plus a study abroad stipend and enrollment in Bellarmine's Honors Program.

Requirements: An essay with the topic "Describe an incident or situation in your life which piqued your intellectual curiosity" | A minimum SAT score of 1390/ACT 30 & 3.4 GPA.

Monsignor Horrigan Scholarship: Award covers tuition costs during the fall and spring semesters.

P.S: The Horrigan Scholarship is reserved for high-achieving students and receiving this award demonstrates the strength of a student's application.

The priority deadline to apply is February 1.

Requirements: Top applicants.

Whitney Young Scholarship Program: This award is combined with federal and state scholarships and grants (PELL, SEOG, CAP, KTG and KEES) to cover full Bellarmine tuition not including room and board or fees.

P.S: You must apply separately for this scholarship by February 1.

Requirements: Top applicants.

Application Deadline: February 1

Application Link:
https://www.bellarmine.edu/financial-aid/institutional/

6 Murray State University

Location: Murray, Kentucky
Setting: Rural (253 Acres)
Undergraduate Enrollment: 7,756
Type: Public

Trustee Scholarship: Awards Full tuition plus a $1,500 Stipend.

Requirements: 33-36 ACT (OR 1450-1600 SAT), and 3.70 – 4.00 GPA.

Kentucky GSP and GSA Scholarship: Awards Full tuition.

P.S: Applicant must be majoring in Art, Music or Theatre.

Requirements: A minimum 3.5 cumulative high school GPA | A minimum 25 ACT composite score.

The Murray State Promise Tuition Program is also available to Kentucky resident's.

Application Deadline: February 1

Application Link:
https://www.murraystate.edu/admissions/scholarships/newfreshmen.aspx

7 Northern Kentucky University

Location: Highland Heights, Kentucky
Setting: Suburban (428 Acres)
Undergraduate Enrollment: 10,776
Type: Public

Presidential Scholarship: Awards Full tuition plus $6,000 for students living in NKU housing.

Requirements: 34+ ACT (OR 1490+ SAT), and 3.75+ Weighted HS GPA.

Kentucky Governor's Scholars Program (GSP): Awards up to Full tuition (to students who have participated in the Kentucky Governor's Scholars Program (GSP)

Kentucky Governor's School for the Arts Program (GSA): Awards up to Full tuition (to students who have participated in the Kentucky Governor's School for the Arts Program (GSA)

Kentucky Governor's School for Entrepreneurs Program (GSE): Awards up to Full tuition (to students who have participated in the Kentucky Governor's School for Entrepreneurs Program (GSE)

Requirements: A minimum 3.0 cumulative high school GPA | 24+ ACT/1160+ SAT.

William H. Greaves Scholarship: Awards Full in-state tuition and books. (Available to incoming freshmen students majoring in STEM disciplines)

Requirements: 25+ ACT | Applicant must rank in the top 25% of their high school class.

Application Deadline: February 15

Application Link:
https://inside.nku.edu/financialaid/programs/scholarships.html

8 Eastern Kentucky University

Location: Richmond, Kentucky
Setting: Rural (892 Acres)
Undergraduate Enrollment: 12,072
Type: Public

Merit Tier 1: Awards Full tuition (***to in-state students only***)

Requirements: Top applicants.

The "Colonel Commitment" Scholarship: Awards up to full tuition and fees.

Eligibility: This scholarship is awarded to Kentucky residents who are Pell Grant-eligible.

Requirements: A minimum high school GPA of 3.0

Governor's Scholar Program: Awards Full tuition.

P.S: Students who completed the Governor's Scholar Program will receive this full tuition award.

Requirements: An ACT composite score from 25 – 28 | 3.75+ high school GPA.

Application Deadline: August 1

Application Link:
https://www.eku.edu/scholarships/

9 Western Kentucky University

Location: Bowling Green, Kentucky
Setting: City (200 Acres)
Undergraduate Enrollment: 14,440
Type: Public

Cherry Presidential Scholarship: Awards up to $16,000 ($64,000 over a four year period)

Cherry Presidential Finalists: Receives an annual Award of up to $10,000 ($40,000 over a four year period)

This covers the total cost of tuition for in-state students.

Requirements: A minimum 29 ACT (1350 SAT) and a minimum 3.8 (unweighted) high school GPA.

Targeted Gatton & Craft Academy Graduates: Awards up to $10,000 ($40,000 over a four year period). This covers the total cost of tuition for in-state students.

Eligibility: This scholarship is awarded to Graduates of Gatton Academy or Craft Academy with a minimum 3.0 unweighted GPA.

P.S: The Hilltopper Guarantee is also available to Kentucky resident's. (Applicant must be a Pell grant recipient)

Application Deadline: January 4

Application Link:
https://www.wku.edu/financialaid/scholarships/freshmen.php

10 Campbellsville University

Location: Campbellsville, Kentucky
Setting: Rural (95 Acres)
Undergraduate Enrollment: 5,880
Type: Private

Presidential Scholarship: Awards Full tuition.

Requirements: 30-32 on ACT/1980-2160 SAT and a 3.5 high school GPA.

Governor's Scholar Scholarship: Awards Full tuition.

P.S: This scholarship is awarded to students who have participated in the Kentucky Governor's Scholars Program. Application is required and will be awarded to students based on GPA, ACT/SAT, and quality and content of essay.

Requirements: A minimum 3.5 cumulative high school GPA | 25 ACT (1720 SAT)

Governor's Scholar for the Arts Scholarship: Awards Full tuition.

P.S: This scholarship is awarded to students who have participated in the Kentucky Governor's Scholars for the Arts Program.

Requirements: A minimum 3.0 cumulative high school GPA | 25 ACT and audition with the School of Music.

Application Deadline: November 1

Application Link:
https://www.campbellsville.edu/admission-and-aid/scholarships-and-grants/

Lindsey Wilson College

Location: Columbia, Kentucky
Setting: Rural (200 Acres)
Undergraduate Enrollment: 1,753
Type: Private

Trustee Scholarship: Awards up to full tuition.

Requirements: A minimum high school GPA of 3.0 | A minimum ACT composite score of 30.

Walter S. Reuling Presidential Scholarship: Awards up to full tuition.

Requirements: Valedictorian (No other student(s) may share the same honor.) | A minimum high school GPA of 3.0 | A minimum ACT composite score of 24.

Award for Excellence: Awards up to full tuition.

Eligibility: Applicant must be a National Merit Semifinalists or National Achievement Semifinalists.

Kentucky Governor's Scholar Scholarship: Awards up to full tuition.

Eligibility: Kentucky Governor's Scholar, Kentucky Governor's School for the Arts, Kentucky Governor's School for Entrepreneurship.

Requirements: A minimum high school GPA of 3.0 | A minimum ACT composite score of 24.

Roger Scholar Scholarship: Awards up to full tuition.

Eligibility: Rogers Scholar.

Requirements: A minimum high school GPA of 3.0 | A minimum ACT composite score of 24.

Application Deadline: Check the website for more details.

Application Link: https://www.lindsey.edu/admissions/cost-and-financial-aid/Academic-Scholarships.cfm

University of Louisville

Location: Louisville, Kentucky
Setting: Urban (287 Acres)
Undergraduate Enrollment: 15,921
Type: Public

GSP, GSA, GSE Award/Gratton & Craft Academy/Rogers Scholars: Awards Full in-state tuition.

Requirements: A minimum 3.5 cumulative high school GPA | A minimum 31 ACT or 1390 SAT.

National Merit Finalist: Awards Full in-state tuition plus an $8,000 educational allowance to National Merit Finalist.

National Merit Semifinalist: Awards Full in-state tuition.

Requirements: A minimum 3.5 cumulative high school GPA.

Martin Luther King Scholars Program: Awards Full in-state tuition plus an $8,000 stipend to cover other university expenses.

Requirements: A minimum 3.5 cumulative high school GPA | A minimum ACT score of 26 or 1230 SAT.

P.S: This scholarship is awarded to Black/African American or Latino high school graduates from Kentucky or Southern Indiana.

Mentored Scholarships

Brown Fellows Program: Awards Full in-state tuition plus additional education allowance.

Requirements: A minimum 3.5 cumulative high school GPA | A minimum 29 ACT or 1330 SAT.

Grawemeyer Scholarship: Awards Full in-state tuition plus $8,000/year educational allowance.

Requirements: A minimum 3.5 cumulative high school GPA | A minimum 29 ACT or 1330 SAT.

McConnell Scholars: Awards Full tuition, plus educational allowance ***(to Kentucky residents)***

Requirements: A minimum 3.5 cumulative high school GPA | Academic merit and leadership potential.

Application Deadline: January 15

Application Link: https://louisville.edu/admissions/cost-aid/scholarships

13

University of Kentucky

Location: Lexington, Kentucky
Setting: City (918 Acres)
Undergraduate Enrollment: 22,735
Type: Public

Presidential Scholarship: Awards Full in-state tuition to in-state residents and a Full out-of-state tuition to Non-resident students.

Requirements: A minimum 3.50 unweighted high school GPA | 31 ACT or 1390 SAT.

Kentucky Governor's Scholar: Awards Full in-state tuition.

Requirements: A minimum 3.50 unweighted high school GPA | 31 ACT or 1390 SAT | Completion of Governor's Scholars, School for the Arts or School for Entrepreneurs program.

Application Deadline: December 1

Application Link: https://www.uky.edu/financialaid/scholarship-incoming-freshmen

1 Southeastern Louisiana University

Location: Hammond, Louisiana
Setting: Rural (365 Acres)
Undergraduate Enrollment: 12,451
Type: Public

Priority Scholarships: Awards Full tuition and fees.

Requirements: A minimum cumulative high school GPA of 3.5 | 27+ ACT

Application Deadline: January 15

Application Link:
https://www.dillard.edu/financialaid/institutional-scholarships.php

2 Dillard University

Location: New Orleans, Louisiana
Setting: City (55 Acres)
Undergraduate Enrollment: 1,224
Type: Private

Presidential Scholarship: Awards Full tuition.

Requirements: A minimum 3.6 cumulative high school GPA (4.0 scale) | A minimum 25 ACT composite score or 1220 SAT combined score.

Application Deadline: March 15

Application Link:
https://www.dillard.edu/financialaid/institutional-scholarships.php

3 University of Louisiana at Monroe

Location: Monroe, Louisiana
Setting: City (238 Acres)
Undergraduate Enrollment: 6,472
Type: Public

President's Distinguished: Awards up to $14,588. This amount covers the total cost of tuition and fees for in-state students.

P.S: Students with a 31-32 ACT score will be awarded a laptop, and students with a 33-36 ACT score will be awarded a laptop and a study abroad stipend (up to $4,500) sponsored by the President's Top Hawks Fund.

Requirements: A minimum ACT score of 27 or SAT equivalent.

Application Deadline: January 31

Application Link:
https://www.ulm.edu/scholarships/freshmen.html

4 Louisiana Tech University

Location: Ruston, Louisiana
Setting: Rural (2,277 Acres)
Undergraduate Enrollment: 10,083
Type: Public

Bulldog Out-of-State Scholarship: Awards Full tuition and fees (*to non-residents of Louisiana*)

Requirements: A minimum 2.5 cumulative high school GPA (on a 4.0 unweighted scale) | A minimum ACT score of 23 or 1130 SAT.

P.S: International students may be eligible for this scholarship if they meet the *specific requirements*.

Application Deadline: January 5

Application Link:
https://www.latech.edu/admissions/freshman-scholarships/

5 Xavier University

Location: New Orleans, Louisiana
Setting: Urban (66 Acres)
Undergraduate Enrollment: 2,696
Type: Private

Presidential Scholarship: Full tuition and fees.

Saint Katharine Drexel Scholarship: Awards full tuition and fees to students who attend a Catholic high school within the United States and are the Valedictorian or Salutatorian of their high school graduating class.

Norman C. Francis Scholarship: Awards full tuition and fees to students who attend a public high school within Orleans or Jefferson Parishes and are the Valedictorian or Salutatorian of their high school graduating class.

Requirements: A minimum 3.3 GPA | 22 ACT/1140 SAT.

Application Deadline: January 31

Application Link: https://www.xula.edu/financialaid/scholarships/index.html

6 Tulane University of Louisiana

Location: New Orleans, Louisiana
Setting: Urban (110 Acres)
Undergraduate Enrollment: 7,350
Type: Private

Paul Tulane Award: Awards Full tuition.

Requirements: Top applicants.

P.S: Typical awardees are in the top 5% of their class and have a long resume of extra activities outside of just normal schoolwork.

Founders Scholarship: Awards Full tuition.

Requirements: Top applicants.

P.S: Typical awardees are in the top 10% of their class.

Dean' Honor Scholarships (DHS): Awards Full tuition.

Requirements: Top applicants.

P.S: To be considered, applicants must submit the Deans' Honor Scholarship Application, included with their application for admission, by December 15.

Application Deadline: January 15

Application Link: https://admission.tulane.edu/tuition-aid

7

Louisiana Christian University

Location: Pineville, Louisiana
Setting: Suburban (81 Acres)
Undergraduate Enrollment: 832
Type: Private

STEM to STEAM Scholarship: Awards Full tuition to select students from STEM accredited High Schools.

Requirements: A minimum 3.0 GPA | A minimum ACT score of 28 and 3 letters of recommendation.

P.S: Applicants must major in a Science/Arts program.

Jimmie Davis Scholarship: Awards full tuition.

Eligibility: Applicants must be PELL eligible, have a FASFA EFC of less than 1000, and be a TOPS recipient.

President's Leadership Award: Awards full tuition.

Requirements: A minimum 3.0 GPA | A minimum ACT score of 28.

P.S: Applicants must be recommended by a Pastor or High School Principal, and demonstration of proven leadership on and off campus.

IMB Dependent Scholarship: Awards full tuition.

Eligibility: Spouses or unmarried children (23 years of age and younger) of active or retired International Mission Board missionaries are eligible for this scholarship.

Application Deadline: Check the website for more details.

Application Link: https://lcuniversity.edu/admissions/grants-scholarships/

1 University of Southern Maine

Location: Portland, Maine
Setting: City (142 Acres)
Undergraduate Enrollment: 5,956
Type: Public

President's Scholar Award: Award range from $5,000 to $12,000. This amount covers the total cost of tuition and fees for in-state students.

Requirements: A minimum high school GPA of 3.5 (on a 4.0 scale)

Dirigo Scholar Award: Award range from $3,000 to $10,000. This amount covers the total cost of tuition for in-state students.

Requirements: A minimum high school GPA of 3.0 (on a 4.0 scale)

Application Deadline: April 1

Application Link: https://usm.maine.edu/scholarships/

2 University of Maine

Location: Orono, Maine
Setting: Rural (660 Acres)
Undergraduate Enrollment: 9,774
Type: Public

Scholarship Programs for *Maine Residents*

Maine's Top Scholar: Awards Full tuition and fees.

P.S: Students are given the opportunity to participate in scholarly activity/research in their field and are invited to join the Honors College.

Requirements: Top applicants.

Scholarship Programs for *Out-of-State Residents*

Presidential Flagship: Award range from $20,000 up to Full tuition and fees.

Requirements: Top applicants.

P.S: Semi-finalists with the National Merit Scholarship Corporation are eligible for the highest awards in this category, including: 100% Tuition and fees, up to 15 credits per semester, & standard room and board.

Application Deadline: December 1

Application Link: https://go.umaine.edu/apply-2022/scholarships/

1 University of Maryland

Location: College park, Maryland
Setting: Suburban (1,340 Acres)
Undergraduate Enrollment: 30,353
Type: Private

President's Scholarship: Award range from $2,000 to $12,500 per year. This amount covers the total cost of tuition and fees for in-state students.

Requirements: Top applicants.

Application Deadline: December 1

Application Link:
https://academiccatalog.umd.edu/undergraduate/fees-expenses-financial-aid/merit-based-financial-assistance/

2 Mount St. Mary's University

Location: Emmitsburg, Maryland
Setting: Rural (1,500 Acres)
Undergraduate Enrollment: 1,896
Type: Private

Full-Tuition Founder's Scholarships: Awards Full tuition.

Requirements: A minimum 3.75 weighted high school GPA.

ROTC Scholarships: Awards Full tuition plus a monthly stipend.

Application Deadline: December 1

Application Link:
https://msmary.edu/admissions/financial-aid/first-year-student.html

3 Coppin State University

Location: Baltimore, Maryland
Setting: Urban (38 Acres)
Undergraduate Enrollment: 1,757
Type: Public

Eagle Honors Program Scholarship: Awards in-state tuition and fees.

Requirements: A minimum cumulative high school GPA of 3.0 | 1080 SAT/ACT 21

Application Deadline: October 1

Application Link:
https://www.coppin.edu/tuition-and-aid/scholarships-and-scholars-programs

4 Stevenson University

Location: Baltimore County, Maryland
Setting: Suburban (145 Acres)
Undergraduate Enrollment: 2,985
Type: Private

Presidential Fellowship: Awards Full tuition.

Requirements: A minimum cumulative high school GPA of 3.7 (on a 4.0 scale) or a 93 on a 100-point scale (weighted or unweighted.)

Check the website for more details.

Application Deadline: December 1

Application Link:
https://www.stevenson.edu/admissions-aid/scholarships-financial-aid/

5 McDaniel College

Location: Westminster, Maryland
Setting: Suburban (160 Acres)
Undergraduate Enrollment: 1,762
Type: Private

Presidential Scholarships: Award ranges from $1000 per year all the way up to full tuition.

Requirements: A minimum high school GPA of 3.85 | Top applicants.

Application Deadline: November 15

Application Link:
https://www.mcdaniel.edu/admissions-cost/cost-financial-aid/types-financial-aid/mcdaniel-scholarships

6 Washington College

Location: Chestertown, Maryland
Setting: Rural (112 Acres)
Undergraduate Enrollment: 955
Type: Private

Presidential Scholarships

George Washington Signature Scholarship: Awards Full tuition.

P.S: *Presidential Fellows programs and scholarships are invitation only.*

Requirements: Top Applicants.

Application Deadline: November 15

Application Link:
https://www.washcoll.edu/admissions/admitted/available-scholarships.php

7 Washington Adventist University

Location: Takoma Park, Maryland
Setting: Suburban (19 Acres)
Undergraduate Enrollment: 582
Type: Private

National Merit Finalist: Awards Full tuition for 4 years.

Eligibility: National Merit Finalists.

Check the website for more details.

Application Deadline: February 1

Application Link:
https://www.wau.edu/admissions-aid/financial-aid/financial-assistance/scholarships/

8 Notre Dame of Maryland University

Location: Baltimore, Maryland
Setting: Suburban (60 Acres)
Undergraduate Enrollment: 660
Type: Private

Presidential Scholarships: Awards Full tuition.

Requirements: A minimum high school GPA of 3.5 (unweighted).

Knott Scholarships: Awards up to Full tuition (to **Catholic students** residing within the **Archdiocese of Baltimore**)

Eligibility: First-year Women's College Students.

Application Deadline: February 15

Application Link:
https://www.ndm.edu/admissions-aid/financial-aid/scholarships/institutional

9

Loyola University Maryland

Location: Baltimore, Maryland
Setting: Urban (80 Acres)
Undergraduate Enrollment: 3,977
Type: Private

Marion Burk Knott Scholarship: Awards Full tuition.

P.S: This scholarship is awarded on a competitive basis to **Catholic students** residing in the **Archdiocese of Baltimore.**

Requirements: Top applicants.

Maryland Guaranteed Access Grant: The grant value for attendance at Maryland independent colleges and universities is equivalent to the cost of tuition, fees, room and board at the University of Maryland, College Park.

The matching GAPP award may consist of a combination of institutionally-funded need-based grants or merit scholarship assistance and may not exceed **Loyola's full cost of tuition and mandatory fees.**

Check the website for more details.

Eligibility: Grant recipients must be legal residents of Maryland | A minimum high school GPA of 2.5 unweighted (on a 4.0 scale)

P.S: Any Maryland high school senior whose annual total family income is below 130 percent of the Federal poverty level is eligible to apply for this Guaranteed Access Grant.

Application Deadline: January 15

Application Link: https://www.loyola.edu/department/financial-aid/undergraduate/programs/scholarships

1 Bard College at Simon's Rock

Location: Great Barrington, Massachusetts
Setting: Rural (275 Acres)
Undergraduate Enrollment: 304
Type: Private

Elizabeth Blodgett Hall and Livingston Hall Scholarships: Awards Full tuition

Requirements: Top Applicants.

Application Deadline: November 1

Application Link: https://simons-rock.edu/admission/tuition-and-financial-aid/scholarships.php

2 Worcester Polytechnic Institute

Location: Worcester, Massachusetts
Setting: City (95 Acres)
Undergraduate Enrollment: 5,246
Type: Private

Great Minds/CoMPASS Scholars Program: Awards up to the full cost of tuition and fees.

Requirements: Applicants must be Pell-eligible seniors attending a Worcester Public High School.

Application Deadline: February 1

Application Link: https://www.wpi.edu/admissions/tuition-aid/types-of-aid/scholarships-grants/wpi-merit

3 Smith College

Location: Northampton, Massachusetts
Setting: Suburban (147 Acres)
Undergraduate Enrollment: 2,523
Type: Private

Springfield/Holyoke Partnership or the Greenfield/Holyoke Community College Scholarship: Awards Full tuition.

Requirements: Applicants must be students from public schools in Springfield and Holyoke, Massachusetts.

P.S: Transfer students are also eligible to apply.

Application Deadline: November 15

Application Link: https://www.smith.edu/admission-aid/tuition-aid-applicants/first-year-applicants

4 Bentley University

Location: Waltham, Massachusetts
Setting: Suburban (163 Acres)
Undergraduate Enrollment: 4,131
Type: Private

Bentley Trustee Scholarship: Awards Full tuition.

Requirements: Top Applicants.

Application Deadline: January 15

Application Link: https://www.bentley.edu/undergraduate/tuition-financial-aid

5 Westfield State University

Location: Westfield, Massachusetts
Setting: Suburban (256 Acres)
Undergraduate Enrollment: 4,239
Type: Public

Tsongas Scholarship: Awards Full tuition and fees *(to Massachusetts residents)*

Requirements: A minimum SAT score of 1360 or higher in Evidence-Based Reading & Writing and Math | 4.0 high school GPA on a 4.0 scale.

Application Deadline: January 1

Application Link: https://www.westfield.ma.edu/cost-aid/scholarships

7 Mount Holyoke College

Location: South Hadley, Massachusetts
Setting: Suburban (800 Acres)
Undergraduate Enrollment: 2,193
Type: Private

Mount Holyoke's Trustee Scholarship: Awards Full tuition.

Requirements: Top applicants.

Application Deadline: November 15

Application Link: https://www.mtholyoke.edu/admission/apply-undergraduate-first-year/affording-mount-holyoke/financial-aid

6 Lesley University

Location: Cambridge, Massachusetts
Setting: City (5 Acres)
Undergraduate Enrollment: 1,861
Type: Private

Cambridge Rindge & Latin Merit Scholarship: Awards Full tuition.

Requirements: Applicants must be graduating from Massachusetts Cambridge Rindge and Latin High School | A minimum 3.0 HS GPA.

Boston Arts Academy Scholarship: Awards Full tuition.

Requirements: Applicant must be graduating from the Boston Arts Academy's Visual Arts program | A minimum 3.0 HS GPA.

P.S: Applicants for this scholarships would have to be nominated by their high school principal/guidance counsellor or the Boston Arts Academy.

Check the website for more details.

Application Deadline: February 15

Application Link: https://lesley.edu/academics/guide-financial-aid-scholarships-undergraduate-first-year-and-transfer-students

8 University of Massachusetts - Lowell

Location: Lowell, Massachusetts
Setting: City (142 Acres)
Undergraduate Enrollment: 12,391
Type: Public

Chancellor's Scholarship: Awards Full tuition and mandatory fees.

Dean's Scholarship Program: Annual award up to half of tuition and mandatory fees.

Requirements: Top Applicants.

Eligibility: These scholarships are awarded to **permanent residents of Massachusetts.**

Application Deadline: November 5

Application Link:
https://www.uml.edu/thesolutioncenter/financial-aid/scholarships/freshmen.aspx

9 Massachusetts Maritime Academy

Location: Bourne, Massachusetts
Setting: Suburban (54 Acres)
Undergraduate Enrollment: 1,327
Type: Public

Admiral Maurice J Bresnahan Scholarship: Award covers the value for in-state tuition and fees.

Requirements: Top Applicants.

Captain Emery E Rice Scholarship: Award covers the value for in-state tuition and fees.

Requirements: Top Applicants.

P.S: Eligibility criteria can be obtained through the Admissions Office.

Application Deadline: February 1

Application Link:
https://www.maritime.edu/financial-aid/undergraduate-aid/awards

10 College of the Holy Cross

Location: Worcester, Massachusetts
Setting: City (174 Acres)
Undergraduate Enrollment: 3,233
Type: Private

Ellis Scholarship: Awards Full tuition ***(to Worcester residents)***

Eligibility: All applicants who reside in Worcester are considered.

Brooks Scholarship: Awards Full tuition ***(to students who major in music)***

Requirements: Top Applicants.

Bean Scholarship: Awards Full tuition.

Eligibility: Applicant must be a major in the *classics department*.

Requirements: Top Applicants.

P.S: International students from countries in which English is not spoken must submit their TOEFL scores no later than November 15.

Application Deadline: January 15

Application Link:
https://www.holycross.edu/how-aid-works/scholarships-grants

11

Babson College

Location: Wellesley, Massachusetts
Setting: Suburban (370 Acres)
Undergraduate Enrollment: 2,761
Type: Private

Weissman Scholarship: Awards Full tuition plus financial support for scholars to develop their unique talents and pursue their personal passions.

P.S: International students are eligible for this scholarship.

Requirements: Top Applicants.

Global Scholarship: Awards Full tuition **(to international students)**

Eligibility: Citizenship or permanent resident status from countries other than the U.S. or Canada.

Arthur M. Blank School for Entrepreneurial Leadership Scholarship: Awards Full tuition and other benefits.

Requirements: Applicant should possess an Entrepreneurial potential.

Diversity Leadership Award: Awards Full tuition.

Eligibility: Awarded to students with the greatest potential for leadership in creating a diverse community.

Enrico Dallas Scholarship: Awards Full tuition **(to Dallas residents)**

Requirements: Top Applicants.

Application Deadline: December 1

Application Link: https://www.babson.edu/undergraduate/admission/tuition-and-financial-aid/merit-awards/

1 Eastern Michigan University

Location: Ypsilanti, Michigan
Setting: City (460 Acres)
Undergraduate Enrollment: 11,617
Type: Public

Education First Opportunity Scholarship (EFOS): Full tuition minus the Pell Grant.

Requirements: A minimum 3.0 cumulative high school GPA | Applicant must be eligible for the Pell Grant.

Application Deadline: February 15

Application Link: https://www.emich.edu/finaid/types/scholarships/freshman.php

2 Michigan State University

Location: East Lansing, Michigan
Setting: Suburban (5,192 Acres)
Undergraduate Enrollment: 39,201
Type: Public

Distinguished Freshman Scholarship: Full tuition and fees for all four (4) years.

Requirements: Excellent Academic & extracurricular record.

Application Deadline: Contact Admission Office.

Application Link: https://admissions.msu.edu/cost-aid/scholarships/first-year

3 Saginaw Valley State University

Location: University Center, Michigan
Setting: Suburban (782 Acres)
Undergraduate Enrollment: 6,789
Type: Public

President's Scholarship: Awards Full tuition and selective mandatory fees.

Requirements: A minimum 3.9 cumulative high school GPA.

Application Deadline: December 1

Application Link: https://www.svsu.edu/go/scholarships/

4 Davenport University

Location: Grand Rapids, Michigan
Setting: Suburban (77 Acres)
Undergraduate Enrollment: 4,352
Type: Private

Martin Luther King Inherit the Dream Scholarship: Awards up to Full tuition.

Requirements: A minimum 2.0 cumulative high school GPA.

Si Se Puede Cesar E. Chavez Scholarship: Awards up to Full tuition.

Requirements: A minimum 2.00 cumulative high school GPA.

Application Deadline: December 2

Application Link: https://www.davenport.edu/financial-aid/scholarships

5 Oakland University

Location: Oakland County, Michigan
Setting: Suburban (1,444 Acres)
Undergraduate Enrollment: 12,841
Type: Public

Golden Grizzlies Tuition Guarantee: Awards up to Full tuition.

Requirements: Top Applicants.

Application Deadline: March 1

Application Link:
https://oakland.edu/futurestudents/scholarships-cost-aid/

6 Siena Heights University

Location: Adrian, Michigan
Setting: Suburban (140 Acres)
Undergraduate Enrollment: 1,116
Type: Private

Trustee Scholarships: Awards up to Full tuition.

Requirements: A minimum 3.5 cumulative high school GPA.

Application Deadline: December 1

Application Link:
https://www.sienaheights.edu/residential-campus/financial-aid/scholarships-grants/

7 Olivet College

Location: Olivet, Michigan
Setting: Rural (56 Acres)
Undergraduate Enrollment: 978
Type: Private

Global Citizen Honors Program: Awards up to the full cost of tuition plus other benefits.

Requirements: Top Applicants.

Application Deadline: January 1

Application Link:
https://www.uolivet.edu/academics/global-citizen-honors-program/

8 Adrian College

Location: Adrian, Michigan
Setting: City (132 Acres)
Undergraduate Enrollment: 1,747
Type: Private

Full Tuition Scholarships

The combination of the Full-Tuition Scholarship Award, State of Michigan grants or scholarships, Federal grants or scholarships, and private grants or scholarships will equal full tuition at Adrian College.

Check the website for more details.

Application Deadline: August 1

Application Link:
https://www.adrian.edu/financial-aid/undergraduate/overview

9 Lake Superior State University

Location: Sault Ste. Marie, Michigan
Setting: Rural (115 Acres)
Undergraduate Enrollment: 1,655
Type: Public

Laker Gold Scholarship: Awards Full tuition.

Philip A Hart Scholarship: Awards Full tuition *(to Michigan resident's)*

Requirements: A minimum 3.5 cumulative high school GPA.

Application Deadline: December 15

Application Link:
https://www.lssu.edu/financial-aid/types-of-aid/scholarships/

10 Andrews University

Location: Berrien Springs, Michigan
Setting: Rural (300 Acres)
Undergraduate Enrollment: 1,295
Type: Private

George Floyd Scholar Program: Awards up to Full tuition.

Requirements: Applicant must be eligible for a Pell Grant | Submission of an essay (minimum of 500 words)

National Merit/National Achievement Finalist Scholarship: Awards Full tuition to National Merit Finalists.

Application Deadline: June 1

Application Link:
https://www.andrews.edu/services/sfs/general_information/scholarships/index.html

11 Baker College

Location: Owosso, Michigan
Setting: Urban (53 Acres)
Undergraduate Enrollment: 5,680
Type: Private

Presidential Scholarship: Awards Full tuition.

Requirements: A minimum cumulative high school GPA of 3.8 (on a 4.0 scale) | 1390+ SAT score or 30+ ACT score.

Check the website for more details.

Application Deadline: December 15

Application Link:
https://www.baker.edu/admissions-and-aid/tuition-and-aid/scholarships/

12 Alma College

Location: Alma, Michigan
Setting: City (125 Acres)
Undergraduate Enrollment: 1,245
Type: Private

Performance Scholarships: Awards up to Full tuition. (P.S: The value for this scholarship is subject to change)

Eligibility: Awarded to students demonstrating exemplary performance in art, dance, music (both vocal and instrumental), theatre and Scottish Arts.

Visit the website to see a list of other awards.

Application Deadline: February 1

Application Link:
https://www.alma.edu/financial-aid/scholarships/

13 Albion College

Location: Albion, Michigan
Setting: Rural (574 Acres)
Undergraduate Enrollment: 1,454
Type: Private

Albion College Promise: Awards Full tuition and fees *(to Michigan residents)*

Eligibility: This Scholarship is awarded to Michigan families making under $65,000 annually.

Scholarships for Incoming ***Students Residing in Michigan's Upper Peninsula***: Awards Full tuition to students residing in Michigan's Upper Peninsula.

Requirements: Top Applicants.

Application Deadline: December 1

Application Link: https://www.albion.edu/offices/financial-aid/aid-scholarships/scholarships/

14 University of Michigan - Dearborn

Location: Dearborn, Michigan
Setting: Suburban (202 Acres)
Undergraduate Enrollment: 6,117
Type: Public

Wade McCree Incentive Scholarship program: Awards Full tuition ***(to qualified students from the Detroit or Southfield Public School System)***

Requirements: A minimum 3.0 cumulative high school GPA | A minimum composite ACT score of 21 or an SAT score of 1060.

Detroit Promise Scholarship: Awards Full tuition ***(to qualified students who graduated from Detroit high schools)***

Requirements: A minimum 3.0 cumulative high school GPA | A minimum composite ACT score of 21 or an SAT score of 1060.

P.S: Check the website for more details.

Application Deadline: December 1

Application Link: https://umdearborn.edu/financial-aid/types-aid/scholarships

15 Lawrence Technological University

Location: Southfield, Michigan
Setting: Suburban (107 Acres)
Undergraduate Enrollment: 2,298
Type: Private

Buell Honor Scholarship: Awards Full tuition for four years.

Requirements: Top Applicants.

Eligibility: A high school GPA of 4.0 or higher.

Application Deadline: December 1

Application Link: https://www.ltu.edu/financial-aid/scholarships-freshmen

16 Wayne State University

Location: Detroit, Michigan
Setting: Urban (190 Acres)
Undergraduate Enrollment: 16,116
Type: Public

Wayne Access Tuition Pledge: Awards up to the full cost of tuition and standard fees at the in-state rate.

Eligibility: Applicant must demonstrate financial need by filing the Free Application for Federal Student Aid (FAFSA)

Heart of Detroit Tuition Pledge: Awards Full tuition and fees **(to Detroit residents)**

Eligibility: Applicant must graduate from any Detroit high school (public, private, charter, parochial, home school or GED program)

Born to Be a Warrior Tuition Pledge: Awards Full tuition and fees ***(to eligible children of full-time Wayne State University employees)***

Requirements: A minimum 3.5 cumulative high school GPA.

P.S: International students will also be considered for this award.

President's Award for National Merit Scholarship Finalists: Awards $12,000 per year for four consecutive years, $5,000 per year towards on-campus room (double occupancy) and board for up to four years, One-time study abroad funding up to $2,500.

Application Deadline: December 1

Application Link:
https://wayne.edu/scholarships

17 University of Detroit Mercy

Location: Detroit, Michigan
Setting: Urban (80 Acres)
Undergraduate Enrollment: 3,156
Type: Private

McNichols Puritan Lodge Community Counsel (MPLCC) Scholarship: Awards Full tuition.

Requirements: Top Applicants.

P.S: Applicants must be residents of the McNichols Puritan Lodge Community Counsel area, which include the boundaries of West McNichols on the north and Lodge Freeway to the south, with Livernois on the west and Log Cabin and Idaho Streets on the east.

Fellowships: Awards Full tuition plus other benefits.

P.S: Fellowships are awarded to incoming students who have demonstrated excellence prior to **law school** through academics, leadership, professionalism, and service.

Application Deadline: February 1

Application Link:
https://www.udmercy.edu/admission/financial-aid/sources/index.php

1 University of Minnesota Morris

Location: Morris, Minnesota
Setting: Rural (130 Acres)
Undergraduate Enrollment: 1,068
Type: Public

Prairie Scholars: Awards Full tuition.

Requirements: Top Applicants.

National Merit Scholarships: Awards Full tuition.

Eligibility: Awarded to National Merit Finalists.

Application Deadline: December 15

Application Link:
https://morris.umn.edu/costs-financial-aid/financial-aid/scholarships

2 Hamline University

Location: Saint Paul, Minnesota
Setting: Urban (60 Acres)
Undergraduate Enrollment: 1,782
Type: Private

Fulford-Karp Physics Scholarship: Awards up to the full cost of tuition to students who demonstrate interest in pursuing a degree and aptitude in the **field of physics.**

Requirements: Top Applicants.

Application Deadline: February 1

Application Link:
https://www.hamline.edu/admission-aid/financial-aid/grants-scholarships/first-year

3 University of Minnesota Twin Cities

Location: The Twin Cities of Minneapolis and Saint Paul, Minnesota
Setting: Urban (1,204 Acres)
Undergraduate Enrollment: 39,248
Type: Public

College of Science and Engineering

Robert K. Anderson Scholarship: Awards Full tuition.

Eligibility: Awarded to students from ***High Schools in Crow Wing County.***

Requirements: Top Applicants.

Norman Family Scholarship: Awards Full tuition.

Application Deadline: November 1

Application Link:
https://admissions.tc.umn.edu/cost-aid/scholarships

4 Concordia College

Location: Moorhead, Minnesota
Setting: Urban (115 Acres)
Undergraduate Enrollment: 1,827
Type: Private

Act Six Leadership Scholarship: Awards Full tuition.

Requirements: Top Applicants.

P.S: Concordia announced that it would reset its tuition rate effective Fall 2021. This fall (2021) tuition is $27,500 for all new students.

Application Deadline: January 15

Application Link:
https://www.concordiacollege.edu/tuition-aid/scholarships/concordia-scholarships/

5 Gustavus Adolphus College

Location: St. Peter, Minnesota
Setting: Rural (340 Acres)
Undergraduate Enrollment: 2,088
Type: Private

National Merit College-Sponsored Scholarship

National Merit finalists will receive a ***Full Tuition Scholarship.***

Application Deadline: November 1

Application Link: https://gustavus.edu/admission/financial-aid/scholarships.php

6 University of Northwestern – St. Paul

Location: Saint Paul, Minnesota
Setting: Suburban (107 Acres)
Undergraduate Enrollment: 3,161
Type: Private

Act Six Scholarship Program: Awards Full tuition and fees.

Application Deadline: February 1

Application Link: https://unwsp.edu/admissions/financial-aid/unw-scholarships/

7 Bethany Lutheran College

Location: Mankato, Minnesota
Setting: City (50 Acres)
Undergraduate Enrollment: 784
Type: Private

Meyer Scholarship: Awards Full tuition.

Requirements: A minimum 3.6 cumulative high school GPA | A minimum ACT score of 26/ SAT score of 1240+

Aspire MN Grant: Awards up to Full tuition.

P.S: **Minnesota residents** who are eligible for the Minnesota State Grant and the Federal Pell Grant may qualify for the Aspire MN Grant.

Together, these three grants **cover tuition in full**.

Residential students who receive the Aspire MN Grant will also receive a discounted rate for room and board.

Requirements: A minimum 2.75 cumulative high school GPA.

Application Deadline: February 28

Application Link: https://blc.edu/admissions/financial-aid/scholarships/academic-scholarships/

8 Bethel University

Location: Saint Paul, Minnesota
Setting: Suburban (245 Acres)
Undergraduate Enrollment: 2,533
Type: Private

Arts & Humanities Scholarship: Full tuition or $10,000 awarded annually.

Requirements: A minimum 3.0 cumulative high school GPA (4.0 scale) | A minimum ACT score of 25, SAT score of 1200 | Applicant must be a U.S. citizen or permanent resident.

Check the website for more details.

Bethel Physics & Engineering Scholarship: Awards two full-tuition and two $10,000 per year (to students planning to pursue a primary major in the **Department of Physics and Engineering**)

Requirements: A minimum 3.5 cumulative high school GPA (4.0 scale) | Applicant must be a U.S. citizen or permanent resident.

Application Deadline: January 15

Application Link:
https://www.bethel.edu/undergrad/financial-aid/types/scholarships/

9 North Central University

Location: Minneapolis, Minnesota
Setting: Urban (9 Acres)
Undergraduate Enrollment: 809
Type: Private

Regent's Scholarship: Awards Full tuition.

Eligibility: Awarded to an applicant with an active membership and regular attendance at an Assemblies of God church.

Requirements: A minimum 3.5 cumulative high school GPA | A minimum ACT score of 30 (SAT score of 1320)

George Floyd Memorial Scholarship: Awards Full tuition.

Eligibility: Applicant must be of African American origin | Be a United States citizen.

Act Six Scholarship Program: Awards Full tuition.

Application Deadline: March 15

Application Link:
https://www.northcentral.edu/financial-aid/types-of-aid/grants-and-scholarships/

10

University of St. Thomas

Location: Saint Paul, Minnesota
Setting: Urban (78 Acres)
Undergraduate Enrollment: 5,942
Type: Private

Dease Scholarship Program: Awards Full tuition.

Requirements: Top Applicants.

Eligibility: Awarded to underrepresented domestic, first-generation students and/or graduates from urban high schools.

GHR Fellows Program: Awards Full tuition and required fees (to students pursuing ***careers in business***)

Requirements: A minimum 3.7 cumulative high school GPA | Applicant must intend to major in business.

Schulze Innovation Scholarship: Awards Full tuition.

Requirements: A minimum 3.5 cumulative high school GPA | Applicant must intend to ***major in Entrepreneurship.***

Application Deadline: January 8

Science, Mathematics & Engineering Scholarships: Awards two full-tuition scholarships and two $8,000/year Scholarships

Requirements: A minimum 3.5 cumulative high school GPA | Applicant must intend to ***major in Science, Mathematics and/or Engineering field.***

Application Deadline: February 15

Application Link: https://www.stthomas.edu/admissions/undergraduate/financial-aid/scholarships/index.html

1 University of Southern Mississippi

Location: Hattiesburg, Mississippi
Setting: Suburban (1,090 Acres)
Undergraduate Enrollment: 10,258
Type: Public

Presidential National Merit Semifinalist Scholarship: Awards Full tuition and fees.

Eligibility: National Merit Semifinalist.

Application Deadline: January 15

Application Link:
https://catalog.usm.edu/content.php?catoid=9&navoid=515

2 Rust College

Location: Holly Springs, Mississippi
Setting: Rural (126 Acres)
Undergraduate Enrollment: 755
Type: Private

Presidential Scholarship: Awards $12,000, this covers the value for tuition and fees.
Requirements: A minimum 3.25 high school GPA.

Academic Dean Scholarship: Awards $10,000, this covers the value for tuition and fees.
Requirements: A minimum 3.0 high school GPA.

Application Deadline: December 1
Application Link:
https://www.rustcollege.edu/prospective-students/financial-aid/scholarships/

3 Millsaps College

Location: Jackson, Mississippi
Setting: City (100 Acres)
Undergraduate Enrollment: 637
Type: Private

Millsaps Yellow Ribbon Program: Awards Full tuition and fees *(to Veterans)*

P.S: The VA's Yellow Ribbon Program is a benefit in which Millsaps partners with the Department of Veterans Affairs to ensure that Yellow Ribbon 100% eligible recipients receive matching institutional funds to cover tuition and fees.

Application Deadline: March 1

Application Link:
https://www.millsaps.edu/financial-aid-and-scholarships/scholarships-grants-loans-students/

4 Mississippi State University

Location: Starkville, Mississippi
Setting: Rural (4,200 Acres)
Undergraduate Enrollment: 18,305
Type: Public

Provost Scholarship Award: Awards Full tuition, a $4,000 scholarship for study abroad, a research grant of $1,500 for academic research and/or creative discovery, a one-summer optional tuition credit of $1,000 ($2,400 for non-resident) and one summer of free housing in Griffis Hall, an optional $750 travel grant to a conference (to be provided by Honors)

Requirements: A minimum 1330 SAT/ 30 ACT | A minimum 3.75 high school GPA.

Application Deadline: December 1

Application Link:
https://www.admissions.msstate.edu/prospective-students/freshman-students

5 University of Mississippi

Location: Oxford, Mississippi
Setting: Rural (3,693 Acres)
Undergraduate Enrollment: 17,302
Type: Public

University Foundation Scholarship

W. R. Newman Scholarship: Awards $10,000 per year. This covers the total cost of tuition and fees for in-state students.

Eligibility: Mississippi residents | Top Applicants.

Robert M. Carrier Scholarship: Awards $10,000 per year. This covers the total cost of tuition and fees for in-state students.

Eligibility: Mississippi residents | Top Applicants.

School of Business Administration Scholarships

Christine and Clarence Day Business Scholarship: Awards $10,000 per year. This covers the total cost of tuition and fees for in-state students.

Eligibility: Mississippi high-school graduates pursuing ***business degrees*** | Top Applicants.

Application Deadline: January 5

Application Link:
https://finaid.olemiss.edu/scholarships/

6 Jackson State University

Location: Jackson, Mississippi
Setting: Urban (220 Acres)
Undergraduate Enrollment: 4,763
Type: Public

Heritage Academic Scholarship: Awards Full tuition.

Requirements: Incoming Freshmen, College Preparatory curriculum GPA of 3.0 (as calculated by Undergraduate Admissions) | ACT score of 23-24 or SAT score of 1130-1190.

Application Deadline: February 15

Application Link:
https://sites.jsums.edu/scholarships/freshmen.htm

3

Mississippi Valley State University

Location: Itta Bena, Mississippi
Setting: Rural (450 Acres)
Undergraduate Enrollment: 1,654
Type: Public

Vice President's Scholarship: Awards Full tuition, fees, and a book allowance of $300.

Requirements: A minimum 3.0 cumulative high school GPA | An ACT score of 22-23 (SAT equivalent)

Valedictorian/Salutatorian Academic Scholarship: Awards Full tuition, fees, and a book allowance of $200.

Eligibility: Awarded to freshmen who have attained the honor of being the Valedictorian or Salutatorian of the their high school graduating class.

University Scholarship: Award covers half tuition and fees and a book allowance of $200.

Requirements: A minimum 3.0 cumulative high school GPA | An ACT score of 20-21 (SAT equivalent)

Application Deadline: February 1

Application Link: https://www.mvsu.edu/prospective-students/scholarships

1 Fontbonne University

Location: St. Louis, Missouri
Setting: Suburban (16 Acres)
Undergraduate Enrollment: 682
Type: Private

Presidential Award: Awards Full tuition.

Eligibility: Applicants are notified by Invitation.

Requirements: Top Applicants.

Application Deadline: January 15

Application Link:
https://www.fontbonne.edu/admission-aid/scholarships-tuition/scholarships-grants-loans/freshman-scholarships-institutional-aid/

2 Park University

Location: Parkville, Missouri
Setting: Suburban (700 Acres)
Undergraduate Enrollment: 7,387
Type: Private

McAfee Scholarship: Awards Full tuition.

Requirements: Two letters of recommendation from high school teachers | GPA 3.75+ | ACT 28/ SAT 1310 Recommended – Not Required | 300-500 word personal statement as described within application.

Application Deadline: November 1

Application Link:
https://www.park.edu/academics/honors-academy/scholarships/

3 Culver-Stockton College

Location: Canton, Missouri
Setting: Rural (143 Acres)
Undergraduate Enrollment: 900
Type: Private

Pillars for Excellence: Awards Full tuition.

Requirements: A minimum cumulative high school GPA of 3.75 (4.0 scale) | 1230+ SAT/ 26+ ACT

Application Deadline: Check the website for more details.

Application Link:
https://culver.edu/admissions/scholarships-grants/

4 Columbia College

Location: Columbia, Missouri
Setting: Urban (231 Acres)
Undergraduate Enrollment: 7,861
Type: Private

Presidential Scholarship: Awards Full tuition.

Requirements: Top Applicants | A minimum 3.0 cumulative high school GPA.

Application Deadline: Check the website for more details.

Application Link:
https://www.ccis.edu/tuition-financial-aid/scholarships/traditional

5 Rockhurst University

Location: Kansas City, Missouri
Setting: Urban (55 Acres)
Undergraduate Enrollment: 2,545
Type: Private

Trustees' Scholarship: Awards Full tuition.

Requirements: Top Applicants.

Check the website for more details.

Application Deadline: January 1

Application Link: https://www.rockhurst.edu/admissions/freshman/scholarships

7 Central Christian College Of The Bible

Location: Moberly, Missouri
Setting: City (40 Acres)
Undergraduate Enrollment: 82
Type: Private

Full-Tuition Torch Scholarship: Awards Full tuition.

Requirements: Student must have a minimum of 3.5 high school GPA and a minium of 22 ACT (OR SAT Equivalent)

Application Deadline: January 1

Application Link: https://cccb.edu/financial-aid/scholarships

6 University of Missouri – Kansas City

Location: Kansas City, Missouri
Setting: Urban (150 Acres)
Undergraduate Enrollment: 10,190
Type: Public

Henry W. Bloch Scholars: Awards Full tuition and fees.

Eligibility: Applicant must live in one of these five area counties – Clay, Jackson or Platte in Missouri, or Johnson or Wyandotte in Kansas | U.S. citizen or permanent resident | Demonstrate financial need – eligible or nearly eligible for the Pell Grant.

Marion H. Bloch Scholars: Awards Full tuition and fees.

Eligibility: Applicant must live in one of these five area counties – Clay, Jackson or Platte in Missouri, or Johnson or Wyandotte in Kansas | U.S. citizen or permanent resident

Requirements: A minimum ACT score of 29 or SAT equivalent | 3.6+ GPA.

Application Deadline: November 15

Application Link: https://finaid.umkc.edu/financial-aid/scholarships/

8 Webster University

Location: Webster Groves, Missouri
Setting: Suburban (47 Acres)
Undergraduate Enrollment: 1,909
Type: Private

Chancellor's Scholarship: Awards Full tuition.

Requirements: A minimum 3.75 cumulative high school GPA (on a 4.0 scale) | A minimum 1260+ SAT | Rank in the top 20% of your high school graduating class.

Dr. Donald M. Suggs Scholarship: Awards Full tuition.

Requirements: A minimum 3.5 cumulative high school GPA (on a 4.0 scale) | A minimum ACT composite score of 25 or 1200+ SAT | Rank in the top 20% of your high school graduating class.

Check the website for more details.

Application Deadline: January 18

Application Link: https://www.webster.edu/financialaid/programs.php

9 Washington University in St. Louis

Location: St. Louis, Missouri
Setting: City (169 Acres)
Undergraduate Enrollment: 8,132
Type: Private

John B. Ervin Scholars Program: Awards Full tuition plus a $2,500 stipend.

Eligibility: Open to U.S. Citizens, permanent residents, and undocumented or DACA students living in the U.S.

Annika Rodriguez Scholars Program: Awards Full tuition plus a $2,500 stipend.

Eligibility: Students who apply to any undergraduate division of Washington University may apply for the Annika Rodriguez Scholars Program.

College of Arts & Sciences

Arthur Holly Compton Fellowship Program: Awards Full tuition plus a $1,000 stipend.

McKelvey School of Engineering

Alexander S. Langsdorf Fellowships: Awards Full tuition plus a $1,000 stipend.

Sam Fox School of Design & Visual Arts

James W. Fitzgibbon Scholarships in Architecture: Awards Full tuition.

Requirements: Top Applicants.

Application Deadline: November 1

Application Link: https://admissions.wustl.edu/cost-aid/scholarships/

10 University of Missouri, Columbia

Location: Columbia, Missouri
Setting: City (1,262 Acres)
Undergraduate Enrollment: 23,752
Type: Public

National Merit Finalist & Semifinalist Scholarship: Awards Full tuition and fees + $3,500 additional stipend + $10,964 one year on-campus housing and dining + one-time payments $2,000 for research/study abroad and a $1,000 for tech enrichment.

Eligibility: National Merit Finalist or Semifinalist | Awarded to ***Missouri residents***.

Missouri Land Grant: Awards 100% of unmet need for tuition and fees.

Eligibility: Awarded to ***Missouri residents*** who are Pell-eligible students.

Application Deadline: November 15

Application Link:
https://admissions.missouri.edu/costs-aid/scholarships/

11 Maryville University

Location: St. Louis, Missouri
Setting: Suburban (130 Acres)
Undergraduate Enrollment: 5,809
Type: Private

Trustee Scholarship: Awards Full tuition.

Requirements: A minimum 3.75 cumulative high school GPA | 1290+ SAT / 27+ ACT

Melissa Brickey Scholarship: Awards Full tuition.

Eligibility: Applicant must be a graduate of De La Salle Middle School (St. Louis, Mo.) and/or one of the public or private high schools within the boundaries of Saint Louis City.

Requirements: Top Applicants.

Application Deadline: December 1

Application Link:
https://www.maryville.edu/admissions/financial-aid/scholarships/

1 Montana State University

Location: Bozeman, Montana
Setting: City (956 Acres)
Undergraduate Enrollment: 14,648
Type: Public

Presidential Scholarship: Full tuition waiver and a generous stipend renewable for up to four years.

P.S: Finalists who do not receive the Presidential Scholarship will be considered for the Provost Scholarship, which also provides a full tuition waiver and a stipend.

Requirements: Top Applicants.

Application Deadline: December 1

Application Link:
https://www.montana.edu/admissions/scholarships/additional.html

2 University of Providence

Location: Great Falls, Montana
Setting: City (44 Acres)
Undergraduate Enrollment: 665
Type: Private

University of Providence Leadership Scholars: Award ranges from $18,000 to full tuition.

Requirements: A minimum 3.0 cumulative high school GPA.

University of Providence Catholic Scholars: Award ranges from $18,000 to full tuition.

Requirements: A minimum 3.0 cumulative high school GPA.

P.S: A separate application is required and includes an essay, resume, letter of recommendation from high school counselor, principal or teacher, and a campus interview.

Endowed Scholarships

Awards cover up to the cost of tuition.

Check the website for more details.

Application Deadline: December 18

Application Link:
https://www.uprovidence.edu/financial-services/scholarships/

1 Union College

Location: Lincoln, Nebraska
Setting: Suburban (50 Acres)
Undergraduate Enrollment: 483
Type: Private

Board of Trustees Scholarship: Awards Full tuition.

Requirements: A minimum 3.9 cumulative high school GPA | 33+ ACT (1500 SAT)

Application Deadline: February 15

Application Link:
https://ucollege.edu/financial

2 Nebraska Wesleyan University

Location: Lincoln, Nebraska
Setting: City (50 Acres)
Undergraduate Enrollment: 1,545
Type: Private

TeamMates Access Scholarship: Awards Full tuition.

Requirements: A minimum 3.0 cumulative high school GPA (on a 4.0 scale) | 25+ ACT, and be Federal Pell rant eligible as determined by a completed FAFSA (Free Application for Federal Student Aid) submitted to NWU.

Application Deadline: January 5

Application Link:
https://www.nebrwesleyan.edu/admissions/financial-aid-office/undergraduate-aid/first-year-scholarships

3 Chadron State College

Location: Chadron, Nebraska
Setting: Rural (281 Acres)
Undergraduate Enrollment: 1,444
Type: Public

Gold Presidential Scholarship: Awards Full tuition.

Requirements: Top Applicants.

Application Deadline: January 15

Application Link:
https://www.csc.edu/start/financial-aid/scholarships/

4 Creighton University

Location: Omaha, Nebraska
Setting: Urban (118 Acres)
Undergraduate Enrollment: 4,290
Type: Private

Markoe First Generation Scholarship: Awards Full tuition.

Requirements: A minimum 3.3 cumulative high school GPA (on a 4.0 scale) | Applicants must be defined as Federal Pell Grant eligible | Must be a first-generation student.

Application Deadline: January 15

Application Link:
https://www.creighton.edu/admission-aid/admissions-information/scholarships

5 University of Nebraska at Kearney

Location: Kearney, Nebraska
Setting: City (501 Acres)
Undergraduate Enrollment: 4,269
Type: Public

In-State Scholarships

Board of Regents Scholarship: Awards Full tuition.

Requirements: Top Applicants.

Kearney Law Opportunities Program (KLOP): Awards Full tuition.

Requirements: A minimum 3.5 cumulative high school GPA | 27+ ACT

P.S: This scholarship is designed to recruit students from rural areas and train them to become **lawyers** who will return and practice in their communities.

Kearney Health Opportunities Program (KHOP): Awards Full tuition.

P.S: The purpose of the program is to recruit and educate students from rural Nebraska who are committed to returning to rural Nebraska to practice **healthcare**.

Out-of-State Scholarships

Blue and Gold Scholarship: Awards Full tuition.

Requirements: Top Applicants.

Application Deadline: November 1

Application Link:
https://www.unk.edu/scholarships.php

6 University of Nebraska – Lincoln

Location: Lincoln, Nebraska
Setting: Urban (861 Acres)
Undergraduate Enrollment: 19,189
Type: Public

Chancellor's Tuition Scholarship: Awards Full tuition.

Eligibility: Awarded to finalists in nationally recognized scholar competitions, such as the National Merit and National Hispanic Recognition programs.

Regents Scholar Tuition Commitment: Awards Full tuition (**to in-state students**)

Requirements: Top Applicants.

Application Deadline: February 1

Application Link:
https://admissions.unl.edu/cost/

7 Wayne State College

Location: Wayne, Nebraska
Setting: Rural (128 Acres)
Undergraduate Enrollment: 3,860
Type: Public

Neihardt Scholars Program: Full tuition, renewable double occupancy room waiver, and a $500 annual stipend for four years.

Requirements: A minimum 3.5 cumulative high school GPA (on a 4.0 scale) | 25+ ACT or an SAT score of at least 1200.

Presidential Scholarship: Awards Full tuition and half of the housing costs, renewable for 4 years.

Requirements: 30+ ACT or an SAT score of at least 1390.

NSCS Board of Trustees Scholarship: Awards Full tuition (**to Nebraska residents**)

Requirements: 25+ ACT or an SAT score of at least 1200.

Rural Health Opportunities Program (RHOP): Awards Full tuition.

Eligibility: Awarded to students from rural areas of Nebraska who demonstrate academic potential and a desire to practice medical laboratory science, dental hygiene, dentistry, medicine, nursing, pharmacy, physical therapy, physician assistant, or radiography in rural Nebraska.

Rural Law Opportunities Program (RLOP): Awards Full tuition (to students from rural areas of **Nebraska**)

Application Deadline: December 1

Application Link:
https://www.wsc.edu/scholarships

8 Peru State College

Location: Peru, Nebraska
Setting: Rural (104 Acres)
Undergraduate Enrollment: 1,156
Type: Public

Board of Trustees Scholarship: Awards Full tuition.

Eligibility: Applicant must be a Nebraska high school graduate or resident.

Requirements: Top Applicants.

No Boundaries Scholarship: Awards Full tuition.

Eligibility: Applicant must be a **non-resident** of the state of Nebraska.

Requirements: Top Applicants.

Rural Health Opportunities Program (RHOP): Awards Full tuition.

Eligibility: Students admitted into the RHOP program must be from a rural background.

P.S: The application deadline for this scholarship is by December 1 | The purpose of the program is to recruit and educate students from rural communities who plan to return to rural areas to practice.

Application Deadline: January 15

Application Link:
https://www.peru.edu/affordability/competitive.html

1 University of Nevada, Reno

Location: Reno, Nevada
Setting: City (200 Acres)
Undergraduate Enrollment: 16,973
Type: Public

Presidential Scholarship: Awards $8,000 per year. This covers the cost for ***in-state tuition***.

Requirements: Have a minimum high school GPA of 3.5

National Merit Scholarship: Awards $16,000 per year. This covers ***twice*** the cost for ***in-state tuition***.

Eligibility: Applicant must be a National Merit Finalist.

Application Deadline: February 1

Application Link:
https://www.unr.edu/financial-aid/scholarships

2 University of Nevada, Las Vegas

Location: Las Vegas, Nevada
Setting: Urban (358 Acres)
Undergraduate Enrollment: 25,365
Type: Public

University of Nevada, Las Vegas offers so many scholarship opportunities to incoming freshmen who wish to pursue an undergraduate degree in the instuition.

P.S: Check the schools website for an extensive list of scholarship opportunities.

Application Link:
https://www.unlv.edu/finaid/scholarships

1 University of New Hampshire

Location: Durham, New Hampshire
Setting: Suburban (2,600 Acres)
Undergraduate Enrollment: 11,480
Type: Public

Granite Guarantee: Awards Full tuition (***to in-state students***)

Eligibility: Applicants must be New Hampshire residents who are first-time, first-year, Pell Grant – eligible.

Guard and Reserve Forces Duty Scholarships: Awards Full tuition and fees; monthly drill pay; monthly cadet stipend.

Application Deadline: November 15

Application Link:
https://www.unh.edu/financialaid/types-aid/scholarships

2 Southern New Hampshire University

Location: Manchester, New Hampshire
Setting: Suburban (338 Acres)
Undergraduate Enrollment: 2,601
Type: Private

Southern New Hampshire University Sets Out to Reimagine Campus-Based Learning, Offers ***Full Tuition*** Scholarships for Incoming Freshmen.

P.S: Check the website for more details.

Application Link:
https://www.snhu.edu/tuition-and-financial-aid/paying-for-college/ways-to-save

1 Saint Elizabeth University

Location: Morris Township, New Jersey
Setting: Suburban (200 Acres)
Undergraduate Enrollment: 737
Type: Private

Presidential Scholarship: Awards Full tuition to **in-state** residents.

Requirements: Top Applicants.

Application Deadline: March 1 (Fall Semester scholarships) | November 1 (Spring Semester scholarships)

Application Link:
https://www.steu.edu/admissions/financial-aid/types-of-scholarships

2 Caldwell University

Location: Caldwell, New Jersey
Setting: Suburban (70 Acres)
Undergraduate Enrollment: 1,605
Type: Private

Presidential Scholarship: Awards range from $20,000 to Full tuition.

Requirements: Awarded to top applicants with SAT scores exceeding 1270.

Application Deadline: December 1

Application Link:
https://www.caldwell.edu/admissions/financial-aid/scholarships-and-grants/

3 Centenary University

Location: Hackettstown, New Jersey
Setting: Suburban (42 Acres)
Undergraduate Enrollment: 1,128
Type: Private

Hackettstown Partnership Scholarship: Awards Full tuition.

Eligibility: Awarded to a student who will be graduating from Hackettstown High School in the current school year.

P.S: Check the website for more details.

Application Link:
https://www.centenaryuniversity.edu/admission-aid/tuition-financial-aid/incoming-freshmen/

4 Stevens Institute of Technology

Location: Hoboken, New Jersey
Setting: City (55 Acres)
Undergraduate Enrollment: 3,988
Type: Private

The Ann P. Neupauer Scholarship: Awards Full tuition.

Requirements: Top Applicants.

Application Deadline: December 1

Application Link:
https://www.stevens.edu/page-basic/stevens-scholarships

5 Seton Hall University

Location: South Orange, New Jersey
Setting: Suburban (58 Acres)
Undergraduate Enrollment: 6,012
Type: Private

ROTC Scholarships: Awards range from full tuition and fees or room and board.

Eligibility: Check the website for more details.

Requirements: Top Applicants.

Application Deadline: January 15

Application Link:
https://www.shu.edu/undergraduate-admissions/scholarships.html

6 The College of New Jersey

Location: Ewing, New Jersey
Setting: Suburban (289 Acres)
Undergraduate Enrollment: 7,039
Type: Public

Bonner Community Scholarship: Award value can cover from 50% to 100% of the cost of in-state tuition (financial need may be considered).

Requirements: Top Applicants.

Application Deadline: January 15

Application Link:
https://admissions.tcnj.edu/scholarships/instatescholarships/

7 Saint Peter's University

Location: Jersey City, New Jersey
Setting: Urban (25 Acres)
Undergraduate Enrollment: 2,068
Type: Private

Academic Award: Awards range from $9,000 to Full tuition.

Requirements: Top Applicants.

Application Deadline: March 15

Application Link:
https://catalogs.saintpeters.edu/undergraduate/generalinformation/studentfinancialaid/

8 Drew University

Location: Madison, New Jersey
Setting: Suburban (186 Acres)
Undergraduate Enrollment: 1,549
Type: Private

Army ROTC

Awards Full tuition, $1,200 book allowance per academic year and a monthly stipend.

Requirements: A minimum cumulative high school GPA of 2.50 | U.S. citizen between the ages of 17 and 26 | A minimum SAT score of 920 or 19 on the ACT.

Application Deadline: January 10

Application Link:
https://drew.edu/admissions-and-aid/student-financial-services/financial-aid-scholarships/grants-scholarships/

9 New Jersey Institute of Technology

Location: Newark, New Jersey
Setting: Urban (48 Acres)
Undergraduate Enrollment: 9,019
Type: Public

National Merit Scholarship: Awards full tuition and fees to students who have been selected by the National Merit Scholarship Corporation (NMSC)

Requirements: To enter the competition, applicant must be either a U.S. citizen or a U.S. lawful permanent resident.

Honors Merit Awards: Awards up to full tuition and fees.

Requirements: Applicant must be accepted into the Albert Dorman Honors College to be eligible for this award.

Faculty Scholarships: Awards up to full tuition minus other tuition-based award.

Requirements: Top Applicants.

Architecture Design Competition Scholarships: Awards Half to Full tuition.

P.S: This is a 5-year scholarship for freshmen majoring in Architecture.

Requirements: Applicant must be accepted into the New Jersey School of Architecture.

Application Deadline: September 30

Application Link:
https://www.njit.edu/financialaid/merit-based-scholarships

10 Fairleigh Dickinson University

Location: Teaneck, New Jersey
Setting: Suburban (266 Acres)
Undergraduate Enrollment: 7,432
Type: Private

Athletic Scholarships: Award varies up to Full tuition and housing.

P.S: Only available to ***International students***.

Requirements: Recognizes superior athletic ability of students participating in the National Collegiate Athletic Association (NCAA) Division I | Only available at the Metropolitan Campus | Subject to Division I rules and regulations of the NCAA.

Application Deadline: December 1

Application Link:
https://www.fdu.edu/admissions/international/scholarships/

11 Rutgers University

Location: New Brunswick, New Jersey
Setting: City (2,656 Acres)
Undergraduate Enrollment: 36,344
Type: Public

Rutgers University – New Brunswick

Scarlet Guarantee: Offers a "Last dollar" financial aid award that covers the cost of in-state tuition and mandatory fees.

Eligibility for the Scarlet Guarantee is based on your family's adjusted gross income (AGI) as reported on your FAFSA or NJAFAA and will be offered as part of your financial aid package.

Harvey Schwartz Scholarship: Awards full tuition.

Requirements: Top Applicants.

Rutgers University – Newark

TheDream.US: Awards up to $33,000 for high school graduate applicants obtaining a bachelor's degree. This covers the cost of Domestic tuition.

Application Deadline: February 28

This scholarship opportunity is for undocumented students and DREAMers!

Application Deadline: December 1

Application Link:
https://admissions.rutgers.edu/costs-and-aid/scholarships

12 Bloomfield College

Location: Bloomfield, New Jersey
Setting: Suburban (12 Acres)
Undergraduate Enrollment: 1,533
Type: Private

Bloomfield High School Scholarship: Awards Full tuition and books to ***Bloomfield High School graduates.***

Requirements: A minimum 3.5 cumulative high school GPA (90) | SAT score of at least 1100 | Top five rank in class.

Trustees Scholar Awards: Awards range from $9,000 – Full tuition.

Requirements: A minimum 3.6 cumulative high school GPA (90) | 980+ SAT (Reading, Writing and Math sections) | College Prep Curriculum 4 + AP and/or Honor courses | Applicants must be U.S. citizens or permanent residents of the United States.

Presidential Scholar Awards: Awards range from $7,000 – Full tuition.

Requirements: A minimum 3.0 cumulative high school GPA (90) | 980+ SAT (Reading, Writing and Math sections) | College Prep Curriculum 2 + AP and/or Honor courses | Applicants must be U.S. citizens or permanent residents of the United States.

Application Deadline: October 1

Application Link:
https://bloomfield.edu/courses/policy/scholarships-financial-aid

Kean University

Location: Union, New Jersey
Setting: Urban (240 Acres)
Undergraduate Enrollment: 10,845
Type: Public

Kean Scholar: Awards up to $20,000 per year. This covers the total cost of tuition.

Trustee Scholar: Awards up to $14,000. This covers the total cost of tuition for ***in-state students***.

Requirements: Top Applicants.

New Jersey Center for Science, Technology and Mathematics (NJSTM) Scholarship: Awards 100% ***in-state tuition*** only.

Eligibility: Awarded to incoming freshmen who matriculate directly into five-year, combined bachelor/master's degree honors program.

Requirements: 3.7 – 4.0 HS GPA

Check the website for more details.

Michael Graves College of Architecture and Design Scholarship: Awards Full ***in-state tuition***.

Eligibility: Awarded to incoming freshmen who pursue undergraduate degrees in **Architecture or Design**.

Requirements: 3.0 unweighted high school GPA.

School of Fine and Performing Arts Scholarship: Awards Full ***in-state tuition***.

Eligibility: Awarded to incoming freshmen who pursue undergraduate degrees in **Fine arts, Music or Theatre**.

Requirements: 3.0 unweighted HS GPA.

Kean Tuition Promise: Award may cover up to the full cost of tuition and fees.

Eligibility: Household adjusted gross income (AGI) is a maximum of $65k | Applicant must be a U.S. citizen or eligible noncitizen | Be a resident of New Jersey for at least one year before the first day of class.

Requirements: 3.2+ High school GPA.

Application Deadline: January 1

Application Link: https://www.kean.edu/offices/financial-aid/scholarship-services/merit-scholarships-new-incoming-students

1 University of New Mexico

Location: Albuquerque, New Mexico
Setting: Urban (769 Acres)
Undergraduate Enrollment: 15,914
Type: Public

Freshmen New Mexico Resident Scholarships

Presidential Scholarship: Awards up to $10,000 per year. This covers the total cost of tuition.

Requirements: A minimum 3.75 cumulative high school GPA.

National African American Scholars: Awards up to $11,000 per year. This covers the total cost of tuition.

Eligibility: National African American Scholars.

National American Indian Scholars: Awards up to $11,000 per year. This covers the total cost of tuition.

Eligibility: National American Indian Scholars.

National Hispanic Scholars: Awards up to $11,000 per year. This covers the total cost of tuition.

Eligibility: National Hispanic Scholars.

Lobo First-Year Promise: Award covers 100% base tuition and fees.

Eligibility: Applicant must graduate from a New Mexico high school and have an annual family income of $50,000 or less.

Application Deadline: December 1

Application Link:
https://scholarship.unm.edu/

2 New Mexico Institute of Mining & Technology

Location: Socorro, New Mexico
Setting: Rural (320 Acres)
Undergraduate Enrollment: 1,218
Type: Public

S-STEM Scholarship for New Freshman students Computer Science and Information Technology Majors:

Awards up to $10,000 per year.

Requirements: High school GPA of at least 3.6 (from transcripts), or ranked in the top 15% of graduating high school class | U.S. citizen or permanent resident.

Application Deadline: May 31

Application Link:
https://www.nmt.edu/finaid/scholarships.php

3 New Mexico State University

Location: Las Cruces, New Mexico
Setting: City (900 Acres)
Undergraduate Enrollment: 11,591
Type: Public

Conroy Honors Scholars: Award covers Full tuition and required fees. Recipients are eligible to receive a $2,500 Global Citizen Award to help fund a study abroad experience with guidance from the Honors College.

Requirements: 3.9 GPA or Academic Index of 159 and above.

Application Deadline: December 1

Application Link: https://fa.nmsu.edu/scholarships/

4 New Mexico Highlands University

Location: Las Vegas, New Mexico
Setting: Rural (175 Arces)
Undergraduate Enrollment: 1,699
Type: Public

Regent's New Mexico Scholars Scholarship: Awards full tuition and fees plus $500 per semester.

Eligibility: Applicant must rank in the top 5 percent of graduating class or 25 ACT | Family income of $60,000 or less.

Application Deadline: March 1

Application Link: https://www.nmhu.edu/financial-aid-2/scholarships/

Tuition-Free College for NEW MEXICANS:

New Mexico Higher Education Department has a provision for New Mexicans to attend College Tuition Free!

With the New Mexico Opportunity Scholarship, the New Mexico Lottery Scholarship, and more than 25 scholarships, grants, and college financial aid programs available, there are options for every New Mexican to pursue higher education without having to worry about the cost of tuition and fees.

P.S: Check the website for more details.

Application Link: https://hed.nm.gov/free-college-for-new-mexico

1 Clarkson University

Location: Potsdam, New York
Setting: Rural (640 Acres)
Undergraduate Enrollment: 2,668
Type: Private

Clarkson Ignite Presidential Fellows Program: Award covers Full tuition.

Requirements: Top Applicants.

Application Deadline: January 15

Application Link:
https://www.clarkson.edu/admissions-aid/undergraduate/tuition-costs

2 SUNY Polytechnic Institute

Location: Albany, New York
Setting: Suburban (800 Acres)
Undergraduate Enrollment: 1,990
Type: Public

Excelsior Scholarship Program: Award when combined with other grants/scholarships, allows students who are ***New York State residents***, and whose families earn $125,000 or less annually to attend SUNY Polytechnic Institute ***tuition free!***

Application Deadline: December 1

Application Link:
https://sunypoly.edu/admissions/undergraduate/first-year-information/scholarships.html

3 Lehman College, CUNY

Location: The Bronx borough, New York
Setting: Urban (37 Acres)
Undergraduate Enrollment: 12,459
Type: Public

Excelsior Scholarship Program: Award when combined with other grants/scholarships, allows eligible full-time students to attend Lehman College, ***tuition free!***

Eligibility: New York residents.

Application Deadline: December 1

Application Link:
https://www.lehman.edu/financial-aid/scholarships.php

4 Ithaca College

Location: Ithaca, New York
Setting: Suburban (670 Acres)
Undergraduate Enrollment: 4,619
Type: Private

Ithaca Opportunity Grant (IOG): Awards up to the Full cost of tuition.

Eligibility: Applicants must be of African American, Asian/Pacific Island, Hispanic, or Native American origin | Have considerable financial need.

Application Deadline: February 1

Application Link:
https://www.ithaca.edu/tuition-financial-aid

5 SUNY College at Geneseo

Location: Geneseo, New York
Setting: Rural (220 Acres)
Undergraduate Enrollment: 4,136
Type: Public

NYS Excelsior Scholarship: Awards up to Full tuition.

Eligibility: New York resident | Family household adjusted gross income must not exceed $125,000 | Good academic standing.

Application Deadline: January 15

Application Link:
https://www.geneseo.edu/financial_aid/private-state-scholarships

6 CUNY John Jay College of Criminal Justice

Location: New York City, New York
Setting: Urban
Undergraduate Enrollment: 12,019
Type: Public

Excelsior Scholarship: Awards Full tuition.

Requirements: Applicants should file the FAFSA and the NYS Tuition Assistance Program (TAP) application | Have a family income of $125,000 or less.

Application Deadline: February 1

Application Link:
https://new.jjay.cuny.edu/admissions/tuition-financial-aid/scholarships

7 Morrisville State College

Location: Morrisville, New York
Setting: Rural (150 Acres)
Undergraduate Enrollment: 1,803
Type: Public

Excelsior Scholarship: Awards up to Full tuition.

P.S: This is a program designed to provide tuition-free college at New York's public colleges and universities to families making up to $125,000 a year.

Eligibility: New York resident | Family household adjusted gross income must not exceed $125,000 | Good academic standing.

Application Deadline: January 15

Application Link:
https://www.morrisville.edu/attend/scholarships/excelsior-scholarship

8 Hobart and William Smith Colleges

Location: Geneva, New York
Setting: City (170 Acres)
Undergraduate Enrollment: 1,559
Type: Private

Seneca Scholarship: Awards Full tuition.

Requirements: Top Applicants.

P.S: In order to be considered for any scholarship(s), applicants must indicate interest by selecting "yes" to merit scholarship interest in your Common Application questions.

Check the website for more details.

Application Deadline: February 1

Application Link:
https://www.hws.edu/admissions/tuition-scholarships-and-aid/merit-based-awards.aspx

9 Hofstra University

Location: Hempstead, New York
Setting: Suburban (244 Acres)
Undergraduate Enrollment: 6,110
Type: Private

Hofstra University Trustee Scholars Program: Awards Full tuition.

Requirements: An average SAT/ACT equivalent of 1530 on a 1600 scale | Weighted GPA of 4.24 | Top 10% of HS graduating class.

Check out the **Provost Academic Excellence Scholarship** offered by Hofstra University to graduates of Nassau Community College.

Application Deadline: November 15

Application Link: https://www.hofstra.edu/admission/first-year-scholarships.html

10 College of Mount Saint Vincent

Location: New York City, New York
Setting: Urban (70 Acres)
Undergraduate Enrollment: 2,259
Type: Private

Premier Programs

Corazon C. Aquino Scholarship: Awards Full tuition.

Eligibility: Awarded to high achieving incoming first-year students of Filipino descent.

P.S: Applicants will be required to complete an interview with the Aquino Scholarship Committee as a part of their application for this scholarship.

There are Full room and board Scholarships also available under the Premier Programs.

Application Deadline: February 15

Application Link: https://mountsaintvincent.edu/admission/financial-aid/financial-aid-options/scholarships/premier-programs/

11 Alfred State College of Technology

Location: Alfred, New York
Setting: Rural (1,062 Acres)
Undergraduate Enrollment: 3,348
Type: Public

NYS Science, Technology, Engineering and Mathematics (STEM) Incentive Program: Awards up to Full tuition.

P.S: This program provides a full SUNY or CUNY tuition scholarship for the top 10 percent of students in each New York State high school if they pursue a STEM degree in an associate or bachelor degree program and agree to work in a STEM field in New York State for 5 years after graduation.

Eligibility: Applicant must be a New York resident | Be a U.S. citizen or eligible non-citizen | Be ranked in the top 10% of their high school graduating class of a NYS high school.

Excelsior Scholarship: Awards up to Full tuition.

Eligibility: New York resident | Family household adjusted gross income must not exceed $125,000 | Good academic standing.

Application Deadline: May 15

Application Link: https://www.alfredstate.edu/financial-aid/scholarships/new-york-state-scholarships

12 Fordham University

Location: New York City, New York
Setting: Urban (93 Acres)
Undergraduate Enrollment: 10,098
Type: Private

Semifinalist and National Recognition Program Scholarships: Award covers Full tuition.

Requirements: Awarded to students who are designated as Semi-finalists by the National Merit Recognition Program or Scholars by the National Hispanic Recognition Program, African American Recognition Program, or Indigenous Recognition Program (new in 2021)

Excellence in Theatre Scholarship: Award covers Full tuition plus the average cost of a double room or actual charges, whichever is less (excluding meal plans and fees), if the recipient lives on campus.

Requirements: Awarded to top theatre admits.

P.S: This Scholarships is available to out-of-state students and International students.

Fordham University **School of Law** has scholarships that covers up to the full cost of tuition.

Application Deadline: November 1

Application Link:
https://www.fordham.edu/undergraduate-admission/apply/scholarships-and-grants/

13 Roberts Wesleyan College

Location: Rochester, New York
Setting: Suburban (188 Acres)
Undergraduate Enrollment: 1,052
Type: Private

B.T Roberts Scholarship: Awards Full tuition.

Requirements: Top Applicants.

P.S: This scholarship will be awarded based on an interview during the event, an essay, and high school academic performance. Students must attend the **Academic Scholarship Celebration** to be eligible.

National Merit Scholarship: Awards Full tuition.

Eligibility: Awarded to National Merit Scholar Finalists.

Music Scholarship: Awards Full tuition.

Requirements: Awarded each year to the most skilled musicians who audition.

Application Deadline: February 14

Application Link:
https://www.roberts.edu/undergraduate/tuition-and-aid/grants-scholarships/

14 University of Rochester

Location: Rochester, New York
Setting: Urban (707 Acres)
Undergraduate Enrollment: 6,767
Type: Private

International Baccalaureate (IB) Scholarship: Awards Full tuition.

Eligibility: Awarded to students who successfully complete ***the International Baccalaureate diploma at Wilson Magnet High School***.

Regents Scholar Tuition Commitment: Awards Full tuition.

Requirements: Top Applicants.

SAY YES TO EDUCATION: Awards Full tuition.

P.S: Say Yes students who are admitted to the College, including all qualified graduates of the Syracuse and Buffalo City School Districts, and ***whose family income is less than or equal to $100,000, will receive full tuition funding*** through a combination of federal, state and university grants.

Application Deadline: November 1

Application Link: https://www.rochester.edu/financial-aid/scholarships/

15 Elmira College

Location: Elmira, New York
Setting: City (55 Acres)
Undergraduate Enrollment: 609
Type: Private

Elmira Scholars Program: Awards Full tuition.

Requirements: A 3.9 GPA (No SAT or ACT scores required) | A 3.7 GPA as well as 1300 SAT or 28 ACT composite score.

Check out the Phi Theta Kappa Scholarship.

As a Phi Theta Kappa Scholar, you will receive ***a one-term, full-tuition scholarship*** to determine if you would like to earn your four-year degree at a nationally-ranked, private college.

ROTC Scholarships

Scholarship for High School Students: Awards Full tuition, $1200 per year in book money, mandatory fees, and a monthly stipend that increases each academic year.

Requirements: Top Applicants.

Application Deadline: December 12

Application Link: https://www.elmira.edu/affordability/undergraduate-tuition-aid/scholarships/scholarships

16 Oswego State University of New York

Location: Oswego, New York
Setting: Rural (700 Acres)
Undergraduate Enrollment: 5,985
Type: Public

Excelsior Scholarship Program: Awards Full tuition.

Eligibility: New York residents.

Through New York State's Excelsior Scholarship program, a greater number of **New York students and families** will be eligible to earn free tuition at SUNY Oswego.

"Free Tuition Plus" Scholarships: Awards Full tuition.

Eligibility: New York residents.

Check the website for more details.

Application Deadline: November 15 (for spring term applicants) | January 15 (for fall term applicants)

Application Link: https://www.oswego.edu/financial-aid/scholarships

17 D'youville College

Location: Buffalo, New York
Setting: City (17 Acres)
Undergraduate Enrollment: 1,399
Type: Private

Dillon Scholarship: Awards Full tuition.

Diocese of Buffalo Catholic High School Scholarship: Awards Full tuition.

Requirements: Top Applicants.

SAY YES: Awards Full tuition.

D'Youville offers unlimited Say Yes Full-Tuition Scholarships to high school students who graduate from a Say Yes eligible schools.

Requirements: In order to be considered for the Say Yes tuition scholarship, the annual family income cannot exceed $75,000. Family income is determined by the FAFSA and D'Youville's financial aid office.

Check the website for more details.

Application Deadline: February 1

Application Link: https://www.dyu.edu/cost-aid/scholarships/undergraduate-scholarships

Syracuse University

Location: Syracuse, New York
Setting: City (721 Acres)
Undergraduate Enrollment: 15,421
Type: Private

The 1870 Scholarship: Awards Full tuition.

P.S: Prospective recipients are evaluated for academic and creative accomplishments, commitment in community service and demonstrated financial need. The award is offered to students in all colleges.

Coronat Scholars Program: Awards Full tuition plus other benefits.

Requirements: A mean high school GPA of 4.15 | A mean SAT score of 1480 (combined math and verbal)

Junior Achievement Scholarship: Award covers Full tuition.

P.S: This Scholarship is awarded by Syracuse University to outstanding first-year student who has applied ***through Junior Achievement of CNY***. Selection is made jointly by Junior Achievement of CNY and Syracuse University based on academic record, quality of work in JA, personal achievement, and an interview.

NFTE Scholarship: Awards Full tuition and mandatory fees.

Requirements: Students must file for financial aid and submit both the CSS/Financial Aid PROFILE and FAFSA to be considered | Students must be a U.S. citizen or a permanent resident.

P.S: The Office of Financial Aid and Scholarship Programs will identify scholars who are both alumni of the NFTE program and admitted under regular Syracuse University Office of Admissions guidelines.

Refugee Scholarship: Award covers Full tuition and fees.

P.S: This program is administered by the Office of Admissions with the Office of Financial Aid and Scholarship Programs. Students should follow normal admissions and financial aid deadlines.

Say Yes to Education: Award covers Full tuition, fees and books.

Requirements: Applicants must file for financial aid and submit both the CSS/Financial Aid PROFILE and FAFSA to be considered. Check site for more details.

Application Deadline: November 15

Application Link: https://financialaid.syr.edu/scholarships/su/

19

CUNY Bernard M Baruch College

Location: New York City, New York
Setting: Urban (3 Arces)
Undergraduate Enrollment: 15,774
Type: Public

Clark Foundation Student Scholarship: Awards Full and partial tuition scholarships.

Eligibility: Awarded to students in the Marxe School of Public and International Affairs.

P.S: Recipients will be chosen on a merit basis.

Dora and Hyman Rosenzweig Scholarship: Awards Full tuition.

Eligibility: Awarded to incoming freshmen who demonstrate financial need and plan to pursue a major in the ***Zicklin School of Business.***

Karl and Helen Meyer Scholarship: Award covers Full tuition.

Eligibility: Awarded to an incoming freshman who is a first generation American or an immigrant and who demonstrates financial need and academic promise.

Lubov and Elizavet Geiman Scholarship: Awards Full tuition.

Eligibility: Awarded to an incoming freshman who is a first generation American or an immigrant, demonstrates significant financial need and plans to study in the ***Zicklin School of Business***.

P.S: Preference is for students who worked during high school.

Max Brenner Scholarship: Awards Full tuition.

Eligibility: Awarded to applicants who plan to pursue a major in Accounting.

Sarah and Sol Laterman Scholarship: Awards annual Full and partial tuition scholarships.

Eligibility: Awarded to incoming freshmen who are ***graduates of Stuyvesant High School***, currently located at 345 Chambers Street, New York, NY, or its successors in interest, who have outstanding academic credentials.

Baruch Scholars Program: Award covers Full tuition for in-state students and a generous tuition scholarship for out-of-state students.

Requirements: Top Applicants.

Application Deadline: December 1

Application Link: https://enrollmentmanagement.baruch.cuny.edu/international-student-service-center/scholarship/

20 St. Lawrence University

Location: Canton, New York
Setting: Rural (1,100 Acres)
Undergraduate Enrollment: 2,145
Type: Private

Trustee Scholarship: Awards Full tuition.

Requirements: Top Applicants.

This scholarship is awarded to the top first-year students.

Based on academic excellence, character, and leadership.

Kirk Douglas Scholarship: Awards Full tuition and fees.

Eligibility: By Invitation only, the Kirk Douglas Scholarship is for students from under-represented and low-income backgrounds who show ambition and potential to contribute to diversity within the campus community.

Application Deadline: January 1

Application Link:
https://www.stlawu.edu/offices/admissions-office/scholarships

21 Molloy College

Location: Rockville Centre, New York
Setting: Suburban (30 Acres)
Undergraduate Enrollment: 3,271
Type: Private

Molloy College Scholar's Program: Awards Full tuition.

Requirements: Applicants must have a minimum of 95% High school average | A minimum score of 1380 on the SAT combined from critical reading and math or a minimum of 30 on the ACT.

Athletic Grants: Grants up to Full tuition.

P.S: Awarded to full-time students based on athletic ability.

Fine Arts and Performing Arts Scholarships: Awards up to Full tuition.

Eligibility: Awarded to entering full-time freshmen who are judged to have exceptional talent or have achieved proficiency in art, music or communication arts. Qualifications are demonstrated through audition, the submission of a portfolio or other documented experience.

Application Deadline: December 15

Application Link:
https://www.molloy.edu/admissions-aid/financial-aid/scholarships-and-grants

22 University at Buffalo

Location: Buffalo, New York
Setting: Suburban (1,350 Acres)
Undergraduate Enrollment: 20,761
Type: Public

Walter E. Schmid Family Foundation Scholarship: Awards up to Full tuition and fees.

Requirements: Applicant must be an incoming first year student from western New York (WNY) pursuing a degree in the **School of Engineering and Applied Sciences** who has demonstrated high academic achievement in high school and entrepreneurial interests.

Presidential Scholarship: Awards $15,000 Annually. (This covers the total cost of tuition for **in-state students**)

Requirements: Top Applicants.

Application Deadline: December 15

Application Link:
https://admissions.buffalo.edu/costs/scholarships.php

23 New York University

Location: New York City, New York
Setting: Urban (230 Acres)
Undergraduate Enrollment: 29,401
Type: Private

AnBryce Scholarships: Awards Full tuition.

Eligibility: Awarded to students who demonstrate financial need and who are the first generation in their family to attend college.

NYU Wagner Merit Scholarships

Dean's Scholarship: Awards Full tuition.

Requirements: Top Applicants.

Nneka Fritz (WAG '08) Scholarship: Awards up to Full tuition.

Eligibility: Awarded to students from historically underrepresented groups with an interest in economic development.

P.S: Candidates should ideally be committed to using their education to benefit the Newark Area of New Jersey.

Application Deadline: February 20

Application Link:
https://wagner.nyu.edu/admissions/financial-aid/scholarships

24 Vaughn College of Aeronautics and Technology

Location: New York City, New York
Setting: Urban (6 Acres)
Undergraduate Enrollment: 1,175
Type: Private

A "Futureproof" Tuition-Free Education Scholarship Program: Awards Full tuition.

Eligibility: Applicants must reside in Queens County, NY.

Requirements: A minimum cumulative grade point average (GPA) of at least an 80% | Minimum cumulative score of 1,000 on the SAT or 22 on the ACT | Applicant must submit academic accomplishments, intellectual and creative distinctions, extracurricular activities, letters of reference and original essays.

Application Deadline: March 1

Application Link:
https://www.vaughn.edu/blog/a-futureproof-tuition-free-education-could-be-yours-with-the-port-authority-scholarship/

1 Gardner Webb University

Location: Boiling Springs, North Carolina
Setting: Rural (240 Acres)
Undergraduate Enrollment: 1,983
Type: Private

Ignite Excellence Full Tuition Scholarships: Awards Full tuition.

Requirements: Top Applicants.

Application Deadline: January 15

Application Link: https://gardner-webb.edu/admissions-aid/scholarships-and-grants/

2 Elizabeth City State University

Location: Elizabeth City, North Carolina
Setting: Rural (154 Acres)
Undergraduate Enrollment: 2,033
Type: Public

The Jackie Robinson Foundation: Awards $6,000 per year (This covers the total cost of tuition and fees for **in-state students**)

Requirements: Top Applicants.

Application Deadline: January 15

Application Link: https://www.ecsu.edu/financial-aid/types-of-aid.php

3 Lees-McRae College

Location: Banner Elk, North Carolina
Setting: Rural (935 Acres)
Undergraduate Enrollment: 855
Type: Private

Elizabeth McRae Scholarship: Awards Full tuition.

P.S: Recipients are chosen from all students invited to attend Scholars Day-An event in the spring that includes an interview and essay competition.

Requirements: Top Applicants.

Application Deadline: December 15

Application Link: https://www.lmc.edu/admissions/financial-aid/types-of-aid.htm

4 Montreat College

Location: Montreat, North Carolina
Setting: Suburban (89 Acres)
Undergraduate Enrollment: 853
Type: Private

Honors Scholarship: Awards Full tuition.

Requirements: A minimum 3.5 unweighted high school GPA | A minimum qualifying test score of 1200 SAT, 25 ACT, or 78 CLT.

Application Deadline: January 14

Application Link: https://www.montreat.edu/admissions/tuition-aid/undergraduate/scholarships/

5 Meredith College

Location: Raleigh, North Carolina
Setting: Urban (225 Acres)
Undergraduate Enrollment: 1,322
Type: Private

Meredith presidential Scholarship: Awards Full tuition and an opportunity for study abroad experience.

Requirements: A minimum unweighted high school GPA of 3.8 (4.0 grading scale) – 4.3 (weighted) | Superior standardized test scores SAT/ACT - 1480/33

Application Deadline: January 15

Application Link:
https://www.meredith.edu/financial-assistance/financial-assistance-undergraduate-scholarships/

6 North Carolina Wesleyan University

Location: Rocky Mount, North Carolina
Setting: Suburban (200 Acres)
Undergraduate Enrollment: 1,249
Type: Private

Trustee Scholarship: Awards Full tuition and books.

Requirements: A minimum 3.75 weighted GPA | 1200 SAT/ 25 ACT scores.

Application Deadline: December 1

Application Link:
https://ncwu.edu/scholarships/

7 Appalachian State University

Location: Boone, North Carolina
Setting: Rural (1,200 Acres)
Undergraduate Enrollment: 18,558
Type: Public

Signature Scholarships

Dr Willie C. Fleming Scholarship: Award covers Full *In-state* tuition and fees plus other benefits.

Diversity Scholars Program Scholarship: Award covers Full *In-state* tuition and fees plus other benefits.

Requirements: Top Applicants.

Application Deadline: November 15

Application Link:
https://scholarships.appstate.edu/signature-scholarships

8 University of North Carolina – Wilmington

Location: Wilmington, North Carolina
Setting: City (661 Acres)
Undergraduate Enrollment: 14,294
Type: Public

SOAR Ambassador Program: Award covers *in-state* tuition and fees. A supplemental $1,000 award is added during the sophomore, junior and senior years.

Requirements: Top Applicants.

Honors Merit Scholarship: Awards may range from $500 a year to an award equivalent of in-state tuition and fees (~$7,500 per year).

Application Deadline: March 1

Application Link:
https://uncw.edu/seahawk-life/money-matters/financial-aid/types/scholarships/

9 Warren Wilson College

Location: Swannanoa, North Carolina
Setting: Suburban (1,135 Acres)
Undergraduate Enrollment: 723
Type: Private

Milepost One: Awards Full tuition.

Requirements: A minimum 3.0 weighted GPA | Have a Total Family Income equal or less than $125,000.

Application Deadline: February 1

Application Link: https://www.warren-wilson.edu/admission/tuition-and-aid/scholarships/

11 Queens University of Charlotte

Location: Charlotte, North Carolina
Setting: Urban (95 Acres)
Undergraduate Enrollment: 1,317
Type: Private

Presidential Scholarship: Awards Full tuition.

Requirements: Top Applicants.

Application Deadline: February 1

Application Link: https://www.queens.edu/afford/scholarships/

10 University of North Carolina, Charlotte

Location: Charlotte, North Carolina
Setting: Urban (1,000 Acres)
Undergraduate Enrollment: 23,461
Type: Public

Levine Scholars Program: Awards 105,000 four year in-state tuition | 155,000 four year out-of-state tuition.

Requirements: Top Applicants.

Learn more: https://levinescholars.charlotte.edu/

Belk Scholars program in Business Analytics: Award covers *In-state* tuition and fees.

Requirements: Unweighted high school GPA of 3.50-4.00 or a weighted high school GPA of 3.75-4.00.

Freeman Endowed Scholarships: Award covers *In-state* tuition and fees.

Requirements: Unweighted high school GPA of 3.20-4.00.

Johnson Scholarship: Award covers *In-state* tuition and fees.

Requirements: Unweighted high school GPA of 3.20-4.00.

Application Deadline: December 15

Application Link: https://ninercentral.charlotte.edu/financial-aid-loans/types-aid/scholarships

12 East Carolina University

Location: Greenville, North Carolina
Setting: City (1,600 Acres)
Undergraduate Enrollment: 21,688
Type: Public

Chancellor's Fellows: Award covers ***In-state*** tuition.

Requirements: Top Applicants.

The Department of Engineering PIRATES Scholars Program: Awards up to $10,000. (This covers the total cost of tuition and fees for in-state students)

Eligibility: This scholarship will be awarded to high-achieving incoming freshmen in the Department of Engineering with demonstrated financial need.

Requirements: An unweighted high school GPA of 3.0 or better and must intend to earn a B.S. in Engineering from the Department of Engineering at ECU.

Check the website for more details:

https://math.ecu.edu/scholarships/

Application Deadline: October 1

Application Link:
https://news.ecu.edu/2020/12/08/ecu-scholarships-guide/

13 Salem College

Location: Winston-Salem, North Carolina
Setting: City (57 Acres)
Undergraduate Enrollment: 364
Type: Private

Outstanding applicants may receive four years of full tuition or full cost of attendance (tuition, fees, room, and board) through named awards such as the ***Chatham, Elberson, Kick, Womble, and Whitaker, Davis Art*** scholarships.

Scholarships for the FLEER Center

Pat Etheridge Scholarship: Awards Full tuition.

Eligibility: This scholarship is awarded to a full time Fleer student taking up to 24 semester hour who has declared their major of either Religion, Philosophy, History, or English with the preference being Religion.

Requirements: Top Applicants.

Application Deadline: November 1

Application Link:
https://www.salem.edu/admissions/scholarships

14 Davidson College

Location: Davidson, North Carolina
Setting: Suburban (841 Acres)
Undergraduate Enrollment: 1,927
Type: Private

Nomination Scholarships

Lowell L. Bryan Scholarship: Award covers Full tuition and fees.

Eligibility: This scholarship is awarded to students who will contribute in a superlative manner to their sports as well as to academic and co-curricular life at Davidson.

Competition Scholarships

William Holt Terry Scholarship: Award covers Full tuition and fees, and a $3,000 special opportunity stipend.

Eligibility: Applicants should demonstrate exemplary leadership skills and personal qualities through student government, athletics, service, or other activities.

Application Scholarships

James B. Duke Scholarship: Award covers Full tuition and fees plus a $5,000 stipend.

Requirements: Top Applicants.

Application Deadline: November 15

Application Link:
https://www.davidson.edu/admission-and-financial-aid/financial-aid/scholarships

15 Catawba College

Location: Salisbury, North Carolina
Setting: Suburban (276 Acres)
Undergraduate Enrollment: 1,094
Type: Private

Socratic Scholarship: Awards Full tuition.

Requirements: Applicants must have a weighted GPA of 4.0+ or an unweighted GPA of 3.5+

The Spirit of Catawba Scholarship: Awards Full tuition.

Requirements: Top Applicants.

Application Deadline: November 1

Application Link:
https://catawba.edu/scholarships/

16 University of North Carolina - Greensboro

Location: Greensboro, North Carolina
Setting: Urban (266 Acres)
Undergraduate Enrollment: 14,198
Type: Public

First year and transfer applicants are automatically considered for a number of scholarship opportunities based on merit and financial need. Awards range in value and duration, ***including four-year, full-tuition scholarships.***

Requirements: Top Applicants.

P.S: To apply, students should complete their admissions application and submit a FAFSA early, by the priority scholarship deadline.

Application Deadline: December 1

Application Link:
https://www.uncg.edu/costs-aid-scholarships/financial-aid/scholarships/

17 Duke University

Location: Durham, North Carolina
Setting: Suburban (8,693 Acres)
Undergraduate Enrollment: 6,640
Type: Private

Initiative for Students from the Carolinas,
Duke university will provide full tuition grants for admitted undergraduate student residents of North Carolina and South Carolina whose families have a total income of $150,000 or less.

For Duke undergraduate students from North Carolina and South Carolina with a total family income of $65,000 or less, the university will provide full tuition grants, plus financial assistance for housing, meals and some course materials or other campus expenses, without the need for student loans.

Application Deadline: November 1

Application Link:
https://financialaid.duke.edu/initiative-students-carolinas/

1 Mayville State University

Location: Mayville, North Dakota
Setting: Rural (55 Acres)
Undergraduate Enrollment: 1,147
Type: Public

ND Scholars Program: Awards Full tuition scholarships to qualifying ***North Dakota high school graduates*** who choose to stay in North Dakota to earn a first bachelor's degree.

Requirements: Top Applicants.

Application Deadline: July 1

Application Link: https://mayvillestate.edu/paying-school/scholarships/

2 University of North Dakota

Location: Grand Forks, North Dakota
Setting: City (521 Acres)
Undergraduate Enrollment: 9,928
Type: Public

National Merit Scholars

This scholarship is awarded to National Merit Scholar Finalist or Semi-Finalist from North Dakota or Minnesota.

Awards Full tuition and mandatory student fees.

Requirements: National Merit Finalist/Semi-Finalist | Applicant must select UND as first choice on the National merit application.

Hudson & Christine Washburn Scholarship: Awards up to $12,000. (This covers the total cost of tuition and fees for ***in-state students***)

Eligibility: This scholarship will be awarded to incoming freshmen students who are from ***LaMoure County***.

Requirements: A minimum High school GPA of 3.0

Application Deadline: December 15

Application Link: https://und.edu/one-stop/financial-aid/scholarships.html

3 University of Jamestown

Location: Jamestown, North Dakota
Setting: Rural (110 Arces)
Undergraduate Enrollment: 1,018
Type: Private

Wilson Scholarship: Awards Full tuition.

Requirements: A minimum 3.5 High School GPA (on a 4.0 scale) | An ACT composite score of 24 or SAT of 1160 | Candidates participate in on-campus interviews.

P.S: This scholarship is by invitation only.

ND Scholars Program: Awards Full tuition scholarships to qualifying ***North Dakota high school graduates*** who choose to stay in North Dakota to earn a first bachelor's degree.

Requirements: Applicants should score at or above the ninety-fifth percentile among those who took the ACT or SAT prior to July 1st of the calendar year preceding the individual's enrollment in college.

Application Deadline: October 15

Application Link: https://www.uj.edu/admission-aid/financial-aid-scholarships/scholarships/

1 Cedarville University

Location: Cedarville, Ohio
Setting: Rural (850 Acres)
Undergraduate Enrollment: 4,533
Type: Private

Foster Care and Adoption Scholarship: Awards Full tuition.

Eligibility: Awarded to a student who has grown up in the foster care system and is now seeking to enroll at Cedarville.

Application Deadline: March 15

Application Link:
https://www.cedarville.edu/cf/finaid/scholarships/currentaid/

2 Wittenberg University

Location: Springfield, Ohio
Setting: City (114 Acres)
Undergraduate Enrollment: 1,258
Type: Private

Bill Martin Scholarship: Awards Full tuition.

Requirements: Top Applicants.

P.S: Applicants of the Bill Martin Scholarship must reside in Washtenaw, Houghton or Keweenaw County, Michigan.

Application Deadline: December 1

Application Link:
https://www.wittenberg.edu/admission/scholarship-opportunities

3 Xavier University

Location: Cincinnati, Ohio
Setting: Urban (175 Acres)
Undergraduate Enrollment: 4,860
Type: Private

ROTC Scholarships

Army ROTC: Award covers full tuition and educational fees, a $1,200 yearly book allowance and a monthly stipend starting at $300/month during the academic school year.

Requirements: Top Applicants.

Application Deadline: December 1

Application Link:
https://www.xavier.edu/undergraduate-admission/tuition-and-aid/index

4 Marietta College

Location: Marietta, Ohio
Setting: Suburban (90 Acres)
Undergraduate Enrollment: 1,109
Type: Private

Trustee Scholarship: Awards Full tuition.

Rickey Physics Scholarship: Awards Full tuition.

Requirements: Top Applicants.

Charles Summer Harrison: Awards Full tuition.

P.S: Applicants are invited to submit a one-page statement on how they have impacted or promoted social justice and inclusion in their community.

Application Deadline: February 15

Application Link:
https://www.marietta.edu/scholarships

5 Muskingum University

Location: New Concord, Ohio
Setting: Rural (245 Acres)
Undergraduate Enrollment: 1,477
Type: Private

John Glenn Scholarship: Awards Full tuition.

Requirements: Top Applicants.

Check the website for more details...

Application Deadline: November 1

Application Link:
https://www.muskingum.edu/financial-aid/first-year

6 Wilmington College

Location: Wilmington, Ohio
Setting: Rural (65 Acres)
Undergraduate Enrollment: 1,032
Type: Private

Presidential Scholarship: Awards Full tuition.

Requirements: 3.5 – 4.0 cumulative GPA | 25 – 36 ACT composite score (1200 minimum New SAT critical reading and math combined score)

Application Deadline: February 15

Application Link:
https://www.wilmington.edu/financial-aid/scholarships-awards

7 Denison University

Location: Granville, Ohio
Setting: Suburban (850 Acres)
Undergraduate Enrollment: 2,272
Type: Private

Denison annually offers several merit scholarships to first-year students, and scholarships generally range from $5,000 to *full tuition*.

Check the website for more details.

Application Deadline: December 1

Application Link:
https://denison.edu/campus/finances/types-of-scholarships-aid

8 Miami University

Location: Oxford, Ohio
Setting: Rural (2,100 Acres)
Undergraduate Enrollment: 16,865
Type: Public

Ohio's Governor's Scholarship: Awards Full tuition.

Requirements: The scholarship is awarded to top students from each of Ohio's 8 counties.

Application Deadline: December 1

Application Link:
https://miamioh.edu/admission-aid/costs-financial-aid/scholarships.html

9 Baldwin Wallace University

Location: Berea, Ohio
Setting: Suburban (100 Acres)
Undergraduate Enrollment: 2,744
Type: Private

Say Yes Scholarship: Awards up to the Full cost of tuition.

Eligibility: Awarded to students attending eligible schools within the Cleveland Metropolitan School District.

Application Deadline: May 15

Application Link:
https://www.bw.edu/undergraduate-admission/first-year/tuition/

10 Walsh University

Location: North Canton, Ohio
Setting: Suburban (143 Acres)
Undergraduate Enrollment: 1,558
Type: Private

Walsh University Presidential Scholarship: Awards Full tuition.

Requirements: Top Applicants.

Walsh University Founders' Scholarship: Awards Full tuition.

Requirements: Top Applicants.

Application Deadline: December 1

Application Link:
https://www.walsh.edu/scholarships-and-grants.html

11 Capital University

Location: Bexley, Ohio
Setting: Urban (48 Acres)
Undergraduate Enrollment: 1,938
Type: Private

Collegiate Fellowship: Awards Full tuition.

Requirements: A minimum high school GPA of 3.75 (on a 4.0 scale)

Capital Scholars Award: Awards Full tuition.

Requirements: A minimum high school GPA of 3.5 (on a 4.0 scale)

P.S: Applicants will experience an interview and complete an essay for scholarship consideration.

Application Deadline: December 1

Application Link:
https://www.capital.edu/admission-aid/first-year-and-transfer-students/first-year-student-scholarships/

12 Ohio Northern University

Location: Ada, Ohio
Setting: Rural (342 Acres)
Undergraduate Enrollment: 2,569
Type: Private

Mathile Scholarship: Awards Full tuition.
Requirements: A minimum ACT score of 30 (1360 SAT, evidence-based reading and writing plus math) | A minimum high school GPA of 3.50.
James F. Dicke Scholarship: Awards Full tuition.
Requirements: A minimum ACT score of 29 (1330 SAT, evidence-based reading and writing plus math) | A minimum high school GPA of 3.50.
Application Deadline: December 1
Application Link:
https://www.onu.edu/admissions-aid/financial-aid/undergraduate-scholarships

13 Otterbein University

Location: Westerville, Ohio
Setting: Suburban (140 Acres)
Undergraduate Enrollment: 2,173
Type: Private

Tuition Exchange Scholarship: Awards up to Full tuition.

Requirements: Top Applicants.

Full Tuition Scholarships: Otterbein awards three ***full tuition scholarships*** through an essay competition.

P.S: By invitation only.

Requirements: Top Applicants.

Application Deadline: December 15

Application Link: https://www.otterbein.edu/financial-aid/scholarships/

14 University of Mount Union

Location: Alliance, Ohio
Setting: City (123 Acres)
Undergraduate Enrollment: 1,889
Type: Private

Investment Alliance Scholarship: Awards Full tuition.

Eligibility: Awarded to the top 15 students of each Alliance High School graduating class, as identified by the school district.

Requirements: Top Applicants.

Presidential Scholarship: Awards Full tuition.

Requirements: A GPA of at least 3.75 or a GPA of at least 3.6 combined with a minimum ACT score of 30 or SAT score of 1360 (EBRW+Math)

Application Deadline: November 8

Application Link: https://www.mountunion.edu/admission/tuition-and-aid/scholarships-and-grants

15 Case Western Reserve University

Location: Cleveland, Ohio
Setting: Urban (267 Acres)
Undergraduate Enrollment: 6,017
Type: Private

Andrew and Eleanor Squire Scholarship: Awards Full tuition.

P.S: Open to first-year applicants in the arts; humanities; management; accountancy; and natural, social and behavioral sciences.

Louis Stokes Congressional Black Caucus Foundation Scholarship: Awards Full tuition plus a grant of up to $2,500 for computer and book purchases, and assistance securing a paid summer internship.

Alexander A. Treuhaft Memorial Scholarship: Awards Full tuition.

P.S: Open to first-year applicants in Science and Engineering.

Performing Arts Scholarships: Awards Full tuition (to students who exhibit excellence in the ***performing arts***.)

Requirements: Top Applicants.

Application Deadline: January 15

Application Link: https://case.edu/admission/tuition-aid/scholarships

16 Oberlin College

Location: Oberlin, Ohio
Setting: Suburban (440 Acres)
Undergraduate Enrollment: 2,986
Type: Private

Robinson Scholarship: Awards Full tuition.

P.S: This scholarship program is awarded to graduates of Oberlin High School.

Eligibility: Applicants must have resided in the Oberlin School District for at least four years prior to high school graduation, must have attended Oberlin High School for four years, and must continue residence in the area while enrolled at Oberlin College.

Requirements: Top Applicants.

Scholarships for International Students

Eduardo Chivambo Mondlane Scholarship: Awards Full tuition scholarship for up to four years.

Eligibility: Any citizen from a ***sub-Saharan African country*** who is applying to Oberlin College of Arts and Sciences is eligible.

Edwin O. Reischauer Scholarship: Awards Full tuition scholarship for up to four years.

Eligibility: Any ***Japanese national*** who has been accepted for admission to the Oberlin College of Arts and Sciences is eligible for this award.

Application Deadline: November 15

Application Link:
https://www.oberlin.edu/financial-aid/basics/scholarships-offered

17 Bowling Green State University

Location: Bowling Green, Ohio
Setting: Rural (1,338 Acres)
Undergraduate Enrollment: 13,853
Type: Public

Socratic Scholarship: Awards Full tuition.

Presidential Scholars Award: Awards Full in state tuition and fees.

Requirements: 3.8 cumulative high school GPA on a 4.0 scale | 30 ACT composite score or 1390 SAT (Evidence-Based Reading and Writing)

Alumni Laureate Scholarship: Awards Full in state tuition, fees and a $1,000 book award.

Requirements: 3.5 cumulative high school GPA on a 4.0 scale | 27 ACT composite score or 1280 SAT

Learn more:
https://www.bgsu.edu/admissions/scholarships-and-financial-aid.html

Forsyth Award: Awards Full in state tuition and fees.

Requirements: Top Applicants.

Sidney A. Ribeau President's Leadership Academy: Awards Full in state tuition and fees.

Requirements: Top Applicants.

Application Deadline: December 1

Application Link:
https://www.bgsu.edu/honors-college/applying/scholarships-and-awards.html

18 Shawnee State University

Location: Portsmouth, Ohio
Setting: City (62 Acres)
Undergraduate Enrollment: 3,101
Type: Public

Shawnee Scholar Award: Awards Full tuition.

Requirements: A minimum ACT score of 30 or SAT (combined reading/math) score of 1320+ and a high school GPA of at least 3.8/4.0 scale.

Free – Tuition Program: The award provides free undergraduate tuition for qualifying incoming freshmen.

Eligibility: Applicants must qualify for Federal Pell Grant (as determined by the FAFSA) | Residents of Scioto, Lawrence, Adams, Pike, Jackson or Ross Counties in Ohio; or Greenup, Boyd or Lewis Counties in Kentucky.

Requirements: A minimum high school GPA of 3.0 | ACT score of at least 18

Choose Ohio First Computer Engineering Technology Scholarship: Award ranges from $1,500 up to Full tuition.

Choose Ohio First Nursing Scholarship: Award ranges from $1,500 up to Full tuition.

Application Deadline: February 1

Application Link:
https://www.shawnee.edu/financial-aid/scholarships

19 John Carroll University

Location: University Heights, Ohio
Setting: Suburban (62 Acres)
Undergraduate Enrollment: 2,417
Type: Private

Ignatian Heritage Scholarship: Awards up to the full cost of tuition.

Eligibility: First-year students applying for admission from Catholic, Jesuit, and/or Cristo Rey High Schools are eligible to apply.

Requirements: Top Applicants.

Say Yes Scholarship: Awards Full tuition and fees.

Eligibility: This scholarship is available to students attending Say Yes eligible schools in Cleveland, OH.

Castellano Scholarship: Awards Full tuition.

Eligibility: This scholarship is available to students who has studied Latin at the secondary level for at least three years and intends to major in Classical Languages at JCU.

Father Hurtado Scholarship: Awards up to Full tuition.

Eligibility: This scholarship is awarded to an incoming first-year student from St. Martin de Porres High School in Cleveland, OH.

Application Deadline: December 1

Application Link:
https://www.jcu.edu/sefs/financing-jcu-education/new-first-year-sefs/new-first-year-student-scholarships-sefs

20 Cleveland State University

Location: Cleveland, Ohio
Setting: Urban (85 Acres)
Undergraduate Enrollment: 9,950
Type: Public

Honors Program: Awards Full in-state tuition for up to eight semesters.

Requirements: A minimum of 30 ACT composite score or 1380 SAT score | Applicant should rank in the top 10% of their high school class.

Ruth Ann Moyer Scholarship: Awards Full in-state tuition.

Eligibility: Applicant must be an Ohio resident, non-traditional (at least twenty-five years of age) student, has accepted admission and submitted final transcripts by June 15.

P.S: To apply for this scholarship, you must submit a brief personal essay describing yourself, including your future plans, any challenges you may have faced and overcome, and what receiving this scholarship means to you.

Application Deadline: January 15

Application Link:
https://www.csuohio.edu/financial-aid/new-incoming-freshman

21 Bluffton University

Location: Bluffton, Ohio
Setting: Rural (235 Acres)
Undergraduate Enrollment: 664
Type: Private

Presidential Scholarship: Awards Full tuition.

Requirements: A minimum 3.5 High School GPA | 24 ACT/1160 SAT (or higher)

Scholarships Available for Intervention specialist coursework

Full tuition scholarships will be awarded to select teachers to earn intervention specialist endorsements. Grants will be presented to 11 teachers from Education Partner schools.

Application Deadline: November 1

Application Link:
https://www.bluffton.edu/admissions/financialaid/scholarships/index.aspx

22 University of Cincinnati

Location: Cincinnati, Ohio
Setting: Urban (254 Acres)
Undergraduate Enrollment: 29,989
Type: Public

Darwin T. Turner Scholarship Program: Award covers in-state tuition, fees, and book stipend per semester for four years.

Requirements: A minimum cumulative high school GPA of 3.0 (based on an unweighted 4.0 scale) | A minimum 24 composite ACT or 1160 combined SAT-R.

NEXT Innovation Scholars Program: Awards Full tuition and some supplemental educational expenses.

Requirements: Top Applicants.

Application Deadline: December 1

Application Link: https://www.uc.edu/about/financial-aid/aid/scholarships.html

23 Ohio State University

Location: Columbus, Ohio
Setting: Urban (1,714 Acres)
Undergraduate Enrollment: 46,123
Type: Public

Morrill Scholarship Program

Awards Levels:

Prominence (the value of in-state tuition plus the non-resident surcharge for non-residents)

Excellence (the value of in-state tuition for Ohio residents).

Criteria: The Morrill Scholarship is awarded on a competitive basis to students admitted to the Columbus campus for the autumn semester following high school graduation. Applicants must be U.S. citizens or legal permanent residents of the United States.

Requirements: Top Applicants.

Application Deadline: December 1

Application Link: http://undergrad.osu.edu/cost-and-aid/merit-based-scholarships

24 Wright State University

Location: Fairborn, Ohio
Setting: Suburban (651 Acres)
Undergraduate Enrollment: 6,938
Type: Public

Rowdy Raider Scholarship: Award range from $1,000 to the value of in-state tuition.

Requirements: Top Applicants.

ArtsGala Scholarship Department of Music: The award amount ranges from $500 to the value of in-state tuition.

Music Scholarship: The award amount ranges from $500 to the value of in-state tuition.

Eligibility: Based on audition results with the School of Music.

ArtsGala Scholarship Department of Theatre, Dance, and Motion Pictures: The award amount ranges from $500 to the value of in-state tuition.

Eligibility: Based on audition/interview with Department of Theatre, Dance, and Motion Pictures.

Dayton Ballet 11 & Dayton Contemporary Dance Company 11 Scholarships: The award amount ranges from $500 to the value of in-state tuition.

Eligibility: Based on audition/interview with Department of Theatre, Dance, and Motion Pictures.

P.S: Applicant must provide a DVD with B.F.A Admission/Scholarship Applications.

Theatre Arts Talent Scholarships; Tom Hanks Scholarship; Augsburger/Estevez Scholarship (Martin Sheen): The award amount ranges from $500 to the value of in-state tuition.

Eligibility: Based on audition with Department of Theatre, Dance, and Motion Pictures.

Application Deadline: November 1

Application Link: https://www.wright.edu/raiderconnect/financial-aid/first-year-scholarships

1 Southwestern Christian University

Location: Bethany, Oklahoma
Setting: Suburban (10 Acres)
Undergraduate Enrollment: 460
Type: Private

National Merit Scholar: Awards Full tuition.

Requirements: 31+ ACT/SAT equivalent.

Application Deadline: October 15

Application Link:
https://swcu.edu/admissions/financial-assistance/scholarships-and-discounts

2 Oklahoma State University

Location: Stillwater, Oklahoma
Setting: City (1,489 Acres)
Undergraduate Enrollment: 20,801
Type: Public

Cowboy Covenant – An Oklahoma's Promise Partnership: Awards Full tuition (Oklahoma's Promise) and a $1,000 stipend for four years.

Requirements: Applicant must be an Oklahoma resident | Must enroll in the 8th, 9th, 10th or 11th grade | Parents' federal adjusted gross income must not exceed $60k per year.

Application Deadline: November 1

Application Link:
https://go.okstate.edu/scholarships-financial-aid/types-of-aid/scholarships-and-grants/freshman-scholarships/

3 Oklahoma Wesleyan University

Location: Bartlesville, Oklahoma
Setting: Suburban (35 Acres)
Undergraduate Enrollment: 782
Type: Private

Valedictorian Scholarship: Awards Full tuition.

Eligibility: OKWU offers 100% tuition to the Valedictorian of accredited high schools; some restrictions may apply.

National Merit Scholarship: Awards Full tuition to National Merit Finalist.

Eligibility: Applicant must be a National Merit Finalist.

Application Deadline: January 15

Application Link:
https://www.okwu.edu/admissions/financial-aid/traditional/

4 University of Tulsa

Location: Tulsa, Oklahoma
Setting: Urban (209 Acres)
Undergraduate Enrollment: 2,647
Type: Private

Presidential Scholars: Awards Full tuition.

Requirements: Applicants *must meet one or more of the following requirements*: National Merit Semi-finalist's who list The University of Tulsa as School of Choice with National Merit Scholarship Corporation | National Hispanic Scholars who rank in the top 10% of their graduating class | Rank in the top 5% of their graduating class OR Have at least a 4.0 weighted GPA.

Application Deadline: January 15

Application Link:
https://utulsa.edu/financial-aid/scholarships/

5 Oklahoma Christian University

Location: Edmond, Oklahoma
Setting: Urban (200 Acres)
Undergraduate Enrollment: 2,003
Type: Private

Ike's Promise: Awards Full tuition.

Requirements: ACT score of 20+ or SAT of 1020+ or CLT of 66 plus | FAFSA EFC of <$1,000 or full Pell Grant recipient or Oklahoma's Promise scholarship.

Oklahoma Christian University Difference Maker Scholarship

Tier 2 – EPIC Presidential Award: Awards Full tuition.

P.S: A Difference Maker applicant will be chosen to receive the EPIC Presidential Award for a four-year, full-tuition scholarship.

Application Deadline: December 1

Application Link:
https://www.oc.edu/admissions/financial-services/scholarships

6 Oklahoma Baptist University

Location: Shawnee, Oklahoma
Setting: City (300 Acres)
Undergraduate Enrollment: 1,330
Type: Private

Full Tuition Scholarships

University Scholar: Awards Full tuition.

Requirements: High School GPA of at least 3.5 | ACT of at least 29 or an SAT score of at least 1330 or CLT of at least 97 | A Letter of recommendation attesting to your academic accomplishments | Current resume exhibiting leadership, involvement in school, church, community, and work activities | 500 – 1,000 word essay.

Allen Academic Scholar: Awards Full tuition.

Requirements: High School GPA of at least 3.5 | ACT of at least 27 or an SAT score of at least 1260 (Critical Reading and Math only)

Martin Academic Scholar: Awards Full tuition.

Eligibility: Applicants must be Choctaw Indian with a degree of Indian blood recognized by the Choctaw Nation and Oklahoma residents.

Requirements: A cumulative High School GPA of at least 3.0 | ACT of at least 25 or an SAT score of at least 1200 (Critical Reading and Math only)

Application Deadline: January 1

Application Link:
https://www.okbu.edu/financial-aid/scholarships-and-grants.html

7 University of Science & Arts of Oklahoma

Location: Chickasha, Oklahoma
Setting: Rural (75 Acres)
Undergraduate Enrollment: 825
Type: Public

Scholarships for In-State Student's

Academic Scholars Program: Awards $15,280 per year. (This covers the cost of tuition and course related fees for in-state students)

Requirements: Applicant must be named a Presidential Scholar by the U.S. Department of Education | Named a National Merit Scholar or National Merit finalist | Scoring in the 99th percentile on a national ACT.

Regional University Baccalaureate Scholarship: Awards $15,280 per year. (This covers the cost of tuition and course related fees for in-state students)

Requirements: Applicant must be an Oklahoma resident and a U.S. citizen | Minimum national ACT composite score of 30 and a minimum 3.50 GPA on a 4.0 scale.

Regent's Academic Scholar (Institutional Nominee): Award amount covers the cost of tuition and course related fees.

Requirements: Applicant must be an Oklahoma resident and a U.S. citizen | Minimum national ACT composite score of 30 or SAT equivalent and a minimum 3.50 GPA on a 4.0 scale | Rank in the top 4% of their high school class.

Application Deadline: December 1

Application Link: https://usao.edu/financial-aid/financial-aid-options/scholarships.html

8 University of Central Oklahoma

Location: Edmond, Oklahoma
Setting: Suburban (210 Acres)
Undergraduate Enrollment: 11,771
Type: Public

Oklahoma State Regents of Higher Education Scholarships

Oklahoma Academic Scholar Program: Awards Full tuition and $4,000 cash per year.

Requirements: 99.5 percntile on National ACT/SAT

Academic Scholar Institutional Nominee Program: Awards Full tuition and $2,400 cash per year.

Eligibility: Applicant must be an Oklahoma resident.

Requirements: Achieve one of the following- 30 on national ACT/SAT OR 3.8 unweighted GPA and rank in the Top 4% of graduating class.

OSRHE Baccalaureate Scholarship: Awards Full tuition and $3,000 cash per year.

Eligibility: Applicant must be an Oklahoma resident.

Requirements: A mimimum 3.5 unweighted high school GPA | Minimum 30 ACT on national ACT test.

Application Deadline: February 1

Application Link:
https://www.uco.edu/admissions-aid/financial-aid/scholarships/

Oklahoma City University

Location: Oklahoma City, Oklahoma
Setting: Urban (104 Acres)
Undergraduate Enrollment: 1,361
Type: Private

The Meinders Business Leadership Fellows Program: Awards range up to Full tuition.

Eligibility: Awarded to top applicants entering the ***Meinders School of Business at Oklahoma City University.***

Requirements: An ACT score of 28+ (or an SAT equivalent)

Frank G. Brooks Memorial Scholarship: Awards Full tuition.

Eligibility: Awarded to outstanding first-year student who chooses to study biology at Oklahoma City University.

Requirements: Top Applicants | A letter of recommendation from a teacher or mentor, community involvement, and an application essay.

Computer Science Fellows Program: Awards range up to Full tuition.

Eligibility: Awarded to top applicants entering the ***Computer Science program at Oklahoma City University.***

Requirements: A minimum high school cumulative GPA of 3.60

Pre-Engineering B.S. Studies Scholarship: Awards Full tuition.

P.S: Oklahoma City University students wishing to become engineers can do so through the Bachelor's and Master's Degree in Engineering partnership with Washington University in St. Louis.

Check the website for more details.

Requirements: An ACT science and math scores of 27 (or SAT Math score of 640)

Bishop's Scholars Award: Awards Full tuition.

Requirements: The Applicant should hold membership in a United Methodist Church | Obtain recommendation from the senior pastor or youth minister of the student's church.

Application Deadline: March 1

Application Link: https://www.okcu.edu/financialaid/types-of-assistance/scholarships/freshmen

1 Portland State University

Location: Portland, Oregon
Setting: Urban (50 Acres)
Undergraduate Enrollment: 16,864
Type: Public

Scholarships for Oregon Residents

Four Years Free: Award covers base tuition and mandatory fees for up to four years.

Eligibility: Awarded to Oregon residents.

Requirements: Top Applicants.

Transfers Finish Free: Award covers base tuition and mandatory fees for up to four years.

Eligibility: Awarded to qualified incoming transfer students | Oregon residents.

Requirements: Top Applicants.

Application Deadline: June 15

Application Link:
https://www.pdx.edu/student-finance/scholarships

2 Linfield University

Location: McMinnville, Oregon
Setting: Rural (189 Acres)
Undergraduate Enrollment: 1,704
Type: Private

Linfield Merit Award

National Merit Scholarship Corporation Program: Award amounts range from half-tuition on a no-need basis, to **Full tuition** with sufficient financial need.

Eligibility: Awarded to students who are finalists in the National Merit Scholarship Corporation Program, and who list Linfield as their first choice college.

Application Deadline: October 1

Application Link:
https://www.linfield.edu/financial-aid/incoming-students/mcminnville-students/first-year-scholarships.html

1 Elizabethtown College

Location: Elizabethtown, Pennsylvania
Setting: Suburban (203 Acres)
Undergraduate Enrollment: 1,737
Type: Private

Stamps Scholarship: Award covers full tuition as well as an enrichment fund which is funded by the Strive Foundation and Elizabethtown College.

Eligibility: Top Applicants.

Application Deadline: January 15

Application Link:
https://www.etown.edu/admissions/financial-aid/index.aspx

2 Gannon University

Location: Erie, Pennsylvania
Setting: Urban (63 Acres)
Undergraduate Enrollment: 2,991
Type: Private

Presidential Scholarship: 100% tuition for all four (4) years.

Requirements: Top of admission pool academically.

Application Deadline: December 1

Application Link:
https://www.gannon.edu/financial-aid/types-of-financial-aid/gannon-scholarships-and-awards/

3 Gwynedd Mercy University

Location: Gwynedd Valley, Pennsylvania
Setting: Suburban (160 Acres)
Undergraduate Enrollment: 1,412
Type: Private

Presidential Scholarship: Full tuition for all four (4) years.

Requirements: Strong academic record with a GPA of at least 3.75

Application Deadline: Contact Admission Office.

Application Link:
https://www.gmercyu.edu/admissions-aid/financial-aid-tuition/types-aid/scholarships/

4 King's College

Location: Wilkes-Barre, Pennsylvania
Setting: Urban (33 Acres)
Undergraduate Enrollment: 1,671
Type: Private

Army & Airforce ROTC: Scholarships covers full tuition, fees and monthly stipends.

Requirements: Contact Admission Office.

Application Deadline: Contact Admission Office.

Application Link:
https://www.kings.edu/admissions/financial_aid/types-of-aid/scholarships

5 University of Pittsburgh

Location: Pittsburgh, Pennsylvania
Setting: City (146 Acres)
Undergraduate Enrollment: 19,928
Type: Public

Nordenberg Scholars Program: The scholarship covers full tuition for all four (4) years.

Requirements: Pennsylvania residency | U.S. Citizen or Permanent Resident | Complete Nordenberg Scholars application

Application Deadline: December 1

Application Link:
https://financialaid.pitt.edu/types-of-aid/scholarships/

6 Misericordia University

Location: Dallas, Pennsylvania
Setting: Suburban (129 Acres)
Undergraduate Enrollment: 1,777
Type: Private

Sr. Mary Glennon '62 Scholarships: Scholarship offers 100% tuition for all four (4) years.

Requirements: Good academic record with a 3.7 GPA or top 5 percent of graduating class.

Application Deadline: December 15

Application Link:
https://www.misericordia.edu/financial-aid/scholarship/sr-mary-glennon-scholarships

7 Saint Joseph's University

Location: Philadelphia, Pennsylvania
Setting: Suburban (125 Acres)
Undergraduate Enrollment: 5,073
Type: Private

Johm P. Mcnulty Scholars Program: Full tuition for all four (4) years.

Requirements: Strong academic record (3.5+/4.00 High school GPA) | Women who declare major in biology, chemistry, environmental science, physics, mathematics or computer science.

Application Deadline: January 28

Application Link:
https://www.sju.edu/mcnulty-scholars

8 Cedar Crest College

Location: Allentown, Pennsylvania
Setting: Suburban (85 Acres)
Undergraduate Enrollment: 953
Type: Private

Cedar Crest Scholarship: Award covers full tuition for all four (4) years.

Requirements: Excellent academic and extracurricular record.

Application Deadline: Contact Admission Office.

Application Link:
https://www.cedarcrest.edu/admissions-and-aid/scholarships/

9 Messiah College

Location: Mechanicsburg, Pennsylvania
Setting: Suburban (471 Acres)
Undergraduate Enrollment: 2,495
Type: Private

Trustees' Scholarship: Scholarship award covers full tuition.

Requirements: A good academic record of at least 3.4 high school GPA and 1320 SAT (OR 29 ACT OR 88-91 ACT)

Application Deadline: February 1

Application Link: https://www.messiah.edu/honorsscholarships

10 Saint Vincent College

Location: Latrobe, Pennsylvania
Setting: Suburban (200 Acres)
Undergraduate Enrollment: 1,375
Type: Private

Wimmer Scholarship: Full tuition for all four (4) years.

Requirements: A high school GPA of 3.75 or higher and an SAT of 1300 and above (OR ACT score of 28 | OR CLT of 86)

Application Deadline: February 15

Application Link: https://www.stvincent.edu/admission-aid/wimmer-scholarship-competition.html

11 Robert Morris University

Location: Moon Township, Pennsylvania
Setting: Suburban (230 Acres)
Undergraduate Enrollment: 2,782
Type: Private

Presidential Scholarship: 100% tuition for all four (4) years.

Requirements: Candidates should have excellent academic records.

Application Deadline: Contact Admission Office.

Application Link: https://www.rmu.edu/admissions/financial-aid/scholarships

12 Keystone College

Location: Factoryville, Pennsylvania
Setting: Rural (276 Acres)
Undergraduate Enrollment: 1,060
Type: Private

Academic Excellence Scholarship: Full tuition for all four (4) years.

Requirements: Strong academic record (high school GPA and test scores inclusive)

Application Deadline: February 1

Application Link:
https://www.keystone.edu/admissions/tuition-aid/scholarships/

13 DeSales University

Location: Center Valley, Pennsylvania
Setting: Suburban (550 Acres)
Undergraduate Enrollment: 2,231
Type: Private

Leadership Scholarship: Award covers 100% tuition for all four (4) years.

Requirements: Outstanding Leadership and satisfactory academic record.

Application Deadline: December 1

Application Link:
https://www.desales.edu/admissions-financial-aid/undergraduate-admissions-aid/financial-aid-scholarships/desales-scholarships/leadership-scholarship-(6-full-tuition-scholarships)

14 La Salle University

Location: Philadelphia, Pennsylvania
Setting: Urban (133 Acres)
Undergraduate Enrollment: 2,776
Type: Private

Christian Brothers' Scholarship: Full tuition for all four (4) years.

Requirements: Excellent Academic Record like Top 10% of graduating class.

Application Deadline: January 15

Application Link:
https://www.lasalle.edu/financial-aid/financial-aid-for-undergraduates/scholarships/la-salle-scholarships/christian-brothers-scholarship/

15 Harrisburg University of Science and Technology

Location: Harrisburg, Pennsylvania
Setting: Urban (38,000 square-foot)
Undergraduate Enrollment: 745
Type: Private

Harrisburg Partnership Scholarship: 100% tuition for all four (4) years.

Requirements: Student from Harrsiburg School District | Contact admission office for more information.

Application Deadline: May 1

Application Link:
https://www.harrisburgu.edu/tuition-financial-aid/financial-aid/hu-scholarships-and-grants/

16 Lehigh University

Location: Bethlehem, Pennsylvania
Setting: City (2,355 Acres)
Undergraduate Enrollment: 5,624
Type: Private

Founder's and Trustees' Scholarships: These scholarships covers full or half tution for all four (4) years.

Requirements: Student should in the top tier of applicant pool.

Application Deadline: Contact Admission Office.

Application Link:
https://www1.lehigh.edu/admissions/merit-scholarships

17 Rosemont College

Location: Rosemont, Pennsylvania
Setting: Suburban (56 Acres)
Undergraduate Enrollment: 425
Type: Private

Cornelian Scholarship: Award covers full tuition and fees for four (4) years.

Requirements: Strong Academic and extracurricular record – with high school GPA of 3.25 or higher.

Application Deadline: January 18

Application Link:
https://www.rosemont.edu/admissions/tuition-and-aid/

18 Kutztown University

Location: Kutztown, Pennsylvania
Setting: Rural (289 Acres)
Undergraduate Enrollment: 6,508
Type: Public

Merit Scholarships: Awards up to full tuition.

Sesquicentennial Academic Honors Scholarship: 100% tuition for all four (4) years.

Requirements: Students should have a high school GPA of at least 3.5 and a minimum SAT score of 1410 (OR 31 ACT)

Board of Governors Scholarship: Awards covers 100% tuition for all four (4) years.

Requirements: Top Applicants.

Application Deadline: March 1

Application Link:
https://www.kutztown.edu/affordability/guide-to-financial-aid/scholarships.html

19 University of Scranton

Location: Scranton, Pennsylvania
Setting: City (58 Acres)
Undergraduate Enrollment: 3,487
Type: Private

Presidential Scholarship: Scholarship covers full tuition for four (4) academic years.

Requirements: Strong Academic and extracurricular record.

Army ROTC Scholarship: Scholarships covers full tuition, $1,200 for books and monthly stipends.

Requirements: Contact Admission Office.

Application Deadline: Contact Admission Office.

Application Link:
https://www.scranton.edu/financial-aid/merit-based-sch.shtml

20 Temple University

Location: Philadelphia, Pennsylvania
Setting: Urban (406 Acres)
Undergraduate Enrollment: 24,106
Type: Public

The Lambert Foundation Scholarship: Awards Full tuition scholarship to *Pennsylvania residents.*

Requirements: Top Applicants.

Cecil B. Moore Scholarship: Awards in-state Full tuition to ***Pennsylvania residents.***

Requirements: Top Applicants.

P.S: This scholarship is open to first-year undergraduate students who reside in ***specific zip codes*** in North Philadelphia and primarily attend public (district or charter) high schools in the city of Philadelphia.

Check the website for more details.

Mario D. Fantini Scholarship in Education: Awards Full tuition.

Eligibility: Applicants must be graduates of South Philadelphia High School and plan to obtain a career in Education.

Army/Airforce ROTC: 100% tuition for all four (4) years.

Requirements: At least a 2.5 High school GPA | Physically fit | 1100 SAT (Airforce ROTC)

Application Deadline: Contact Admission Office.

Application Link: https://sfs.temple.edu/financial-aid-types/scholarships/scholarship-opportunities-temple/new-incoming-students

21 Drexel University

Location: Philadelphia, Pennsylvania
Setting: Urban (96 Acres)
Undergraduate Enrollment: 12,482
Type: Private

Drexel Athletic Scholarships: Award covers full tuition for all four (4) years.

Requirements: Contact the athletic department.

Drexel Global Scholar Program: Awards 100% tuition for all four (4) years.

Requirements: International freshmen | Satisfactory academic performance and leadership capacity.

Application Deadline: November 15

Drexel Liberty Scholars: Awards covers full tuition and fees for all four (4) years.

Requirements: US Citizen/Permanent Resident with demonstrated financial need (Using CSS/FAFSA)

Application Deadline: November 1

Army/Navy ROTC Scholarship: This scholarship covers 100% tuition for all four (4) years.

Requirements: Army/Navy ROTC Cadets enrolled at Drexel.

Application Deadline: Contact admission office.

Application Link: https://drexel.edu/drexelcentral/finaid/grants/undergraduate-scholarships/

22 Villanova University

Location: Villanova, Pennsylvania
Setting: Suburban (260 Acres)
Undergraduate Enrollment: 6,989
Type: Private

Presidential Scholarship: Full tuition, room, board (up to 21 meals per week plan), general fee, and the cost of textbooks for eight consecutive semesters.

Criteria: In order to be considered for the presidential Scholarship, students must first be nominated by the chief academic officer of their high school (principal, president, headmaster), secondary school counselor, or an official school designee.

St. Martin de Porres Scholarship: Full tuition and general fees.

Eligibility: U.S. citizens or permanent residents from one or more of the most underrepresented groups at the Villanova University.

Anthony Randazzo Endowed Presidential Scholarship: Full tuition, room, board (up to 21 meals per week plan), general fee, and the cost of textbooks for eight consecutive semesters.

Eligibility: Awarded to a first year African American/Black student | Applicant must reside in the city of Philadelphia, Pennsylvania.

Application Deadline: January 2

Application Link: https://www1.villanova.edu/university/undergraduate-admission/Financial-Assistance-and-scholarship/merit-based-scholarships.html

1 University of Rhode Island

Location: South Kingstown, Rhode Island
Settting: Rural (1,245 Acres)
Undergraduate Enrollment: 13,927
Type: Public

Thomas M. Ryan Scholars Program: Awards Full tuition, fees, housing, dining, books, and one Global winter travel J term experience with faculty.

Requirements: Top Applicants.

Alfred J. Verrecchia Business Scholars Program: Awards Full tuition, fees, housing, dining, books, and one Global winter travel J term experience with faculty.

Requirements: Awarded to selected students interested in majoring in Business.

Application Deadline: June 26

URI Narragansett Undergraduate Scholarship: Awards up to full in-tuition and fees, plus $5,000

Requirements: Accepted into URI | Have an official FAFSA on file | A tribal enrollment ID card or an official letter from the tribal administration that confirms membership through a direct family member (parents)

Application Deadline: Contact the ROTC Department for scholarship deadline dates.

Application Link: https://web.uri.edu/admission/scholarships/

2 Providence College

Location: Providence, Rhode Island
Setting: City (105 Acres)
Undergraduate Enrollment: 4,279
Type: Private

Roddy Scholarship: Awards Full tuition, fees, room and board.

Requirements: Applicants must aspire to a career in the medical profession | Consideration is based on outstanding academic achievement in high school | Awarded to first-year students who reside in the United States.

Application Link: https://financial-aid.providence.edu/types-of-assistance/institutional-merit-based/

3

Roger Williams University

Location: Bristol, Rhode Island
Setting: Suburban (140 Acres)
Undergraduate Enrollment: 4,103
Type: Private

Intercultural Leadership Ambassador Program & Scholarship: 100% tuition for all four (4) years.

Requirements: Student must have a 3.0+ GPA and demonstrate go co-curriclar involvements

Harold Payson Memorial Scholarship: 100% tuition for all four (4) years.

Requirements: Student must has resided in Bristol for at least two years | For U.S. Citizens and Permanent Residents Only.

Michael Andrade Memorial Scholarship: 100% tuition and fees for all four (4) years.

Requirements: Student must be a graduate of Mount Hope High School | Have a B averageand an SAT of 1000 +(OR ACT equivalent) | For U.S. Citizens and Permanent Residents Only.

Porthsmouth High School (RI) Scholarship: 100% tuition for all four (4) years.

Requirements: Student must be a graduate of Portsmouth High School (RI) | Have a 3.0+ GPA and an SAT of 1000+ (OR ACT equivalent) | For U.S. Citizens and Permanent Residents Only.

Application Deadline: Contact Admission Office.

Application Link: https://catalog.rwu.edu/content.php?catoid=3&navoid=124

1 Furman University

Location: Greenville, South Carolina
Setting: Suburban (800 Acres)
Undergraduate Enrollment: 2,283
Type: Private

ROTC Scholarships: Awards up to full tuition and fees.

Requirements: Top Applicants.

Application Deadline: Contact the ROTC Department for scholarship deadline dates.

Application Link: https://www.furman.edu/financial-aid/aid-types/other-scholarships/

2 South Carolina State University

Location: Orangeburg, South Carolina
Setting: City (160 Acres)
Undergraduate Enrollment: 2,374
Type: Public

General University Scholarship: 100% tuition for all four (4) years.

Requirements: High school GPA of at least 3.25 | SAT score of 1100+ (OR 24 in ACT)

SC State University Achievers Scholarship: 100% tuition for all four (4) years.

Requirements: Student must already be enrolled on SC State | Achieve a GPA of at least 3.50

Application Deadline: Contact Admissions Office.

Application Link: https://www.scstategives.com/scholarships-and-funds/

3 Anderson University

Location: Anderson, South Carolina
Setting: City (387 Acres)
Undergraduate Enrollment: 3,237
Type: Private

Honors Program Scholarship: 100% tuition for all four (4) years.

Requirements: High school GPA of at least 3.75 | Good test scores | Must accepted into the Anderson University Honors Program.

Application Deadline: Contact Admissions Office.

Application Link: https://anderson.edu/blog-stories/honors-program-scholarship/

1 University of South Dakota

Location: Vermillion, South Dakota
Setting: Rural (274 Acres)
Undergraduate Enrollment: 7,132
Type: Public

Presidential Alumni Scholarship: Award covers 100% in-state tuition and fees for all four (4) years.

Requirements: Excellent Academic & Extracurricular performance. Contact Admission Office for more info.

Walter A. & Lucy Yoshiko Buhler Scholarship: Award covers 100% in-state tuition and fees for all four (4) years.

Requirements: Excellent Academic & Extracurricular performance | Enrolled in a Business or Fine Arts major | Contact Admission Office for more info.

Application Deadline: December 1

Application Link:
https://www.usd.edu/Admissions-and-Aid/Financial-Aid/Types-of-Aid/Scholarships

2 University of Sioux Falls

Location: Sioux Falls, South Dakota
Setting: City (140 Acres)
Undergraduate Enrollment: 1,325
Type: Private

National Merit Scholarship: This Scholarships covers full tuition for four (4) complete years.

Requirements: Applicant must be a national merit scholar.

Application Deadline: Contact Admission Office.

Application Link:
https://www.usiouxfalls.edu/financial-aid/university-scholarships

1 Milligan University

Location: Milligan, Tennessee
Setting: Suburban (355 Acres)
Undergraduate Enrollment: 737
Type: Private

Jeanes Honors Scholarships: This scholarship offer covers 100% tuition for all four (4) years.

Requirements: High school GPA of 3.5 or higher | 1300+ SAT (28+ ACT, 86+ CLT) | Active participation in ecxtracurrcicular activities.

Application Deadline: December 1

Application Link: https://www.milligan.edu/programs/honors-program/

2 Middle Tennessee State University

Location: Murfreesboro, Tennessee
Setting: City (550 Acres)
Undergraduate Enrollment: 17,438
Type: Public

The Buchanan Fellowship: Award covers full tuition for complete four (4) years.

Requirements: Student is expected to have a high school GPA of 3.5 or higher and an SAT of 1360+ (or ACT equivalent)

Application Deadline: December 1

Application Link: https://www.mtsu.edu/honors/buchanan/index.php

3 Maryville College

Location: Maryville, Tennessee
Setting: Suburban (300 Acres)
Undergraduate Enrollment: 1,065
Type: Private

McGill Scholarship/Fellowship: Awards up to Full tuition for all four (4) years.

Requirements: 3.7+ GPA | 1390+ SAT(28+ ACT OR 92+ CLT) | Demonstarted Leadership Abilities.

Application Deadline: January 28

Application Link: https://www.maryvillecollege.edu/admissions/finaid/types-of-aid/scholarships-awards/mcgill/

4 Bryan College

Location: Dayton, Tennessee
Setting: Rural (128 Acres)
Undergraduate Enrollment: 1,376
Type: Private

Bryan Opportunity Scholarship Program: Award covers full tuition for all four (4) years.

Requirements: Applicant(s) must be a first-time freshman | Complete FAFSA by January 31 | Total family income < $36,000 | GPA of 3.0 and ACT 21 or SAT 1060.

Application Deadline: January 31

Application Link: https://www.bryan.edu/scholarship/bryan-opportunity-scholarship-program/

5 Lipscomb University

Location: Nashville, Tennessee
Setting: Suburban (113 Acres)
Undergraduate Enrollment: 2,955
Type: Private

Trustee Scholarship: 100% tuition for all four (4) years.

Requirements: Candidates should have a GPA of 3.5 or higher and an SAT score of 1360 or better (30 or higher of ACT | 92 or higher of the CLT).

Application Deadline: October 15

Application Link:
https://www.lipscomb.edu/admissions/cost-financial-aid/incoming-student-financial-aid/types-aid-incoming-students-0/trustee

7 Carson-Newman University

Location: Jefferson City, Tennessee
Setting: Rural (90 Acres)
Undergraduate Enrollment: 1,528
Type: Private

F. Edward Hebert Armed Forces Health Professions Scholarship Program (HPSP): Full tuition for all four(4) years, plus a monthly stipend of $2,000 and a sign-on bonus of $20,000 in some cases.

Requirements: Specific to health related majors

Application Deadline: Contact Admission Office.

Application Link:
https://www.cn.edu/admissions-and-aid/financial-aid/scholarships/

6 Southern Adventist University

Location: Collegedale, Tennessee
Setting: Suburban (1,000 Acres)
Undergraduate Enrollment: 2,571
Type: Private

Freshman Academic Scholarship: Award covers full tuition.

Freshman Full Tuition Scholarship: Award covers full tuition.

Requirements: Score a minimum of 7,301 points.

To get points: (1) Multiply your high school GPA (over/4.0) by 1000 | (2) Multiply your ACT test score by 100 | (3) Add all points from Step 1 and 2.

P.S: Check site for more details in regards to converting your SAT score to an ACT score in respect of this scholarship(s).

National Merit Scholarship: Award covers full tuition.

Requirements: Applicant must be a National Merit Finalist, accepted in the National Hispanic Recognition Program (Hispanic students) or National Achievement Scholarship Program (African American students)

Application Link:
https://www.southern.edu/undergrad/finances/grants-and-scholarships.html

8 Belmont University

Location: Nashville, Tennessee
Setting: City (93 Acres)
Undergraduate Enrollment: 7,376
Type: Private

Ingram Diversity Leadership Scholarship: This prestigious award covers full tuition for all four (4) years.

Requirements: Student must be from Nashville area | High academic performance and good participation in extracurriccular activities.

E.S. Rose Scholarship: This prestigious award covers full tuition for all four (4) years.

Requirements: Student must live in proximity to E.S. Rose Park in Nashville | High academic performance and good participation in extracurriccular activities.

Application Deadline: December 1

Application Link: https://www.belmont.edu/sfs/scholarships/

9 Vanderbilt University

Location: Nashville, Tennessee
Setting: Urban (333 Acres)
Undergraduate Enrollment: 7,151
Type: Private

Ingram Scholars Program: This scholarship offer covers 100% tuition for all four(4) years, plus a one-time summer stipend.

Cornelius Vanderbilt Scholarship: This scholarship offer covers 100% tuition for all four(4) years, plus a one-time summer stipend.

P.S: Vanderbilt will provide additional need-based financial aid to those Cornelius Vanderilt Scholarship recipient whose demonstrated needs exceeds the amount of full tuition.

Requirements: Student must have excellent academics and extracurricular record.

Application Deadline: December 1

Application Link: https://www.vanderbilt.edu/scholarships/

Texas Christian University

Location: Fort Worth, Texas
Setting: Suburban (307 Acres)
Undergraduate Enrollment: 10,523
Type: Private

Chancellor's Scholarship: Awards 100% tuition & fees for all four (4) years.

Requirements: Top of admission pool academically.

Application Deadline: November 1

Application Link:
https://admissions.tcu.edu/afford/scholarship-aid/index.php

2 Abilene Christian University

Location: Abilene, Texas
Setting: City (272 Acres)
Undergraduate Enrollment: 3,189
Type: Private

National Merit Finalist & Semi-Finalists Schoalrship Award: Full tuition and fees for all four (4) years.

Requirements: Scholar must be a National Merit Finalist or semi-finalist. And must submit a FAFSA.

Application Deadline: November 1

Application Link:
https://acu.edu/admissions-aid/scholarships/first-year/

3 Lamar University

Location: Beaumont, Texas
Setting: Urban (292 Acres)
Undergraduate Enrollment: 8,257
Type: Public

Smith-Hutson Scholarship Program: This scholarship award covers 95% - 100% of recipient's college bill for all four (4) years.

Requirements: Applicant must be an entering freshaman to LU | Texas Resident | Submit FAFSA |

Application Deadline: February 1

Application Link:
https://www.lamar.edu/financial-aid/scholarships/smith-hutson-scholarship.html

4 Howard Payne University

Location: Brownwood, Texas
Setting: Rural (80 Acres)
Undergraduate Enrollment: 773
Type: Private

Gen. MacArthur Honors Scholarship: This scholarship program awards Full tuition for all four (4) years.

Requirements: Top 10% at an Accredited High School or 3.80 GPA) and (ACT 29 or SAT 1350 or CLT 91).

Application Deadline: Contact Admission Office.

Application Link:
https://www.hputx.edu/campus-offices/financial-aid/scholarships/

5 Lubbock Christian University

Location: Lubbock, Texas
Setting: City (155 Acres)
Undergraduate Enrollment: 1,346
Type: Private

National Merit Scholarship: This awards covers Full tution for its recipients across 4-5 years.

Requirements: Student should be a National Merit Scholar to receive award.

Application Deadline: Contact Admission Office.

Application Link: https://lcu.edu/financial-assistance/scholarships

6 University of Houston

Location: Houston, Texas
Setting: Urban (895 Acres)
Undergraduate Enrollment: 37,943
Type: Public

National Merit Scholarship: This awards covers 100% tuition and fees for all four (4) years. Additionally, recipients receive a one-time $1,000 research stipend and a one-time $2,000 study abroad stipend.

Requirements: Applicants must be at the top of admission pool academically.

Army Reserve Officers' Training Corps (AROTC) Scholarship: Award takes care of full tuition for all four (4) years. Funds for books, equipment and supplies may also be provided.

Requirements: Contact Admission Office.

Application Deadline: Contact Admission Office.

Application Link: https://uh.edu/financial/undergraduate/types-aid/scholarships/

7 Trinity University

Location: San Antonio, Texas
Setting: Urban (125 Acres)
Undergraduate Enrollment: 2,512
Type: Private

Trinity Tower Scholarship: This scholarship awards covers full tuition over four (4) years.

Requirements: Excellent Academic and extracurricular record.

Application Deadline: November 1

Semmes Distingusied Scholars Scholarship: This scholarship awards covers full tuition over four (4) years. And a $5,000 stipend for research, travel and supplies.

Requirements: Strong Academic and extracurricular record. Applicant must be studying a STEM field at Trinity.

Application Deadline: November 1

Murchison Scholarship: This scholarship awards covers full tuition over four (4) years.

Requirements: Student should a high academic and extracurricular record.

Application Deadline: February 1

Application Link: https://www.trinity.edu/admissions-aid/tuition-and-financial-aid-admissions-and-aid

8 University of North Texas

Location: Denton, Texas
Setting: City (963 Acres)
Undergraduate Enrollment: 33,024
Type: Public

President's Elite Scholarship: This prestigious award covers full tuition for all four (4) years.

Requirements: High academic performance and good participation in extracurriccular activities.

Application Deadline: March 15

Application Link: https://financialaid.unt.edu/unt-excellence-scholarships

1 Weber State University

Location: Ogden, Utah
Setting: Suburban (490 Acres)
Undergraduate Enrollment: 28,903
Type: Public

Presidential Scholarship: Scholarships covers full in-state tuition for four (4) years and $1,000 housing discount per year.

Requirements: Student should have a GPA of at least 3.2 and a SAT score of 1330 (29 ACT)

Application Deadline: December 1

Application Link:
https://www.weber.edu/FinancialAid/resident.html

2 Southern Utah University

Location: Cedar City, Utah
Setting: Rural (129 Acres)
Undergraduate Enrollment: 12,649
Type: Public

President's Eight Semester Scholarship (For In-state students): Full tuition for all four (4) years.

Requirements: 3.9+ GPA 1390 – 1600 SAT Score, OR 31 – 36 ACT score.

President's Eight Semester Scholarship(For Out-of-State Students): Full tuition for all four (4) years.

Requirements: 3.9+ GPA 1390 – 1600 SAT Score, OR 31 – 36 ACT score.

Application Deadline: December 1

Application Link:
https://www.suu.edu/finaid/scholarships.html

3 University of Utah

Location: Salt Lake City, Utah
Setting: Urban (1,534 Acres)
Undergraduate Enrollment: 26,355
Type: Public

For Utah Scholarship: 100% tuition and fees for all four (4) years.

Requirements: Utah residents who are eligible for PELL GRANT.

Application Deadline: February 1

President's Scholarship for Residents: Scholarships covers full in-state tuition for four (4) years.

Requirements: Based on cumulative GPA at admission, Course rigor considered.

Application Deadline: December 1

Application Link:
https://financialaid.utah.edu/types-of-aid/scholarships/freshman/index.php

4 Utah Valley University

Location: Orem, Utah
Setting: City (524 Acres)
Undergraduate Enrollment: 40,542
Type: Public

Non-resident Presidential Scholarship: Full tuition & general fees for all four(4) years.

Requirements: Student should have atleast 3.9+ GPA and 1400+ SAT (OR 31 ACT).

Resident Presidential Scholarship: Full tuition & general fees for all four(4) years.

Requirements: Student should have at least 3.9+ GPA and 1400+ SAT (OR 31 ACT).

Application Deadline: March 3

Application Link:
https://www.uvu.edu/financialaid/scholarships/

5 Utah State University

Location: Logan & Other Areas, Utah
Setting: City (450 Acres)
Undergraduate Enrollment: 24,835
Type: Public

Presidential Scholarship: Full tuition & fees for all four (4) years.

Requirements: Student should have at least a 3.75+ GPA and 1450+ SAT (OR 33 ACT).

Ambassador Scholarship: Full tuition & fees for all four (4) years.

Requirements: Must apply as a Senior in high school and have a GPA of 3.5 and above. (ACT/SAT not required)

Application Deadline: January 10

Application Link:
https://www.usu.edu/admissions/costs-and-aid/

7 Brigham Young University -- Provo

Location: Provo, Utah
Setting: City (560 Acres)
Undergraduate Enrollment: 31,401
Type: Private

The Russell M. Nelson Scholarship: This scholarship award covers full tuition, fees and more.

Requirements: Strong academic performance, extracurricular record, character and leadership history.

Application Deadline: Contact Admission Office.

National Merit Scholarship: Awards Full LDS tuition for eight semesters.

6 Utah Tech University

Location: Saint George, Utah
Setting: City (117 Acres)
Undergraduate Enrollment: 12,481
Type: Public

Non-resident Presidential Scholarship: This award covers the whole tuition and fees for all four(4) years.

Requirements: Applicants are expected to have a GPA of atleast 3.2 and SAT score of 1300 (OR 28 ACT)

Resident Presidential Scholarship: This award covers the whole tuition and fees for all four(4) years.

Requirements: Applicants are expected to have a GPA of atleast 3.2 and SAT score of 1300 (OR 28 ACT)

Application Deadline: December 15 & July 15

Application Link:
https://scholarships.utahtech.edu/non-resident-freshman-scholarships-2/

Eligibility: National Merit Finalist.

Heritage Scholarship: Awards Full LDS tuition for eight semesters.

Sterling Scholarship Competition: Awards Full LDS tuition for two semesters.

Check site for more details.

Application Deadline: December 15

Application Link:
https://enrollment.byu.edu/scholarship-types

1 Norwich University

Location: Northfield, Vermont
Setting: Rural (1,200 Acres)
Undergraduate Enrollment: 2,854
Type: Private

Naval ROTC Preparatory Scholarship: Full tuition and fees for all four (4) plus years plus additional benefits.

Requirements: Visit scholarship page for detailed information.

Application Deadline: February 1

Application Link: https://home.norwich.edu/on/corps-cadets/rotc/naval-and-marine-reserve-officers-training-corps-nrotc

2 University of Vermont

Location: Burlington, Vermont
Setting: Suburban (460 Acres)
Undergraduate Enrollment: 11,898
Type: Public

Green and Gold Scholars Award: Scholarships covers full in-state tuition for all four years.

Requirements: Student must be nominated by a Vermont high and have high academic/extracurriclar track record.

Application Deadline: January 15

Application Link: https://www.uvm.edu/studentfinancialservices/scholarships_prospective_vermont_resident_students

1 Liberty University

Location: Lynchburg, Virginia
Setting: City (7,000 Acres)
Undergraduate Enrollment: 48,906
Type: Private

Liberty Academic Scholarship: Awards Full tuition.

Requirements: Test score; SAT 1540+ OR ACT 35+ OR CLT 107+ combined with a High school GPA of 3.0+

Application Deadline: Contact Admission Office.

Application Link:
https://www.liberty.edu/student-financial-services/scholarships/

2 Saint Michael's College

Location: Colchester, Virginia
Setting: Suburban (440 Acres)
Undergraduate Enrollment: 1,209
Type: Private

Presidential Scholarship: Awards range from $17,000 up to Full tuition for all four(4) plus years.

Requirements: Student must be nominated by a Vermont high school and meet the following requirements: A- average or higher, Top 10% of class, 1300+ SAT or 27+ ACT test score (test-optional)

Application Deadline: November 1

Application Link:
https://www.smcvt.edu/admission-aid/financial-aid/scholarships-loans-grants-and-work-study/academic-scholarships/

3 Hollins University

Location: Roanoke, Virginia
Setting: Suburban (475 Acres)
Undergraduate Enrollment: 691
Type: Private

Batten Scholar Award: Awards 100% tuition for all four (4) years.

Requirements: Top of admission pool academically.

Application Deadline: December 1

Application Link:
https://www.hollins.edu/admission-aid/undergraduate-financial-aid-scholarships/

4 Bridgewater College

Location: Bridgewater, Virginia
Setting: Rural (190 Acres)
Undergraduate Enrollment: 1,385
Type: Private

President's Merit Award: Full tuition for all four (4) years.

Requirements: Strong academic record.

Application Deadline: January 28

Application Link:
https://www.bridgewater.edu/admissions-aid/tuition-and-financial-aid/financial-aid/

5 Hampden-Sydney College

Location: Hampden Sydney, Virginia
Setting: Rural (1,343 Acres)
Undergraduate Enrollment: 835
Type: Private

The Davis Fellowship: Award covers full tuition.

Requirements: Strong Academic and extracurricular record.

Application Deadline: Contact Admission Office -- Telephone: (800) 755-0733

Application Link: https://www.hsc.edu/admission-and-financial-aid/financial-aid/types-of-aid/academic-and-leadership-awards

6 Virginia Wesleyan University

Location: Virginia Beach, Virginia
Setting: Suburban (300 Acres)
Undergraduate Enrollment: 1,479
Type: Private

The Batten Fellowship: Awards 100% tuition for all four (4) years.

Requirements: High academic performance specifically 1353+ in SAT (or equivalent), 3.5+ high school GPA, and application to Batten Honors College.

Application Deadline: March 9

Application Link: https://www.vwu.edu/enrollment-aid/financial-aid/vwu-grants-and-scholarships.php

7 Bluefield University

Location: Bluefield, Virginia
Setting: Rural (82 Acres)
Undergraduate Enrollment: 718
Type: Private

Presidential Scholarship: Award covers full tuition for all four (4) years.

Requirements: Good academic and extracurriccular record

Application Deadline: Contact Admission Office.

Application Link: https://www.bluefield.edu/bluefield-central/financial-aid/grants-scholarships/

8 University of Virginia

Location: Charlottesville, Virginia
Setting: Suburban (1,682 Acres)
Undergraduate Enrollment: 17,496
Type: Public

Reserved Officers' Training Corps Scholarships: Awards 100% tuition and fees for all four (4) years – recipient could also receive monthly stipends, books allowance and supplies.

Requirements: Varies across Army, Navy & Airforce – Visit scholarship page.

Application Deadline: Visit web page.

Application Link: https://sfs.virginia.edu/financial-aid-new-applicants/financial-aid-basics/types-aid/scholarships-and-grants

9 Virginia Commonwealth University

Location: Richmond, Virginia
Setting: Urban (198 Acres)
Undergraduate Enrollment: 20,958
Type: Public

Provost Scholarship: Full tuition and mandatory fees.

Requirements: A minimum 4.0 GPA and 1200+ in SAT (and it's equivalent in other tests)

Application Deadline: November 1

Application Link:
https://admissions.vcu.edu/cost-aid/scholarships-funding/

10 Christendom College

Location: Front Royal, Virginia
Setting: Suburban (200 Acres)
Undergraduate Enrollment: 550
Type: Private

Padre Pio Full-Tuition Scholarship: Full tuition

Requirements: SAT 1280+ OR ACT 27+ OR CLT 84+ and an admission to Christendom College.

Application Link:
https://www.christendom.edu/admissions/full-tuition-scholarship/

Military Service Scholarship Program: Full Tuition.

Requirements: For more information on how to apply and program eligibility, please contact Christine Schmidt, Financial Aid Officer, at **540-551-9216**.

Application Deadline: Contact admission office.

Application Link:
https://www.christendom.edu/admissions/financial-aid/military-service-scholarship-program/

11 Washington and Lee University

Location: Lexington City, Virginia
Setting: City (430 Acres)
Undergraduate Enrollment: 1,867
Type: Private

Multiple Scholarship Awards: Full Tuition.

Requirements: Student should have excellent academic record and be from one of the following places: Maryland | West Virginia | New Orleans, Louisiana | Houston, Texas | Dallas, Texas | Columbia, South Carolina.

A full tuition scholarship is also available for students of Jewish faith specifically.

Fully funded need based scholarships are also available.

Application Deadline: Visit Scholarship Webpage.

Application Link:
https://www.wlu.edu/admissions/financial-aid/types-of-aid/scholarships/

1 Whitworth University

Location: Spokane, Washington
Setting: Suburban (200 Acres)
Undergraduate Enrollment: 2,045
Type: Private

Whitworth Bound Promise: Awards up to Full tuition.

Requirements: Offered and renewed to Washington residents who are eligible for the College Bound Scholarship and have a minimum 3.0 weighted, cumulative GPA.

Application Deadline: Contact Admission Office.

Application Link:
https://www.whitworth.edu/cms/administration/financial-aid/

2 Pacific Lutheran University

Location: Tacoma, Washington
Setting: Suburban (156 Acres)
Undergraduate Enrollment: 2,301
Type: Private

Regent's Scholarship: Award covers Full tuition.

Requirements: High school seniors with a minimum GPA of 3.8 (weighted), or scored 1310 or higher on the SAT (math and evidence-based reading and writing only), or scored 28 or higher on the ACT.

Application Deadline: December 1

Application Link:
https://www.plu.edu/student-financial-services/types-of-aid/scholarships-and-grants/

3 Walla Walla University

Location: College Place, Washington
Setting: Rural (83 Acres)
Undergraduate Enrollment: 1,314
Type: Private

National Merit Finalists Awards: 100% tuition for two years and 50% tuition for two additional years. P.S: This amount is subject to change and might be further reduced in the next admission cycle.

Requirements: Finalist in the national merit competition.

Application Deadline: Contact Admission Counselor.

Application Link:
https://www.wallawalla.edu/admissions-and-aid/student-financial-services/financial-aid/scholarships

4 Seattle Pacific University

Location: Seattle, Washington
Setting: Urban (44 Acres)
Undergraduate Enrollment: 2,428
Type: Private

Distinguished Scholar Award: Award covers Full tuition.

Requirements: Good academic and extracurricular record (Invitatation only)

Falcon Bound Scholarship: Awards Full tuition.

Requirements: 1220/25 or higher in SAT/ACT, 3.0 high school GPA, eligible for College Bound, etc.

Application Deadline: December 15

Application Link:
https://spu.edu/undergraduate-admissions/scholarships-financial-aid/scholarships-and-grants/

5 Washington State University -- Pullman

Location: Pullman, Washington
Setting: Rural (1,742 Acres)
Undergraduate Enrollment: 22,612
Type: Public

Distinguished Regents Scholars: Full tuition and mandatory fees.

Requirements: Strong academic achievement, co-curricular/civic involvement, academic reference.

Application Deadline: Contact 509-335-9711

National Merit Scholarship: Awards up to Full tuition.

Requirements: National Merit Scholarship and WSU – Pullman admission.

Application Deadline: Admission by Jan 31 and choose WSU as first choice on National Merit Corporation by May 1

Application Link: https://admission.wsu.edu/cost/scholarships/

6 Whitman College

Location: Walla Walla, Washington
Setting: Rural (117 Acres)
Undergraduate Enrollment: 1,493
Type: Private

The Eells Scholarship: Awards Full tuition and fees.

Requirements: Entering student who has financial need and demonstrates high academic achievement and talent in fine/performing arts or humanities.

Application Deadline: January 15

Application Link: https://www.whitman.edu/admission-and-aid/financial-aid-and-costs/merit-and-talent-scholarships

1 Bethany College

Location: Bethany, West Virginia
Setting: Rural (1,100 Acres)
Undergraduate Enrollment: 545
Type: Private

Presidential Scholarship: Awards Full tuition.

Requirements: Contact Admission for more info: 304-829-7611

Application Deadline: Contact Admission for more info: 304-829-7611

Application Link:
https://www.bethanywv.edu/admissions-aid/affording-bethany-college/scholarships/

2 Bluefield State College

Location: Bluefield, West Virginia
Setting: Rural (50 Acres)
Undergraduate Enrollment: 1,281
Type: Public

BOG Auxiliary Scholarship: Full tuition and/or fees.

Requirements: Academic Excellence as determined by ACT/SAT score and GPA.

Application Deadline: Contact admission office.

Application Link:
https://bluefieldstate.edu/tuition/scholarships

1 Carroll University

Location: Waukesha, Wisconsin
Setting: Suburban (137 Acres)
Undergraduate Enrollment: 2,771
Type: Private

MacAllister Scholarship: Awards Full tuition.

Requirements: Applicants must be accepted to Carroll University, good academic performance and extracurricular activities.

Application Deadline: December 2

Application Link:
https://www.carrollu.edu/financial-aid/undergraduate-scholarships/macallister

2 University of Wisconsin, Platteville

Location: Platteville, Wisconsin
Setting: Rural (820 Acres)
Undergraduate Enrollment: 6,266
Type: Public

Pioneer Plegde Award: Awards Full tuition and fees.

Requirements: Be a freshman (full time), submit FAFSA and be Pell eligible, be resident of Wisconsin, Illinois, Iowa or Minnesota.

Application Deadline: May 1

Application Link:
https://www.uwplatt.edu/department/financial-aid-scholarships/scholarships

3 Viterbo University

Location: La Crosse, Wisconsin
Setting: City (21 Acres)
Undergraduate Enrollment: 1,385
Type: Private

Health Science Scholarship: Awards Full tuition (For Health related Majors only)

Requirements: Great academic performance, and strong extracurricular activities, reference from science teacher or school counselor.

Application Deadline: January 15

Application Link:
https://www.viterbo.edu/school-natural-science-mathematics-and-engineering/scholarship-opportunities

4 Milwaukee School of Engineering

Location: Milwaukee, Wisconsin
Setting: Urban (23 Acres)
Undergraduate Enrollment: 2,575
Type: Private

ROTC Programs & Scholarships: Awards range from $18,000 up to Full tuition and fees.

Requirements: Visit scholarship page for more details.

Application Link:
https://www.msoe.edu/admissions-aid/financial-aid-scholarships/scholarships-and-grants/rotc-scholarships/navy-rotc/

5 Alverno College

Location: Milwaukee, Wisconsin
Setting: Urban (47 Acres)
Undergraduate Enrollment: 788
Type: Private

Roosevelt Scholarship: Awards Full tuition.

Requirements: Good academic performance and excellence in leadership/volunteerism.

Application Deadline: December 2

Application Link: https://www.alverno.edu/Financial-Aid-Scholarships

7 University of Wisconsin, Oshkosh

Location: Oshkosh, Wisconsin
Setting: City (166 Acres)
Undergraduate Enrollment: 11,773
Type: Public

Army ROTC Scholarship: Full in-state tuition, books and cash stipends.

Requirements: Visit the scholarship webpage for more information.

Application Deadline: June 20

Application Link: https://uwosh.edu/admissions/costs-and-aid/scholarships/

6 Ripon College

Location: Ripon, Wisconsin
Setting: City (250 Acres)
Undergraduate Enrollment: 766
Type: Private

Knop Science Scholarship: Awards Full tuition.

Requirements: Academic and extracurricular excellence. This scholarship application process is by invitation only. It is open to majors in science and mathematics departments.

Application Deadline: February 1

Application Link: https://ripon.edu/financial-aid/scholarships/

8

Marquette University

Location: Milwaukee, Wisconsin
Setting: Urban (107 Acres)
Undergraduate Enrollment: 7,528
Type: Private

Urban Scholars Program: Awards Full tuition plus housing.

Requirements: 3.0/4.0 GPA, Demostrated leadership and service, Demonstrated financial need (FAFSA or Net price calculator), High school seniors from Milwaukee area.

P.S: Citizenship is not a factor in awarding scholarship.

Application Deadline: February 1

Ronald E. And Kathleen M. Zupko Scholarship: Awards Full tuition.

Requirements: High School Seniors in the Milwaukee Public School System (with 3.0 GPA or higher), Demonstrated financial need (FAFSA or Net Price Calculator)

Burke Scholars Program: Awards Full tuition.

Requirements: Wisconsin high school seniors or entering first-year students, demonstrated community service, demonstrated academic excellence through high GPA, SAT/ACT and application materials.

Opus Scholars Program: Awards Full tuition, plus student fees and lab fees | conditionally housing and meal plans are also awarded.

Requirements: Admission to Opus College of Engineering, community service (e.g. Cristo Rey Network), demonstrated financial need (FAFSA or Net Price Calculator)

Do Great Things Full Tuition Scholarship: Awards Full tuition plus 2 years of room and board.

Requirements: Admission to Marquette University, attended Green Bay West High School, demonstrated financial need (FAFSA or Net Price Calculator)

Global Scholar Scholarship Award: Full tuition.

Requirements: Freshman entering Marquette University, high school located outside United States, 3.25 GPA (on an unweighted 4.0 scale), international student on an F-1 visa.

Application Deadline: December 1

Application Link: https://www.marquette.edu/explore/scholarships.php

9

University of Wisconsin – River Falls

Location: River Falls, Wisconsin
Setting: Rural (303 Acres)
Undergraduate Enrollment: 4,772
Type: Public

Chancellor Scholars Scholarship: Full tuition or Half Tuition + $2,000.

Requirements: Must have a high school GPA of 3.8 or higher **OR** rank in the top 10% of their high school class **OR** have an 28 ACT (1310 SAT) or higher.

- Applicant Must submit one letter of recommendation from a teacher, guidance counselor, coach, mentor, etc. explaining the student's leadership and academic potential.
- Applicant Must write an essay.

Application Deadline: January 5

Mary Barrett Chancellor Scholars Scholarship: Full tuition or Half Tuition + $2,000.

Requirements: Must have a minimum ACT score of 26 and/or a high school GPA of 3.0

This application includes an essay and digital portfolio upload requirement. Finalists will be required to complete an interview and provide a physical portfolio containing work samples.

The award is for four academic years, provided the student continues to pursue a degree in Art: BS Art, BS Art Education, BFA.

Application Deadline: February 1

Application Link: https://www.uwrf.edu/paying-for-college/scholarships

Carthage College

Location: Kenosha, Wisconsin
Setting: Suburban (80 Acres)
Undergraduate Enrollment: 2,600
Type: Private

Presidential Scholarship: $27,000 to Full tuition.

Requirements: Excellent academic performance & extracurricular activities, 250-word essay, submitted Carthage college application, presidential scholarship competition application.

Business Scholarships: Full tuition (for business related majors)

Requirements: Carthage college application, one-page essay, business scholarship competition application, excellent grades, test scores and extracurricular activities.

Kenosha Scholarships: Full tuition (for Kenosha residents only)

Requirements: Carthage college application, 250-word essay, Kenosha scholarship competition application, excellent grades, test scores and extracurricular activities.

Math/Science Scholarships: Full tuition (for Science and math related majors)

Requirements: Carthage college application, one-page essay, math/science scholarship competition application, excellent grades, test scores and extracurricular activities.

Spring Scholarships: Full tuition (for Science and math related majors)

Requirements: Carthage college admission, spring scholarship competition application, excellent grades, test scores and extracurricular activities.

Application Deadline: November

Kenosha Police/Fire Scholarship: Full tuition (for Science and math related majors)

Requirements: Dependent of a city of Kenosha Police officer or firefighter, Carthage college application, scholarship application, good grades, test scores and extracurricular activities.

Application Deadline: December 3

Application Link: https://www.carthage.edu/admissions/undergraduate-students/undergraduate-scholarships/

1

Wyoming Catholic College

Location: Lander, Wyoming
Setting: Town (600 Acres)
Undergraduate Enrollment: 189
Type: Private

Founder's Scholarship: Awards Full tuition.

Requirements: High school senior(s) who applied to Wyoming Catholic College. Students who exhibit academic excellence throughout the application eassy, letters of reference, and high school (unofficial) transcript.

Application Deadline: October 1 (for Fall) & February 1 (for spring)

Application Link: https://wyomingcatholic.edu/admissions/scholarships/

CHAPTER 5

OTHER $CHOLARSHIP$ FUNDS

- **Fukunaga Scholarship Foundation**

Amount: Awards **$20,000** over a period of four years. (**$5,000** per year)

Eligibility: Awarded to high school students in the **State of Hawaii** who intend to have a **career in business** | Applicant must be an entering freshman at any accredited four-year college or university | High School GPA of 3.0 or higher.

Deadline: February 21

Application Link:
https://www.servco.com/giving-back/scholarships/

- **HBCU Week and FOSSI STEM Scholarship**

Amount: Awards **$40,000** over a period of four years. (**$10,000** per year) and other benefits.

Eligibility: Applicants must be high school seniors accepted as a full-time student at a historically Black College or University for the upcoming academic year, planning to pursue studies in a field associated with **STEM, MIQA, technical or operation manufacturing** | A minimum high school GPA of 3.0 | Be a U.S. Citizen or permanent resident.

Deadline: January 31

Application Link:
https://futureofstemscholars.org/FOSSI/apply

- **Golden Door Scholars**

Amount: Awards up to **$30,000**

Eligibility: A minimum (unweighted) high school GPA of 3.2 | Applicant must possess a DACA or TPS immigration status | Strong preference given to applicants with high financial need.

Deadline: October 1

Application Link:
https://www.goldendoorscholars.org/

- **National Space Club and Foundation Keynote Scholars Program**

Amount: **$15,000** plus other benefits.

Eligibility: High school seniors entering College | Applicant must be a U.S. Citizen intending to pursue a career in any STEM discipline | Check the website for more details.

Deadline: December 4

Application Link:
https://www.spaceclub.org/scholarship/index.html

- **Amazon Future Engineer Scholarship**

Amount: Awards **$40,000** over a period of four years. (**$10,000** per year) plus other benefits.

Eligibility: U.S. Citizen or permanent resident | High school seniors entering College | Must demonstrate financial need | Be planning to attain a bachelor's degree in computer science, Engineering, or robotics | A minimum cumulative GPA of 2.3 on a 4.0 scale.

Deadline: December 15

Application Link:
https://www.amazonfutureengineer.com/scholarships

- **Society of Women Engineers – Lehigh Valley Section**

Amount: **$5,000**

Eligibility: Female high school seniors who intend to major in engineering at the respective college or university | Applicants must be females graduating from high school who reside in areas with zip codes beginning in 177-187 and 195-196.

Deadline: January 28

Application Link:
http://lv.swe.org/scholarships.html

- **WSOS Baccalaureate Scholarship**

Amount: $22,500 plus other benefits.

Eligibility: Awarded to students pursuing bachelor's degrees in high-demand STEM and health care majors in Washington State.

Deadline: February 15

Application Link:
https://waopportunityscholarship.org/applicants/baccalaureate/

- **The Elevating Futures Scholarship Fund**

Amount: Awards **$22,000**

Eligibility: Applicants must be **Chicago Public School students** from low income households, pursuing a STEM four year college degree and launching a career in the construction or engineering industries | A minimum high school GPA of 3.0

Deadline: March 1

Application Link:
https://chicagoscholars.org/scholarship/the-elevating-futures-scholarship-fund/

- **American Association of Blacks in Energy Scholarship**

Amount: $20,000

Eligibility: A minimum high school GPA of 3.0 | Applicant must be a graduating high school senior who intends to enroll next semester in an

Application Link:
https://www.aabe.org/index.php/index.php?component=pages&id=99

- **Lockheed Martin Vocational Scholarship**

Amount: $5,000

Eligibility: High school seniors entering College or currently enrolled undergraduates | Applicant must be a U.S. Citizen | Check the website for a list of specific majors and fields of study eligible for this scholarship.

Deadline: March 31

Application Link:
https://www.lockheedmartin.com/en-us/who-we-are/communities/stem-education/lockheed-martin-vocational-scholarship.html

- **California Capital Airshow STEM Scholarship**

Amount: $8,000

Eligibility: Graduating high school seniors from Sacramento, El Dorado, Yolo Placer, Yuba, Sutter, or Solano counties planning to pursue a degree in one of the careers listed on the website | A minimum cumulative GPA of 3.5

Deadline: March 10

Application Link:
https://sacregcf.academicworks.com/opportunities/1344

- **Unitil Scholarship Fund**

Amount: $5,000

Eligibility: Awarded to high school seniors from New Hampshire, Maine and Massachusetts who are pursuing degrees in science, technology, engineering, or math | Generally, top applicants are selected.

Deadline: January 28

Application Link:
https://unitil.com/community/stem-education/teachers-students/stem-scholarships

- **Edison Scholars Program**

Amount: $50,000

Eligibility: Applicants must live in Southern California Edison's service area | High School Senior planning to pursue studies in the STEM fields at a four-year accredited college or university | Minimum cumulative GPA of 3.0 | Demonstrate financial need.

Deadline: January 23

Application Link:
https://www.edison.com/community/edison-scholars

- **HSF Scholarship**

Amount: $5,000

Eligibility: Applicants must be **Hispanic/Latino** | Minimum high school GPA of 3.0 | U.S. citizen, permanent resident, DACA or eligible non-citizens.

Deadline: February 15

Application Link:
https://www.hsf.net/scholarship

- **MathWorks Math Modeling (M3 Challenge)**

Amount: $20,000

Eligibility: High schools in the U.S. (including US territories and DoDEA schools) | Schools with sixth form students (age 16-19) in England and Wales (including British Schools Overseas) are eligible | A maximum of two teams per school, each consisting of three to five students with one coach, may register for M3 Challenge, so long as the school, students and coach all meet the eligibility criteria. P.S: Check the website for more details on this scholarship.

Deadline: February 23

Application Link: https://m3challenge.siam.org/

- **DGV Scholarship Program**

Amount: $20,000

Eligibility: High school seniors entering College or currently enrolled undergraduates | Must be pursuing, or planning to pursue, a degree in STEM, finance or business | U.S. citizen, permanent resident, DACA or eligible non-citizen | Minimum cumulative GPA of 3.0

Deadline: March 31

Application Link:
https://www.dgvlp.com/scholarship

- **Penn State Braddock Scholarship**

Amount: $10,000 annually for four years.

Eligibility: Graduating high school seniors who are interested in the study of Astronomy & Astrophysics, Biochemistry, Biology, Biotechnology, Chemistry, Forensic Science, Microbiology, Molecular Biology, Physics, or Pre-Medicine at Penn State's University Park campus.

Deadline: January 20

Application Link: https://science.psu.edu/future-students/undergraduates/scholarships/braddock-scholarship

- **United States Geospatial Intelligence Foundation Scholarships**

Amount: $10,000

Eligibility: Students from a variety of educational institutions including community colleges, technical colleges, traditional four year universities, and other post-secondary institutions are eligible. P.S: Check the website for more details.

Deadline: May 31

Application Link: https://usgif.org/usgif-scholarship-program/

- **JMU Second Century STEM Scholarship**

Amount: $54,300

Eligibility: GPA of 3.75+ (performance in science, technology and mathematics courses will receive additional consideration) | Demonstrate interest and commitment to study in a STEM field.

Deadline: November 1

Application Link:
https://www.jmu.edu/admissions/apply/scholarships/stem.shtml

- **Thomas K. Evans Memorial Scholarship**

Amount: $5,000

Eligibility: Applicant must be graduating from a high school whose physical address is located in the Quad-Cities (Check the website for a list eligible locations) | Plan to pursue an education with a major or specific focus in science, technology, engineering and/or math.

Deadline: February 26

Application Link:
https://www.americanpowerinc.com/about/scholarships/

- **Micron Science and Technology Scholars Program**

Amount: $25,000

Eligibility: Applicant must be a resident of and be a high school senior who attends a public or private school in either of these three states: Idaho, Utah and Virginia | A combined SAT score of at least 1350 | 3.50 unweighted GPA (on a 4.0 scale) | Plan to major in Engineering field, Physics or Chemistry.

Deadline: September 30

Application Link: https://www.micron.com/gives

- **Boren Scholarships**

Amount: Maximum award of **$25,000**

Eligibility: U.S. citizens | A high school graduate. This scholarship is designed for U.S. undergraduate students to study less commonly taught languages in world regions critical to U.S. interests. P.S: Check the website for more details.

Deadline: January 31

Application Link:
https://www.borenawards.org/

- **Davidson Fellows Scholarship**

Amount: $50,000

Eligibility: Applicant must be 18 years and under, who have completed a significant piece of work. Application categories are: STEM fields, Literature, Music, Philosophy and Outside the Box | Be a U.S. citizen residing in the United States, or a Permanent Resident.

Deadline: February 14

Application Link:
https://www.davidsongifted.org/gifted-programs/fellows-scholarship/

- **Black American Engineering Scholarship Award**

Amount: $10,000

Eligibility: High school seniors entering College | Applicant must be Black American | U.S. citizen, national, or permanent resident | Able to show proven financial need | Good academic standing | Pursuing a degree in Civil, Electrical, Mechanical, or Chemical Engineering, including any subfield of those disciplines.

Deadline: January 31

Application Link:
https://thehelpingproject.org/scholarship/

- **Health Professions Scholarship Program**

Amount: Full tuition & fees **($20,000)**

Eligibility: Must be accepted to or enrolled in an accredited medical school | Be a U.S. Citizen| Have at least a 3.2 GPA |Check the website for other specific requirements.

Deadline: Deadline varies

Application Link:
https://www.medicineandthemilitary.com/applying-and-what-to-expect/medical-school-programs/hpsp

- **Frito Lay Community Builder Scholarship**

Amount: $25,000

Eligibility: Live in the U.S.| Be a high school senior or graduate or current college undergraduate who plans to enroll in full-time undergraduate study in the U.S.| Minimum GPA of 2.5/4.0

Deadline: November 20

Application Link:
https://learnmore.scholarsapply.org/frito-lay/

- **Equitable Excellence Scholarship**

Amount: $20,000

Eligibility: Current high school senior who plans to enroll in college| Demonstrate ambition and have strong extracurricular records| Have a 2.5 GPA on a 4.0 scale.

Deadline: December 18

Application Link:
https://learnmore.scholarsapply.org/equitableexcellence/

- **National Forum for Black Public Administrators Scholarship**

Amount: $10,000

Eligibility: This scholarship is specifically to honor exceptional scholastic achievements and leadership among African American and minority students | check application portal for other requirements.

Deadline: January 22

Application Link:
https://www.nfbpa.org/programs/scholarship-program

- **McDonald's HACER National Scholarship**

Amount: $100,000

Eligibility: Applicants must be a high school senior with at least one parent of Hispanic/Latino heritage| Legal U.S. resident who is younger than 21 years old| Minimum of 2.8 GPA.

Deadline: Check the website for more details.

Application Link:
https://www.mcdonalds.com/us/en-us/community/hacer.html

- **Goya Foods Culinary Arts Scholarship Program**

Amount: $20,000

Eligibility: Applicant must be majoring in a full-time Culinary Arts or a Food Sciences program | A minimum GPA of 3.0/4.0 | Be a U.S. Citizen, permanent resident or student granted DACA.

Deadline: March 1

Application Link:
https://learnmore.scholarsapply.org/goyaculinary/

● SEG Scholarships

Amount: $10,000

Eligibility: High school senior planning to attend college next year or an undergraduate| Above average grades | Intending or pursuing a college curriculum directed toward a career in applied geophysics.

Deadline: March 1

Application Link: https://seg.org/programs/student-programs/scholarships/

● NRF Foundation Next Generation Scholarship

Amount: $10,000 - $25,000

Eligibility: Students interested in pursuing careers in retail | This opportunity was created for students of various academic backgrounds who have demonstrated leadership skills, previous retail experience, and a passion for making an impact.

Deadline: May 23

Application Link: https://nrffoundation.org/campus/scholarships/next-generation/how-to-apply

● Colgate-Palmolive Haz La U Scholarship

Amount: $100,000

Eligibility: Graduating high school seniors | Have a minimum of 3.0/4.0 GPA| Be of Hispanic heritage (includes Spain, Brazil, Philippines)

Deadline: November 13

Application Link: https://www.colgate.com/en-us/make-the-u

● UNCF Chevron Corporate Scholars Program

Amount: $15,000

Eligibility: Graduating high school seniors who have been accepted to an accredited four-year Historically Black College/University (HBCU) | Have a 2.8 GPA | U.S. Citizen or legal resident| Interested in a STEM major or relevant field.

Deadline: August 14

Application Link: https://uncf.org/programs/uncf-chevron-corporate-scholars-program

● Daniels Scholarship Program

Amount: $100,000

Eligibility: Must be citizen or permanent resident of the U.S.; and be resident of Colorado, New Mexico, Utah, or Wyoming | Have a minimum GPA of 3.0 | Minimum SAT math score of 490 and minimum reading & writing of 490 | Or minimum ACT score of 18 in each category.

Deadline: October 15

Application Link: https://www.danielsfund.org/scholarships/daniels-scholarship-program/overview

● Perryman Family Foundation Scholarships

Amount: $15,000

Eligibility: U.S. Citizen | 3.0 GPA and above | Must live within 150 miles of Houston, PA | Check the website for other requirements (There are 3 different scholarships).

Deadline: March 31

Application Link: https://perrymanfoundation.org/

• NACME Scholarship Programs

Amount: $5,000

Eligibility: NACME partners with like-minded entities to provide scholarships, resources, and opportunities for high-achieving, underrepresented minority college students pursuing careers in engineering and computer science.

Deadline: Varies

Application Link: https://www.nacme.org/scholarships

• WTS Foundation Scholarships

Amount: $5,000 - $6,000

Eligibility: Female students pursuing careers in transportation through undergraduate and graduate programs. The scholarships are competitive and based on the applicant's specific transportation goals, academic record and transportation-related activities.

Deadline: November 27

Application Link: https://www.wtsinternational.org/wts-foundation/scholarships

• John J. McKetta Undergraduate Scholarship

Amount: $5,000

Eligibility: Awarded to a chemical engineering undergraduate students (incoming junior or senior only), planning a career in the chemical engineering process industries | must be AIChE student members at the time of the nomination (free of charge) and have a 3.0 GPA.

Deadline: June 15

Application Link: https://www.aiche.org/community/awards/john-j-mcketta-undergraduate-scholarship

• Helen Brett Scholarship

Amount: $5,000

Eligibility: Must be a full-time student enrolled at an accredited | Minimum 3.0/4.0 GPA | Must be enrolled in a degree program focusing on exhibition/event management.

Deadline: May 1

Application Link: https://www.iaee.com/helen-brett-scholarship/

• Exceptional Youth Scholarship

Amount: $10,000

Eligibility: Be a high school junior or senior planning to attend an accredited four year college or university in the U.S. | Have a minimum 3.0 GPA | Have participated in some form of community service, volunteerism or mentorship activities | Be a U.S. citizen or legal permanent resident.

Deadline: April 15

Application Link: https://globalsportsdevelopment.org/exceptional-youth-scholarship-blog/

• General James H. Doolittle Scholarship Fund

Amount: $5,000

Eligibility: Must have a minimum 2.75 GPA | Must be citizens of the United States | Must be pursuing aerospace science, aeronautical engineering or related degree (College juniors or seniors)

Deadline: April 1

Application Link: https://www.cftexas.org/scholarships/scholarship-opportunities/general-james-h-doolittle-scholarship-fund

- **PMMI Foundation Scholarships**

Amount: $5,000

Eligibility: Currently enrolled at a North American 4-year college or university | GPA 3.0 or higher | Check website for other requirements (There are 11 different scholarships).

Deadline: March 31

Application Link: https://www.pmmifoundation.org/scholarships

- **GVTC Foundation – Ritchie T. Sorrells Scholarship**

Amount: $25,000

Eligibility: Awarded to well-deserving high school seniors from households that subscribe to at least one GVTC service in pursuit of their higher education.

Deadline: March 1

Application Link: https://gvtc.com/foundation/impact/scholarships

- **Linly Heflin Scholarship**

Amount: $40,000

Eligibility: Applicants must have significant economic need and sound academic records (such as an ACT score of 23) | Must be Alabama residents and U.S. citizens who attend or plan to attend a four-year Alabama college or university.

Deadline: January 10

Application Link: https://www.linlyheflin.org/apply/

- **Emerson's ASCO Engineering Scholarship Program**

Amount: $5,000

Eligibility: Applicants must have completed their freshman year in a bachelor's degree program | Must be studying STEM major | Must be a U.S. citizen or legal U.S. resident.

Deadline: July 31

Application Link: https://go.emersonautomation.com/asco-scholarship-2023

- **SAE Heinz C. Prechter Automotive Excellence Scholarship**

Amount: $10,000

Eligibility: Must be a U.S. resident | Must be pursuing a STEM degree | Applicants should be visionaries who can implement ideas.

Deadline: February 28

Application Link: https://www.sae.org/participate/scholarships/sae-heinz-c-prechter-automotive-excellence-scholarship

- **National Honor Society Scholarship**

Amount: $25,000

Eligibility: A high school senior expecting to receive a high school diploma during the current academic year | An active member in good standing of a National Honor Society chapter | Planning to pursue a degree at an accredited U.S. college or university.

Deadline: November 30

Application Link: https://www.nationalhonorsociety.org/advisers/the-nhs-scholarship/

- **George M. Pullman Educational Foundation Scholarship**

Amount: $40,000

Eligibility: Applicants must be a graduating high school senior | Be a Cook County, Illinois resident who will be enrolling as a full-time student, for the first time, to receive a bachelor's degree | Demonstrate strong financial need | A minimum 3.0 high school GPA.

Deadline: February 1

Application Link:
https://www.pullmanfoundation.org/apply/

- **Washington State Baccalaureate Scholarship**

Amount: $22,500

Eligibility: A minimum 2.75 GPA | This scholarship supports low and middle income students pursuing eligible high-demand majors in STEM or health care and encourages recipients to work in Washington state once they complete their degrees.

Deadline: February 29

Application Link:
https://waopportunityscholarship.org/applicants/baccalaureate/

- **Single Parent Household Scholarship for a Bright Future**

Amount: $10,000

Eligibility: Applicants must be minority high school or college students who reside and study in the United States, are underprivileged.

Deadline: May 31

Application Link:
https://app.goingmerry.com/scholarships/for-a-bright-future---the-single-parent-household-scholarship/18969

- **STEAM Scholarship for a Bright Future**

Amount: $10,000

Eligibility: Applicants must be minority high school or college students who reside and study in the United States, are underprivileged.

Deadline: May 31

Application Link:
https://app.goingmerry.com/scholarships/for-a-bright-future---steam-scholarship/18967

- **Dr. Emma Lerew Scholarship for a Bright Future**

Amount: $10,000

Eligibility: Applicants must be minority high school or college students who reside and study in the United States, are underprivileged | Have graduated high school with a minimum 3.0 GPA. This scholarship supports underrepresented and underprivileged, and exceptional students focused on careers in Education.

Deadline: May 31

Application Link:
https://app.goingmerry.com/scholarships/for-a-bright-future---the-dr-emma-lerew-scholarship/18968

- **CrowdStrike NextGen Scholarship Program**

Amount: $10,000

Eligibility: Graduating high school seniors who will be enrolling in college/university in the United States or Canada, majoring in Cybersecurity or AI | A minimum high school GPA of 3.0

Deadline: June 2

Application Link:
https://www.crowdstrike.com/about-crowdstrike/nextgen-scholarship-program/

- **NANOG Scholarship Program**

Amount: $10,000

Eligibility: Applicants must be current post-secondary undergraduate or graduate student pursuing a degree in one of the following fields of study: Computer Engineering, Computer Science, Electrical Engineering, Network Engineering | A minimum GPA of 3.0 on a 4.0 scale.

Deadline: January 31

Application Link:
https://www.nanog.org/outreach/higher-education/nanog-scholarship-program/

- **The Dream.US Opportunity Scholarship**

Amount: $20,000 per year for 4 years

Eligibility: This scholarship is designed for undocumented students living in locked-out states, where accessing higher education seems like an insurmountable obstacle.

Deadline: January 31

Application Link:
https://www.thedream.us/scholarships/opportunity-scholarship/

- **George and Mary Josephine Hamman Foundation Scholarship**

Amount: $20,000

Eligibility: Applicants must be Graduating high school seniors from Houston area high schools or homeschooled | U.S. citizens | Good academic standing and demonstrate financial need.

Deadline: February 16

Application Link:
https://hammanfoundation.org/

- **Gordon A. Rich Memorial Scholarship**

Amount: $12,500 per year

Eligibility: Applicants must be Graduating high school seniors | A minimum high school GPA of 3.5 (on a 4.0 scale) and rank in the top 20% of their class | Demonstrate financial need | U.S. citizen or legal resident | Must be dependent children of full-time employees in the financial services industry.

Deadline: February 20

Application Link:
http://www.gordonrich.org/html/index.html

- **J & J Trujillo Memorial Scholarship**

Amount: $12,500

Eligibility: Applicants must be residents of Arizona, New Mexico, or Minnesota | Graduating high school seniors or current post-secondary undergraduates | Good academic records.

Deadline: February 17

Application Link:
https://learnmore.scholarsapply.org/trujillomemorial/

- **Connecticut Roberta B. Willis Need-Based Grant**

Amount: $18,000

Eligibility: Applicants must be Connecticut residents who will attend a Connecticut public or non-profit private college | Graduating high school seniors | Demonstrate financial need.

Deadline: January 15

Application Link:
https://www.ohe.ct.gov/SFA/WillisScholarship.shtml

- **Education and Training Vouchers for Youths Aging out of Foster Care in Texas**

Amount: $20,000

Eligibility: Applicants must be at least 16 and are likely to remain in foster care until age 18; aged out of foster care but have not yet turned 21 | Have a high school diploma or equivalent, or is exempt from required school attendance.

Deadline: Check the website for more details.

Application Link: http://www.collegeforalltexans.com/apps/financialaid/tofa2.cfm?ID=480

- **Odyssey Scholarships**

Amount: $340,000

Eligibility: Qualifying students who apply to and are accepted to attend the University of Chicago need not worry about tuition payments. With this Full-tuition scholarship, applicants will be able to focus on their studies without worrying about post secondary education cost.

Deadline: Check the website for more details.

Application Link: https://odyssey.uchicago.edu/

- **Puckett Scholars Program**

Amount: $10,000

Eligibility: Applicants must be high school seniors graduating from a school in the state of Minnesota | Admission as a full-time student to the University of Minnesota, Twin Cities | Pursuing a bachelor's degree and have a Good academic standing.

Deadline: Check the website for more details.

Application Link: https://diversity.umn.edu/puckett

- **The Sweet Feet Foundation Scholarship**

Amount: $10,000

Eligibility: Impending Acceptance into a college or university or current student | Family income of $60,000 or less | Must be either Active in the community, Volunteer, have a job or play sport | Applicants must be from the New England Area.

Deadline: Check the website for more details.

Application Link: https://www.sweetfeet28.com/the-sweet-feet-foundation

- **Soroptimist's Live Your Dream Award**

Amount: $16,000

Eligibility: A woman who: Provides the primary financial support for yourself and your dependents | Has financial need | Is motivated to achieve your education and career goals | Is enrolled in or has been accepted to a vocational/skills training program or an undergraduate degree program | Resides in one of Soroptimist International of the Americas' member countries/territories.

Deadline: November 15

Application Link: https://www.liveyourdream.org/get-help/apply-for-an-educational-grant/index.html

- **Good Tidings Community Service Scholarship**

Amount: $10,000

Eligibility: Graduating high school seniors | Resident of one of the select California counties.

Deadline: November 8

Application Link: https://goodtidings.org/impact/education-and-scholarships/

- **New Futures Scholars Program**

Amount: $7,800

Eligibility: Applicants must be nominated by a school or organization | Demonstrate financial need | Plan to pursue an associate degree or professional certification | Be between the ages of 17 and 29 | Live in the Washington, DC metropolitan region | Aspire to a career as listed on the website.

Deadline: March 15

Application Link: https://newfuturesdc.org/

- **Achieve Atlanta Scholarship**

Amount: $20,000

Eligibility: Applicant must be a senior at an Atlanta Public High School | Demonstrate financial need | Graduate from an APS high school (includes charters) with a minimum cumulative weighted GPA of 2.0 | Be enrolled full time at an accredited, nonprofit private or public college or technical program in Georgia.

Deadline: May 31

Application Link: https://achieveatlanta.org/scholarship/current-aps-students/

- **The Trotter Project's Pursuit of Excellence Scholarship**

Amount: $10,000

Eligibility: Awarded to incoming nontraditional or current culinary arts/hospitality students who demonstrate financial need and enrolled in an accredited college/university in the U.S. | Applicants must have a minimum 2.5 GPA.

Deadline: May 15

Application Link: https://www.thetrotterproject.org/scholarships

- **NIH Undergraduate Scholarship Program**

Amount: $80,000

Eligibility: U.S. citizen or permanent resident | Be enrolled or accepted for enrollment as a full-time undergraduate student at an accredited four-year college or university | A minimum GPA of 3.3 on a 4.0 scale or rank within the top five percent of your class | Demonstrate exceptional financial need certified by your undergraduate institution's financial aid office.

Deadline: April 3

Application Link: https://www.training.nih.gov/

- **Lee E. Schauer Scholarship**

Amount: $48,000

Eligibility: College-bound Shelby County high school senior | A minimum 2.5 GPA | Applicants who are members and also volunteered at the YMCA will receive additional consideration; demonstrate caring, honesty, respect and responsibility in daily life.

Deadline: April 7

Application Link: https://brokescholar.com/scholarship/lee-e-schauer-scholarship

- **Burger King Scholars**

Amount: $60,000

Eligibility: Applicants must be living in the United States, Puerto Rico, Guam or Canada | Be graduating high school seniors (U.S., Puerto Rico and Guam) | A minimum cumulative high school GPA of 2.0 (on a 4.0 scale)

Deadline: December 15

Application Link: https://www.burgerkingfoundation.org/programs/burger-king-sm-scholars

- **The Rezvan Foundation for Excellence Scholarship**

Amount: $100,000

Eligibility: A minor now or formerly in foster care; a minor who has been orphaned; or a minor who has been adopted after time spent in foster care | A U.S. resident | Graduating high school senior or currently enrolled in an accredited high school | 3.5+ GPA

Deadline: February 9

Application Link: https://www.rezvanfoundation.org/

- **Life Happens Life Lessons Scholarship**

Amount: $15,000

Eligibility: Applicant must be between the ages of 17 – 24 | Have experienced the death of a parent or legal guardian | Will be attending college, university or trade school in the U.S. or Puerto Rico in the upcoming semester | Legal residents of the United States or Puerto Rico.

Deadline: March 1

Application Link: https://lifehappens.org/life-lessons-scholarship-program/

- **The Annual Venus Morris Griffin Scholarship Fund**

Amount: $10,000

Eligibility: Applicant must have a biological parent that is currently incarcerated | Graduating high school seniors in the United States entering college | Good academic standing.

Deadline: February 15

Application Link: https://vmgfoundation.org/

- **SVCF on Your own Scholarship**

Amount: $16,000

Eligibility: Applicant must be accepted to or attending San Jose State University for the upcoming academic term and must have been in foster care at least one day since their 13th birthday | Demonstrate financial need | A minimum cumulative high school GPA of 2.50

Deadline: February 29

Application Link: https://www.siliconvalleycf.org/scholarships/find-scholarships

- **American Legion Legacy Scholarship**

Amount: $20,000

Eligibility: This scholarship is designed for children of U.S. Military members (entering college/universities) who died while on active duty on or after Sept. 11, 2001.

P.S: Check the website for more details.

Deadline: April 1

Application Link: https://www.legion.org/scholarships/legacy

- **Life on Purpose Scholarship**

Amount: $40,000

Eligibility: High school seniors applying to four-year colleges | Minimum unweighted GPA of 3.0 | Demonstrate an interest in fostering the well being of yourself and others.

Deadline: March 1

Application Link: https://www.lifeonpurposescholars.org/

- **The Social Shifters Global Innovation Challenge**

Amount: $10,000

Eligibility: To enter the Social Shifters Global Innovation Challenge, your idea must be unique and contribute towards at least one of the UN's 17 Sustainable Development Goals.

Deadline: August 20

Application Link:
https://socialshifters.innovationchallenge.com/skild2/socialshifters/registerLeader.action

- **Women With Promise Scholarship**

Amount: $5,000

Eligibility: Women who are accepted into an accredited course of study at an accredited institution (College, University, Trade/Vocational School) | Demonstrate a need for financial assistance | Exhibits a strong desire, ability and determination to complete the academic course | Has partnered with a non-profit organization or social agency for at least six months. P.S: Check the website for more details.

Application Link:
https://www.womenwithpromise.org/scholarship

- **Sahara Hope Scholarship for women Empowered to change the world**

Amount: $5,000

Eligibility: Women who are currently enrolled in an undergraduate degree at an accredited university | A minimum cumulative GPA of 3.0 | Residing in the United States.

Deadline: November 15

Application Link:
https://cosmoforge.io/sahara-hope-scholarship-for-women-empowered-to-change-the-world/

- **Brave of Heart Scholarship**

Amount: Awards up to **$25,000** per year.

Eligibility: Applicant must be a child, spouse or domestic partner of a frontline healthcare worker who lost their life to a COVID-19 related cause | Plan to enroll full-time or part time in an undergraduate or graduate program.

Deadline: Application opens by February and August of each year.

Application Link:
https://learnmore.scholarsapply.org/braveofheart/

- **Bristol-Meyers Squibb Scholarship for Cancer Survivors**

Amount: $10,000

Eligibility: Applicants must be cancer survivors, age 25 and under, who are high school seniors or graduates, or current postsecondary undergraduates | Applicant must be planning to enroll in full time undergraduate study at an accredited college/ university or vocational-technical school.

Deadline: April 1

Application Link:
https://learnmore.scholarsapply.org/cancer-survivors/

- **The Graydon and Myrth Fox Scholarship**

Amount: $5,000 per year for four years.

Eligibility: This scholarship is offered to U.S. Armed Services veterans, their surviving spouses, and their dependent children and grandchildren. Preference for the award is given to wounded personnel, or the dependent children of personnel's.

Deadline: March 15

Application Link:
https://www.tun.com/scholarships/graydon-myrth-fox-scholarship/

- **ATSSA Roadway Worker Memorial Scholarship Program**

Amount: $10,000

Eligibility: This scholarship program provides financial assistance for post-high school education to dependents (children and spouses) of roadway workers killed or permanently disabled in work zone incidents.

Deadline: February 15

Application Link: https://foundation.atssa.com/our-programs/scholarship-programs/

- **Women's Independence Scholarship Program (WISP)**

Amount: $6,000

Eligibility: The applicant must be a woman who is a direct survivor of intimate partner abuse | Be physically separated from her abuser a minimum of one year but not more than ten. P.S: Check the website for more information.

Deadline: March 1

Application Link: https://wispinc.org/

- **Hendrick Scholarship Foundation**

Amount: $15,000

Eligibility: Be a Plano ISD (Texas) high school senior | Have at least a 3.0 weighted high school GPA | Demonstrate financial need | U.S. citizens.

Deadline: March 15

Application Link: https://hendrickscholarship.org/

- **Chick and Sophie Major Memorial Duck Calling Contest**

Amount: $5,000

Eligibility: Applicant must be a high school graduating senior | The contest is associated with the World's Champion Duck Calling Contest and will take place on the Main Street Stage beside the Stuttgart Chamber of Commerce. P.S: Seniors will be required to blow a Main Street duck calling routine.

Deadline: November 24

Application Link: https://www.stuttgartduckfest.com/scholarship-contest

- **Samuel A. Green Scholarship Program**

Amount: $25,000

Eligibility: Applicants must be high school graduating senior/rising college freshmen from public, private, parochial or charter school, or home-schooled student, who plans to be a full-time student at a community or four-year, not for profit, accredited college or university.

Deadline: March 1

Application Link: https://www.greenfamilyfoundation.org/samuel-a-green-scholarship

- **Gloria Barron Prizes for Young Heroes**

Amount: $10,000

Eligibility: Applicants must be between the ages of 8 and 18 | Permanent residents of and currently residing in the U.S.A. or Canada | Currently working on an inspiring service project or have done so within the past 12 months.

Deadline: April 15

Application Link: https://barronprize.org/

● SVCF Krishnan-Shah Family Scholarship

Amount: $40,000

Eligibility: Applicant must be graduating high school seniors residing in the greater Silicon Valley Region | First generation college students pursuing first undergraduate degree | A cumulative GPA of 3.75+ on a 4.0 scale.

Deadline: February 28

Application Link:
https://www.siliconvalleycf.org/scholarships/krishnan-shah-family-scholarship

● Diversity Scholars Program

Amount: $20,000

Eligibility: U.S citizens or lawful permanent resident of the United States | United States high school community college; student of African-American, Native American, or Hispanic/Latino heritage | Intended or declared major in transportation engineering, planning, or a related field | Minimum high school GPA of 3.0

Deadline: March 15

Application Link:
https://www.ite.org/membership/diversity-scholars-program/

● Sigma Alpha Epsilon Scholarships

Amount: Awards up to **$5,000**

Eligibility: Freshmen who complete the application form, submit all required recommendations and transcripts, and are enrolled in a business or scientific degree. Members may apply for as many scholarships as they wish.

Deadline: March 1

Application Link:
https://www.sae.net/foundation/scholarship-program/

● Rotary Scholarships Grants and Fellowships

Amount: Awards up to **$26,000**

Eligibility: Clubs and districts offer scholarships for secondary, undergraduate, or graduate study. These scholarships can be supported with funds raised locally or with Rotary Foundation district or global grants. Contact your local club for application information and eligibility requirements.

Deadline: The application deadline varies from one Club/District to another.

Application Link: https://www.rotary.org/en/our-programs/scholarships

● EEqual Scholarship Awards Program

Amount: $8,000

Eligibility: Applicant is a legal resident of the 50 United States and the District of Columbia (D.C.) who is at least 16 years of age and no older than 23 years | A minimum unweighted GPA of 2.0 | Have succeeded in spite of poverty or homelessness | A graduating high school senior and have participated in activities that are helpful to others.

Deadline: March 1

Application Link: https://eequal.org/scholarships/

● Lake Erie College Twins Scholarship

Amount: $25,000 (Half tuition for each twin)

Eligibility: This full-tuition scholarship is awarded 50/50 if both students are enrolled full-time at Lake Erie College. In essence, both twins can attend Lake Erie College for the tuition of only one.

If a twin is eligible for a higher merit award, that will be given. P.S: Check the website for more details.

Deadline: Varies.

Application Link: https://www.lec.edu/financial-aid/freshman-aid/

- **Tech for Mental Health Scholarship**

Amount: $10,000

Eligibility: U.S. Citizens planning to pursue a degree at an accredited Indiana or Ohio post secondary institution | A minimum 3.8 high school GPA.

Deadline: December 1

Application Link:
https://www.arisehealthclinic.com/careers

- **Wells Fargo Scholarship Program for People with Disabilities**

Amount: $10,000

Eligibility: Applicant must have an identified disability | Be a high school senior or graduate planning to enroll, or who are already enrolled, in full – or half time undergraduate study at an accredited two or four year college or university in the United States, and have a minimum GPA of 3.0 on a 4.0 scale.

Deadline: December 15

Application Link:
https://learnmore.scholarsapply.org/pwdscholarship/

- **Tennessee Step Up Scholarship**

Amount: $10,000

Eligibility: Have been a Tennessee resident | Complete high school in a Tennessee high school | Not be ineligible for the scholarship under § 49-4-904 | Check website for detailed requirements.

Deadline: Varies year-round

Application Link:
https://www.collegefortn.org/tennessee-step-up-scholarship/

- **Raytheon Underrepresented Minorities in Cybersecurity Scholarship**

Amount: $10,000

Eligibility: Applicants must be a U.S. citizen | Belong to a historically underrepresented minority in STEM | Persons with disabilities | Have a 3.3 GPA | Be a high school senior or undergraduate pursuing a degree in cybersecurity, information security or similar field.

Deadline: May 1

Application Link:
https://www.iamcybersafe.org/s/raytheon-cyber-security-scholarship

- **Beat the Odds Scholarship Program**

Amount: $10,000

Eligibility: Applicants must be graduating high school seniors from an Oregon public high school | Have a 3.0 GPA | Plan to earn a Bachelor's degree from an accredited four year college in the United States | Demonstrate financial need.

Deadline: May 12

Application Link: https://stand.org/blog/apply-for-the-beat-the-odds-scholarship/

- **TMCF Bridging the Dream Scholarship Program for High School Seniors**

Amount: $10,000

Eligibility: Applicants must be a U.S. citizen or legal permanent resident | Be a graduating high school senior | NOT a resident of Utah or attending an accredited post secondary domestic institution in Utah. Check the website for more details.

Deadline: March 25

Application Link: https://www.tmcf.org/students-alumni/scholarship/tmcf-bridging-the-dream-scholarship-program-for-high-school-seniors/

● Autism Can Do Scholarship

Amount: $5,000

Eligibility: Applicants must be on the autism spectrum and live in the United States or Canada | Be a graduating high school senior.

Deadline: March 15

Application Link:
https://johnscrazysocks.com/blogs/news/enter-the-2023-autism-can-do-scholarship

● Komen College Scholarship Program

Amount: $10,000

Eligibility: Applicant must have lost a parent/guardian to breast cancer OR must be a breast cancer survivor diagnosed at 25 years or younger | Must be no older than 25 years old | Must be a high school senior, college freshman | Plan to attend a state-supported college or university in the state where they permanently reside | Must have a minimum high school and/or college GPA of 2.8 on a 4.0 scale | U.S. citizen, or documented permanent resident.

Deadline: October 15

Application Link:
http://tow.pub30.convio.net/grants/college-scholarships/

● Holly Scanlan Foundation Scholarship

Amount: $5,000

Eligibility: Applicant must have an immediate family member (or be the family member) with a serious cancer diagnosis | A resident of Connecticut or Minnesota entering College.

Deadline: May 31

Application Link:
http://www.hollyscanlanfoundation.org/scholarship/

● Cure Cancer Support Scholarship

Amount: $5,000

Eligibility: Applicants must be a U.S. citizen residing in the USA; demonstrate academic achievement through evidence of working to one's potential. This scholarship is designated for students who were diagnosed with cancer and whose disease and related treatments placed a significant financial burden on them and their families.

Deadline: June 1

Application Link:
https://www.petersons.com/scholarship/cure---cancer-support-scholarship-111_216161.aspx

● Northwestern Mutual Childhood Cancer Survivor

Amount: $10,000

Eligibility: Applicants must be U.S. Citizens or permanent residents | A minimum GPA of 2.5 (on a 4.0 scale) | Be pediatric cancer survivors, age 25 and under, who have been diagnosed by a physician as having had treatment for and survived cancer, or in current treatment.

Deadline: February 1

Application Link:
https://learnmore.scholarsapply.org/nmsurvivors/

● ACPA Randall/LaRossa Scholarships

Amount: $10,000

Eligibility: Have a diagnosis of cleft lip and/or cleft palate or other congenital craniofacial difference | Be enrolled full time in an accredited post secondary institution or program in the U.S during the year of the award.

Deadline: January 31

Application Link: https://acpacares.org/college-scholarships/

● The Vertex Foundation Scholarship

Amount: $5,000

Eligibility: Applicants must have been diagnosed with Cystic fibrosis (CF) | Open to all legal residents of the U.S. or Canada who are full time or part-time students in good academic standing at an accredited institution.

Deadline: February 3

Application Link:
https://www.vertexfoundation.org/healthy-families

● Anne Ford Scholarship

Amount: $10,000

Eligibility: Graduating high school senior with a documented learning disability (LD) and/or ADHD | GPA of 3.0 or higher, be US citizen.

Deadline: April 5

Application Link: https://ncld.org/scholarships-awards/anne-ford-scholarship/

Google Lime Scholarship

Amount: $10,000

Eligibility: Awarded to computer science students with disabilities | Applicants must be a
Deadline: April 30

Application Link:
https://buildyourfuture.withgoogle.com/scholarships/google-lime-scholarship

● AbbVie Cystic Fibrosis Scholarship

Amount: $25,000

Eligibility: Applicants must be U.S. citizens or a legal and permanent resident of the United States | Diagnosed with Cystic Fibrosis by a physician | Enrolled in or awaiting acceptance from an accredited institution.

Deadline: May 25

Application Link:
https://www.ncjwny.org/programs/

● NCJW NY Jackson-Stricks Scholarships

Amount: $10,000

Eligibility: Available to students with physical challenges that affect mobility, vision or hearing who are currently enrolled in an undergraduate or graduate program in the New York Metropolitan Area.

Deadline: February 29

Application Link:
https://www.ncjwny.org/programs/

● Team Type 1 Global Ambassador Scholarship Program

Amount: $10,000

Eligibility: The Applicant(s) lives with Type 1 diabetes | Attends an accredited NAIA or NCAA school and plays a sanctioned sport for that school | Would utilize their sport as a platform to inspire others with diabetes.

Deadline: March 31

Application Link:
https://www.teamtype1.org/global-ambassador-scholarship-program/

- **The Matthews & Swift Educational Trust Scholarship**

Amount: $100,000

Eligibility: Children of members in good standing who are killed or permanently disabled, by hostile action, while serving in the U.S. armed forces. | Also, the children of fulltime firefighters and law enforcement officers, who while in the lawful performance of their duties, died as a result of criminal violence directed at them.

Deadline: Varies

Application Link:
https://www.kofc.org/en/what-we-do/scholarships/educational-trust-scholarship.html

- **Salix Gastrointestinal Health Scholars Awards**

Amount: $10,000

Eligibility: Applicant must have been diagnosed with and treated for a gastrointestinal condition | United States citizen living in the United States.

Deadline: May 15

Application Link:
https://www.salix.com/scholarship/

- **UCB Family Epilepsy Scholarship**

Amount: $10,000

Eligibility: U.S. citizen or legal resident of the United States | Diagnosed with epilepsy by a physician or the immediate family member | An incoming freshman or a graduate student | Demonstrate academic and personal achievement.

Deadline: April 14

Application Link:
https://www.ucbepilepsyscholarship.com/

- **Dollars 4 Tic Scholars Tourette Syndrome Scholarship**

Amount: $5,000

Eligibility: Awarded to students who have Tourette Syndrome | Applicants must be seeking vocational education in technical fields | A minimum GPA of 2.5

Deadline: April 15

Application Link:
https://www.dollars4ticscholars.org/

- **Lighthouse Guild Scholarship Program**

Amount: $10,000

Eligibility: Applicants must provide proof of legal blindness | U.S. citizen or legal residents | Provide a documentation of academic achievement via copies of school transcripts.

Deadline: April 15

Application Link:
https://lighthouseguild.org/support-services/academic-and-career-services/scholarships/

- **Microsoft Disability Scholarship**

Amount: $20,000 (**$5000** for 4 years)

Eligibility: High school seniors living with a disability who plan to study engineering, computer science, business, law, or related fields at a two- or four-year college/university/technical school | Must have a 2.5 GPA or higher and demonstrate financial need.

Deadline: March 15

Application Link:
https://www.kofc.org/en/what-we-do/scholarships/educational-trust-scholarship.html

● CLT Scholarships

Amount: Awards up to **$30,000**

Eligibility: The CLT is the new standard for college entrance exams and standardized testing. Over 150+ CLT partner colleges tie scholarship dollars directly to CLT scores. If you score in the top 50% of CLT test-takers, you're eligible to win up to $30,000.

Deadline: April 5

Application Link:
https://www.cltexam.com/scholarships/

● Alabama Golf Association Women's Scholarship Fund

Amount: $20,000 ($5,000 per year)

Eligibility: A female bona fide resident of the state of Alabama | A high school graduate entering college | Demonstrate financial need | Have an interest in the game of Golf.

Deadline: March 2

Application Link:
https://www.alabamagolf.org/aga-womens-scholarship-information/

● Corvias Foundation Scholarship for Children of Active-Duty Service Members

Amount: Awards up to **$50,000**

Eligibility: High school seniors or students between the ages of 16 – 19 | Must be a child of an active-duty service members and plan to attend an accredited four year college or university | A minimum high school GPA of 3.0

Deadline: February 15

Application Link:
https://www.corvias.com/news/corvias-foundations-2022-scholarship-applications-open-military-spouses-and-children-active

● Executive Women International Scholarship Program

Amount: $10,000

Eligibility: High school seniors enrolled in a public, private, charter or parochial school located within the boundaries of a participating EWI Chapter or persons who are homeschooled | A minimum 3.0 GPA on a (4.0 scale) | Demonstrate financial need.

Deadline: March 15

Application Link:
https://ewiconnect.com/page/scholarships

● Dorrance Scholarship

Amount: $48,000 ($12,000 per year)

Eligibility: Applicants must be high school seniors who are Arizona residents, first-generation college students, admitted to one of Arizona's three residential public universities | Demonstrate financial need | A minimum high school GPA of 3.0, SAT 1110 or ACT 22.

Deadline: February 1

Application Link:
https://dorrancescholarship.org/

● SVCF Bright Futures Scholarship

Amount: $10,000

Eligibility: Graduating high school seniors residing in California | A minimum cumulative GPA of 2.0 | Planning to enroll at a two-or four year institution in the fall.

Deadline: February 28

Application Link:
https://www.siliconvalleycf.org/scholarships/the-bright-futures-scholarship

- **California Hispanic Education Endowment Fund (HEEF)**

Amount: $10,000

Eligibility: Open to students pursuing educational goals. HEEF embraces undocumented students and provides a range of scholarships considering financial need, academic excellence, and involvement in extracurricular activities, community service, work experience, and home life. P.S: Check the website for more details.

Deadline: December 31

Application Link: https://www.heef.org/

- **Richard J. Bea Nursing Scholarship**

Amount: Awards up to **$7,500**

Eligibility: Applicant must be a resident of the Grossmont Healthcare District (and have been so for a minimum of one year) | Have graduated from a high school within the Grossmont Healthcare District. P.S: Check the website for more details.

Deadline: February 2

Application Link:
https://www.grossmonthealthcare.org/community/scholarships/richard-j-bea-nursing-scholarship/

- **Colorado Masons' Benevolent Fund Scholarships**

Amount: $28,000 ($7,000 per year)

Eligibility: Applicant must be a graduating senior in a public high school in Colorado and must attend an institution of higher learning within the state of Colorado.

Deadline: March 7

Application Link:
https://grandlodgeofcolorado.org/

- **Grossman Scholarship Program**

Amount: $10,000

Eligibility: Applicant must be a Colorado resident | Has demonstrated a commitment to caring for our environment's natural resources within their personal, educational, or professional time | Intend to pursue post-secondary education through an accredited environmental, natural resource, climate, or outdoor industry related education program in Colorado.

Deadline: March 26

Application Link:
https://www.voc.org/grossman-scholarship

- **Roothbert Fund Scholarships**

Amount: Undergraduates who have completed at least 1 year of study, preference will be given to those who can satisfy high scholastic requirements and are considering careers in education. Preference is given to candidates who reside in or attend schools in certain states. P.S: Check the website for more details.

Deadline: February 1

Application Link:
https://www.roothbertfund.org/scholarships

- **UNICO Scholarship Program**

Amount: $10,000

Eligibility: The applicant must reside in or have a UNICO Chapter/District sponsor who reside in specific states | U.S. citizens | A 3.0 minimum GPA

P.S: Check the website for more details.

Deadline: April 15

Application Link:
https://accessscholarships.com/scholarship/unico-foundation-scholarships/

- **Herman M. Holloway, Sr. Memorial Scholarship**

Amount: $28,150 (covers full tuition)

Eligibility: Applicants must reside in Delaware; be a legal U.S. resident; a graduating high school senior | A minimum 3.0 GPA; SAT composite score of 1000 or an equivalent ACT composite score.

Deadline: February 20

Application Link: https://education.delaware.gov/families/college-career-life/college-scholarship-financial-aid/

- **Sunshine Opportunity Scholarships**

Amount: $25,000

Eligibility: Applicant must have a GPA of 3.0 or higher; must have overcome significant obstacles in life and must attend public or private high schools in specific geographic areas of Florida, South Carolina and North Carolina | Demonstrate financial need.

Deadline: March 2

Application Link: https://sunshineopportunityscholarships.com/

- **ROJ Postsecondary Scholarship**

Amount: $10,000

Eligibility: Open to all Pinellas County High School seniors with an expected spring graduation or equivalent. Applications are evaluated by the CFY Scholarship Committee based on a variety of criteria including extracurricular activity, community service, and an essay.

Deadline: January 15

Application Link: https://cfypinellas.org/scholarships/

- **C. Valentine Bates Memorial Hope Scholarship**

Amount: $20,000

Eligibility: Applicant must be a high school senior attending school in Florida | GPA between 2.30 – 3.59 | U.S. citizen | Demonstrate financial need.

P.S: Preference is given to students who have shouldered extra responsibilities such as working throughout their high school career to help provide support for siblings or family.

Deadline: January 12

Application Link: https://www.floridaelks.org/hope-scholarship

- **Watson Brown Foundation Scholarships**

Amount: $6,000

Eligibility: Awarded to select Georgia and South Carolina students attending accredited four year colleges and universities in the United States | Graduating high school seniors and current undergraduate students may apply for the scholarship.

Deadline: February 8

Application Link: https://watson-brown.org/scholarship/

- **Greenhouse Scholars Whole Person College Program**

Amount: $20,000

Eligibility: U.S. citizen, a permanent resident and a legal resident of California, Colorado, Georgia, Illinois, New York or North Carolina.

P.S: Check the website for more details.

Deadline: November 21

Application Link: https://greenhousescholars.org/our-program/

● Hawaii Pacific University Esports Scholarship

Amount: $24,000

Eligibility: Awarded to a select number of incoming undergraduate students interested in joining Hawaii Pacific University's eSports team. Only those who have submitted both a complete admissions application and a eSports scholarship application will be considered.

Deadline: May 1

Application Link:
https://www.hpu.edu/esports/index.html

● Idaho Governor's Cup Scholarship

Amount: $20,000

Eligibility: Applicant must be a resident of Idaho | A graduating senior of an Idaho high school or home school | A minimum cumulative GPA of 2.8 | Applicant must write a 500-word personal essay about your goals and interests.

Deadline: March 1

Application Link:
https://boardofed.idaho.gov/scholarships/idaho-governors-cup-scholarship/

● Principia College Scholarships

Amount: Ranges from $14,000 - $24,000

Eligibility: Open to incoming freshmen admitted into Principia College | A minimum 3.9 GPA, 26 ACT / 1240 SAT. Scholarship decisions are made at the time of admittance, which means you will receive a scholarship decision alongside your admittance letter.

Deadline: January 15

Application Link:
https://www.principiacollege.edu/admissions/scholarships

● Next Generation Hoosier Educators Scholarship

Amount: $40,000 ($10,000 per year) – In exchange, students agree to teach for five years at an eligible Indiana school or **repay** the corresponding, prorated amount of the scholarship.

Eligibility: Applicant must be an Indiana resident, a U.S. citizen or eligible non-citizen | Rank in the top 20% of high school graduating class | Have a top 20% ACT or SAT score; or a minimum cumulative GPA of 3.0 (4.0 scale)

Deadline: January 31

Application Link:
https://www.indstate.edu/financial-aid/next-gen

● Hagan Scholarship Foundation

Amount: $60,000

Eligibility: Applicant must be a U.S. citizen, attending a traditional public high school located in the U.S. that is governed by a school district | A minimum GPA of 3.50 | Must enrol at an eligible four-year college or university the first semester following high school graduation.

Deadline: December 1

Application Link: https://haganscholarships.org/

● Phillips University Legacy Foundation Scholarship

Amount: $34,000 ($8,500 per year)

Eligibility: Applicant must be well rounded, with a proven track record of academic success, involvement, and leadership roles in their schools and the broader community | Be incoming first-year college students.

Deadline: March 21

Application Link:
https://pulf.secure2.agroup.com/undergraduate-program/

- **Logan Thomas Family Memorial Scholarship**

Amount: $20,000

Eligibility: Awarded to high school seniors attending Lee County high school in Beattyville, Kentucky who demonstrate financial need and have a cumulative GPA of 3.0 or higher. Students must attend a college or university within the state of Kentucky.

Deadline: March 4

Application Link:
https://www.bgcf.org/scholarships-available/

- **McNeese State University Freshman Academic Scholarships**

Amount: $28,000

Eligibility: Applicant must be an incoming freshman at McNeese State University | High test scores (SAT/ACT), an above average GPA and class standing.

Deadline: March 1

Application Link:
https://www.mcneese.edu/scholarships/freshman_academic_scholarships/

- **Grambling Technology Scholarship**

Amount: Awards up to **$30,000**

Eligibility: Open to incoming freshmen who have intent or interest in majoring in cyber security, computer science, computer information systems, and engineering technology | A minimum high school GPA of 3.0. Applicants are expected to write a 500 word essay about their career goals.

Deadline: January 14

Application Link:
https://www.gram.edu/news/index.php/technology-scholars-tour/

- **Richard H. Pierce Memorial Scholarship**

Amount: $20,000

Eligibility: Applicants must be Maine residents entering their first year of a post secondary education | Academic excellence demonstrated by the content of the applicant's transcript and GPA | Demonstrated financial need | Contributions to school, community and/or work environment.

Deadline: April 1

Application Link:
https://www.famemaine.com/scholarships/the-richard-h-pierce-memorial-scholarship/

- **Worthington Scholarship**

Amount: $20,000

Eligibility: Applicant must be a U.S. citizen | A Maine resident | A graduating senior at one of the participating high schools with plans to enrol full time at one of the partner colleges or universities.

Deadline: April 15

Application Link:
https://worthingtonscholars.org/

- **Center for Women in Technology (CWIT) Scholars Program at UMBC**

Amount: Award ranges from **$5,000 - $15,000** per year for in-state students, and from **$10,000 - $22,000** per year for out-of-state students.

Eligibility: This merit based scholarship program is designed for talented incoming female undergraduates majoring in computer science, information systems, business technology administration, computer engineering...

Deadline: January 15

Application Link:
https://cwit.umbc.edu/cwitscholars/

- **Association for Iron and Steel Technology Scholarships**

Amount: $12,000

Eligibility: Awarded to incoming students majoring in engineering, engineering technology, computer science, data science, safety or industrial hygiene programs | Minimum cumulative GPA of 2.5 on a 4.0 scale | Applicants must be a citizen of an USMCA country (USA, Canada, Mexico)

Deadline: October 2

Application Link:
https://www.aist.org/students-faculty/scholarships/

- **Henry David Thoreau Scholarship Program**

Amount: $25,000

Eligibility: Applicant must be a resident of Massachusetts and be in your final year at a Massachusetts high school | Demonstrate strong academic qualifications and a commitment to an environmental field.

Deadline: February 1

Application Link:
https://www.thoreauscholar.org/undergraduate-scholarships/application

- **The Martha's Vineyard Community Foundation Scholarships**

Amount: Awards up to **$15,000**

Eligibility: The goal of this scholarship is to put charitable contributions to work for the people of Martha's Vineyard by making grants that address community priorities; funding scholarships…

Deadline: March 15

Application Link:
https://marthasvineyardcf.org/scholarships/scholarship-funds/

- **Massport Memorial and Diversity STEM Scholarships**

Amount: $5,000

Eligibility: Applicants must be graduating minority high school seniors from the city of Boston or Massports Neighboring Communities | A 3.0 minimum high school GPA | Must be interested in pursuing a degree in areas of study including Aviation, business administration, accounting, architecture, engineering, finance, and human resource.

Deadline: April 30

Application Link:
https://www.massport.com/community/scholarships-and-internships

- **Gerber Foundation Medallion Scholarship**

Amount: $11,500

Eligibility: Applicant must be a U.S. citizen or lawful permanent resident of the U.S and planning to attend a college, University or post-secondary program within the U.S | Graduating from select high schools in Newaygo, Muskegon, or Oceana Counties in West Michigan.

Deadline: February 28

Application Link:
https://www.gerberfoundation.org/scholarships-programs/

- **National Cherry Queen Program**

Amount: $12,500

Eligibility: Young women between the ages of 19-25. Check the website for more details.

Deadline: May 15

Application Link:
https://www.cherryfestival.org/p/other/national-cherry-queen-program

- **Catch a Break! Scholarship**

Amount: $44,000 ($11,000 per year**)**

Eligibility: This scholarship program was established to assist highly motivated Minnesota residents who have faced challenges in life and learned from them, and are now enrolling for the first time in post-secondary education | A minimum ACT composite score of 24

Deadline: March 31

Application Link:
https://catchabreakscholar.org/

- **Jennings Scholarship**

Amount: Awards up to **$10,000**

Eligibility: Graduating high school students planning to enroll in a post-secondary education | This scholarship program was designed to provide opportunities for students who had demonstrated achievement in anti fraud related studies.

Deadline: February 5

Application Link:
https://www.acfe.com/scholarship.aspx

- **Tupelo Elvis Fan Club Scholarship**

Amount: $5,000

Eligibility: Applicant must be a resident of Mississippi and enrolled as a senior at a Mississippi high school | You must sing, dance, or play a musical instrument and submit a performance video for review by the selection committee by uploading to YouTube (Do NOT mail in DVDs)

Check the website for more details.

Deadline: February 14

Application Link:
https://www.tupeloelvisfestival.com/scholarships

- **Jimmy Rane Foundation Scholarship**

Amount: $5,000

Eligibility: Graduating high school senior (including homeschooled students/GED recipients) or full-time college freshmen (no older than 20 years of age) | A minimum GPA of 3.0 for graduating high school seniors or 2.75 for college applicants.

Deadline: February 8

Application Link:
https://www.jimmyranefoundation.org/

- **Build Your Dreams Scholarship**

Amount: $5,000

Eligibility: Applicants of the Build Your Dreams Scholarship must submit an essay that describes how they have chosen their career path for life after high school, and explain how winning this scholarship will assist in their goals.

P.S: There are no lengthy requirements required. Check the website for more information.

Deadline: January 15

Application Link:
https://performanceeyecare.com/scholarship/

- **Boeing Engineering Internship Program**

Amount: $15,000

Eligibility: Boeing provides internship opportunities in careers such as Engineering, Business, IT, and Data Analytics. When you join the internship program, you'll grow skills, create lasting connections and work on projects and products that few industries can match.

Deadline: Varies by location.

Application Link:
https://jobs.boeing.com/internships

● Davis Memorial Foundation Scholarship

Amount: $5,000

Eligibility: Applicants of the Davis Memorial Foundation Scholarship must be provisionally accepted as students into undergraduate or graduate degree programs for the coming academic year by accredited colleges, universities or vocational education programs | Residents of the states covered in the WSRCA service area.

Deadline: April 21

Application Link:
https://wsrca.com/mpage/home

● NEHRA's Diversity and Inclusion Scholarship

Amount: $7,500

Eligibility: Applicant must be a graduating high school senior with proven academic success (High test scores and GPA) and dedication to positive impact.

Deadline: February 17

Application Link:
https://www.nehra.com/page/AnnualScholarship

● Adventure Ted Scholars Program

Amount: $16,000

Eligibility: Applicants must be individuals living in the state of New Jersey who have previously battled or are currently battling cancer or a hematological disorder | Complete the Adventurer Application and create an Instagram post responding to the prompts on the post.

Deadline: May 8

Application Link:
https://www.childhoodcancersociety.org/adventure-ted-program/

● NYWICI Scholarship Program

Amount: $10,000

Eligibility: Applicants must be pursuing a career/major in the field of communications | Must reside in New York, New Jersey, Connecticut, or Pennsylvania or go to college or university in one of those states.

Deadline: February 28

Application Link:
https://nywici.org/advance/students/scholarships/

● Herb it Forward Scholarship

Amount: $5,000

Eligibility: Applicants must be residents of Philadelphia, Pennsylvania, or the Greater Philadelphia Area, who are applying to or are students of accredited programs at colleges, vocational, or technical schools anywhere in the United States | Must be 17-21 years of age | Graduating high school seniors or home schooled students, or those who previously graduated high school or completed home-schooling.

Deadline: February 4

Application Link: https://www.herbie.com/hif-scholarship/

● Dayton-Montgomery County Scholarship Fund

Amount: $20,000

Eligibility: Applicant must be Pell Grant eligible | GPA – 3.0 or higher | Senior graduating from a participating Montgomery County high school | Resident of Montgomery County | Plan to attend an accredited college or university.

Deadline: March 15

Application Link:
https://dmcsp.org/scholarship/

- **Ron Brown Scholar Program**

Amount: $40,000 ($10,000 per year)

Eligibility: Applicants MUST be Black/African American, U.S. citizens or permanent residents, and a current high school senior at the time of their application.

Deadline: December 1

Application Link: https://ronbrown.org/

- **Smith Diversity Scholarship**

Amount: $100,000 ($25,000 per year)

Eligibility: Applicant must be a graduating Nebraska high school senior living in Nebraska | Annual household income should be less than $65,000 | Students from marginalized racial and ethnic groups are encouraged to apply.

Deadline: February 28

Application Link: https://www.onelfs.org/sds/

- **Jackie Robinson Foundation Scholarship**

Amount: Awards up to **$35,000**

Eligibility: Applicant must be a graduating minority high school senior | U.S. citizen demonstrating evidence of financial need | Demonstrate a record of academic excellence

Deadline: January 10

Application Link: https://jackierobinson.org/apply/

- **ELC Scholarship Program**

Amount: Awards up to **$60,000**

Eligibility: High achieving Black students.

Deadline: January 15

Application Link: https://elcscholars.com/scholarships/

- **Architecture Foundation Diversity Advancement Scholarship**

Amount: $20,000

Eligibility: Applicants must be a U.S. citizen or permanent resident | A high school student planning to enroll in a NAAB-accredited architecture degree program. P.S: Applications from Minority students are prioritized.

Deadline: January 19

Application Link: https://architectsfoundation.org/our-programs/architecture-scholarships/the-diversity-advancement-scholarship/

- **Advantage Iowa Award**

Amount: $32,000

Eligibility: Applicants must be students that are from historically underrepresented populations (Alaskan Native, American Indian/Native American, Black/African American, Hispanic/Latinx, Native Hawaiian or other Pacific Islander, two or more underrepresented races) at the University of Iowa or participation in a federally funded Upward Bound Program.

Deadline: December 15

Application Link: https://risefirst.org/resources/resource-directory/advantage-iowa-award

- **UNCF Edna Blum Scholarship**

Amount: $5,000

Eligibility: Applicant must be an African-American residing in New York City with an unmet financial need | U.S. citizen or permanent resident.

Deadline: March 1

Application Link: https://uncf.org/the-latest/scholarships-for-february-at-uncf

- **Fontana Transport Inc. Scholars Program**

Amount: $5,000

Eligibility: Applicants do not have to be U.S. citizen, but they must have a minimum 3.5 weighted GPA and graduate a US high school in Spring or Summer | First generation high school seniors who are underrepresented, need financial assistance and are passionate about furthering their education.

Deadline: March 14

Application Link: https://www.cfnc.org/pay-for-college/scholarship-search/fontana-transport-inc-scholars-program/

- **University of Washington Diversity Scholarship**

Amount: $40,000

Eligibility: High achieving high need students entering the University of Washington as freshmen from communities that are traditionally underserved in education | Washington resident | Demonstrate financial need. P.S: Check the website for more details.

Deadline: January 15

Application Link: https://admit.washington.edu/costs/scholarships/

- **Blacks at Microsoft Scholarship**

Amount: $20,000 ($5,000 per year)

Eligibility: Applicants must be high school seniors of African descent (e.g., African-American, African, or Ethiopian) | Plan to pursue a bachelor's degree in engineering, computer science, computer information systems, or select business programs.

Deadline: January 10

Application Link: https://www.microsoft.com/en-us/diversity/programs/bam-scholarship.aspx

- **Sachs Foundation Undergraduate Scholarship**

Amount: $40,000 - $50,000 ($10,000 - $12,500 per year)

Eligibility: A Black high school student in their senior year | A full-time Colorado resident for a minimum of three years. Residence due to military orders to Colorado may be accepted on a case-by-case basis.

Deadline: March 15

Application Link: https://www.sachsfoundation.org/undergraduate-scholarships/

- **Reverend Pinckney Scholarship**

Amount: $40,000 ($10,000 per year)

Eligibility: African American high school seniors entering college from Beaufort, Charleston and Jasper counties | demonstrate financial need | Good academic performance.

Deadline: March 15

Application Link: https://coastalcommunityfoundation.org/grants-scholarships/reverend-pinckney-college-readiness-scholars-programs/

- **The Dawna J Colbert and John Fitzpatrick Scholarship**

Amount: $10,000

Eligibility: Applicants must be Black Female high school seniors who will be attending a two or four-year institution majoring in technology and computing | Applicants must be a resident of Delaware, New York, New Jersey, Pennsylvania or Washington D.C.

Deadline: March 1

Application Link: https://uncf.org/the-latest/scholarships-for-february-at-uncf

Saint Robert Bellarmine Fund Scholarship

Amount: $32,000 (**$8,000** per year)

Eligibility: Catholic students who plan on attending a Catholic university/college that is listed on the Newman Guide | Students who are looking to use their gifts for the sake of building up the Kingdom of God are encouraged to apply.

Deadline: January 31

Application Link: https://www.saintrobertbellarminefund.org/apply

Dr. James Earl Massey Intercultural Leadership Scholarship

Amount: $40,000 (**$10,000** per year)

Eligibility: First time entering freshmen | A minimum high school GPA of 2.75 | Application and essay are required. P.S: Check the website for more details.

Deadline: February 1

Application Link: https://anderson.edu/blog-stories/massey-scholarship/

University of Dayton First-year Merit Scholarships

Amount: $124,000 (**$31,000** per year)

Eligibility: Applicants must be entering freshmen | Scholarships are awarded based on a variety of criteria including GPA, test scores (if submitted) and academic rigor.

Deadline: February 15

Application Link: https://udayton.edu/affordability/undergraduate/types-of-aid/scholarships/merit.php

Pepperdine University Helen Young Scholarship

Amount: $20,000 (**$5,000** per year)

Eligibility: Applicants must be entering freshmen | A current active member of a Church of Christ Congregation | This scholarship desires to strengthen churches by financially supporting Christian students at Pepperdine University in their education and spiritual walk.

Deadline: November 1

Application Link: https://seaver.pepperdine.edu/admission/financial-aid/undergraduate/assistance/plp-scholarship.htm

Cynthia H. Kuo Scholarship

Amount: $5,000

Eligibility: Applicants must be Chinese students who are either first-generation in the U.S. or born overseas, planning to attend a four-year college in the U.S. on a full time basis | Graduating high school seniors or current college students | A minimum GPA of 3.0 on a 4.0 scale.

Deadline: March 25

Application Link: https://www.siliconvalleycf.org/scholarships/cynthia-h-kuo-scholarship

National Association of the Church of God Scholarship

Amount: Awards Full tuition for four years.

Eligibility: Applicants must be an existing member of the National Association of the Church of God prior to applying for this scholarship | Must be an entering freshman admitted to Anderson University.

Deadline: February 1

Application Link: https://anderson.edu/start-your-story/nachog/

• Dr. Abdus Saleem Family Scholarship

Amount: $10,000

Eligibility: Entering freshman in College | GPA of 3.5 or higher | Majoring in the areas, but not limited to medical technology, oil and energy, computer science, journalism, or business administration | U.S. citizen or permanent residency.

Deadline: March 1

Application Link: https://isna.net/dr-abdus-saleem-family-scholarship/

• Diller Teen Tikkun Olam Award

Amount: $36,000

Eligibility: This award honors Jewish teens who demonstrate remarkable leadership and engagement in community service projects that embody the values of tikkun olam – "Repairing the world" | Teens (13 – 19 years old) who self-identify as Jewish and live in the United States.

Deadline: January 5

Application Link: https://dillerteenawards.org/

• JFLA Brawerman Fellowship

Amount: $40,000 (**$10,000** per year)

Eligibility: Applicants must be Jewish graduating seniors who are entering freshmen at an accredited four-year college/university | Residents of Los Angeles County | A minimum GPA of 3.5 | Demonstrate financial need, P.S: Check the website for more details.

Deadline: February 15

Application Link: https://www.jewishla.org/program/brawerman-fellowship/

• JCF Gail Karp Orgell Scholarship

Amount: $7,000

Eligibility: Applicants must be Jewish female high school seniors or graduates who are beginning their first year of an undergraduate program at a four-year college or university in California | A minimum cumulative high school GPA of 3.5 (on a 4.0 scale) | Applicants must have a permanent resident in the greater San Francisco Bay Area.

Check the website for more details.

Deadline: March 31

Application Link: https://jewishfed.org/how-we-help/scholarships/college-scholarships

• JCF Helen B. Lewis E. Goldstein Scholarship

Amount: $10,000

Eligibility: Applicants must be Jewish high school seniors or graduates who are planning to enroll or already enrolled in a full-time undergraduate program | Demonstrate financial need | Preference will be given to someone enrolled in a professional school such as a law school, business, or library/information science.

Deadline: March 31

Application Link: https://jewishfed.org/how-we-help/scholarships/college-scholarships

• Valparaiso University Ed Voelz Endowed Scholarship

Amount: Ranges from **$5,000** to **$7,000** per year.

Eligibility: Graduates of St. Peter's Lutheran School in Columbus, IN | Applicants must complete undergraduate admission application.

Deadline: January 15

Application Link: https://www.valpo.edu/student-financial-services/planning/scholarships/lutheran/

- **Foot Locker Scholar Athletes Program**

Amount: $20,000

Eligibility: Freshman entering college by fall, currently involved in high school sports, intramural sports, or community based sports | Have a minimum GPA of 3.0 | A U.S. citizen or permanent legal resident.

Deadline: January 20

Application Link:
https://www.footlockerscholarathletes.com/

- **Brad Fowler Memorial Scholarship**

Amount: $12,000 + Laptop Computer

Eligibility: San Diego County high school senior entering college, currently involved in high school sports, Intramural sports, or community based sports | Overcome personal obstacle relating to drug/alcohol | No minimum GPA.

Deadline: February 17

Application Link:
https://sandiegosportsassociation.com/project/bfms/

- **The Scott and Kim Verplank Foundation Scholarships**

Amount: $40,000 ($10,000 annually)

Eligibility: High School Senior | Diagnosed with Type 1 Diabetes | Active athletics organization in an organized team| Minimum of 3.0 GPA | A U.S. citizen.

Deadline: April 15

Application Link:
https://verplankfoundation.com/scholarships/

- **USBC Youth Scholarships**

Amount: $5,000 - $6,000

Eligibility: High school senior/College student who competes in sport of bowling entering | Non-professional USBC member.

Deadline: Check the application portal.

Application Link:
https://bowl.com/youth/scholarships-and-awards/usbc-youth-scholarships

- **Gen.G Foundation Scholarship**

Amount: $10,000

Eligibility: All college students interested in gaming, esports, entrepreneurship, journalism, content creation| Both U.S. & international students.

Deadline: October 2

Application Link:
https://geng.gg/pages/foundation

- **The LPGA Foundation Scholarships**

Amount: $10,000

Eligibility: Female high school senior, who participates in Golf | Check the website for other requirements (There are 5 different scholarships).

Deadline: January 31

Application Link:
https://www.girlsgolf.org/about/scholarships

CMP Scholarship

Amount: $20,000

Eligibility: High school seniors who participate in firearms marksmanship competitions| Have a letter of recommendation | A U.S. citizen.

Deadline: March 31

Application Link:
https://thecmp.org/youth/cmp-scholarship-program/

Charles B. Staats Memorial Scholarship

Amount: $10,000

Eligibility: Graduating high school senior who is also a swim coach| One swimming reference letter; A minimum GPA of 3.0.

Deadline: May 27

Application Link:
https://www.cbsmf.org/scholarship.html

PGA WORKS John & Tamara Lundgren Scholars Program

Amount: $32,000 (**$8,000** annually)

Eligibility: High School Seniors/graduates | Pursue a PGA Golf Management degree at one of the 17 accredited PGA Golf Management Universities.

Deadline: February 6

Application Link:
https://www.pgareach.org/pgaworks/scholarship

Women's Western Golf Foundation Scholarship

Amount: $20,000

Eligibility: Female high school senior| Active participant in golf | 3.5/4.0 GPA | Outstanding character and leadership.

Deadline: March 4

Application Link:
https://www.wwga.org/scholarships

U.S. Tennis Association Foundation Scholarships

Amount: $15,000 & More

Eligibility: High school seniors who participate in organized youth tennis programs| Good academic standing.

Deadline: Check the website for more details.

Application Link:
https://www.ustafoundation.com/scholarship_opportunities/

Druid Hills Golf Club Foundations Wayne Reynolds Scholarship

Amount: $12,000

Eligibility: Graduate of a Georgia high school senior, who participates in Golf | Legal resident of Georgia | GPA of 2.5 or more & an ACT/SAT score at or above national average.

Deadline: April 29

Application Link:
https://www.dhgc.org/club/scripts/library/view_document.asp?NS=PUBLIC&DN=REYNOLDS

Francis Ouimet Scholarship Fund

Amount: $60,000

Eligibility: High school seniors or college students who have performed 2+ years service to golf as caddies, or in golf professional or course superintendent operations at any golf course in Massachusetts | Have financial need.

Deadline: December 1.

Application Link: https://www.ouimet.org/how-to-apply/

Heisman High School Scholarship

Amount: $10,000

Eligibility: A weighted GPA of 3.0 (B average) or better | Proven leadership ability | Applicants must participate or have participated in grades 9, 10, or 11 in at least one of the sports recognized by the International Olympic Committee in the Summer and Winter Olympic Games, the Paralympic Games or the National Federation of State High School Associations.

Deadline: 17 October

Application Link: https://heismanscholarship.com/about/how-it-works/

NCAA Division I Degree Completion Award Program

Amount: Cost of tuition plus more…

Eligibility: Student athlete who has exhausted athletics eligibility at an NCAA Division I member institution | Has received athletics-related financial aid | Check the link for other requirements.

Deadline: Varies

Application Link: https://www.ncaa.org/sports/2013/11/21/ncaa-division-i-degree-completion-award-program.aspx

NCAA Division II Degree Completion Award Program

Amount: Cost of tuition and more.

Eligibility: Student athlete who has exhausted athletics eligibility at an NCAA Division II member institution | Has received athletics-related financial aid | Check the website for more details.

Deadline: Varies

Application Link: https://www.ncaa.org/sports/2013/11/21/division-ii-degree-completion-award-program.aspx

More Information About Athletics Scholarships

- How to Get Recruited
- How do you know if you're eligible for an athletic scholarship?
- Can an athletic scholarship be taken away?
- Recruiting myths
- Athletic scholarship facts

Get Full Information Here:

❑ https://www.ncsasports.org/recruiting/how-to-get-recruited/scholarship-facts

❑ https://www.ncaa.org/sports/2014/10/6/scholarships.aspx

- **The Kim and Harold Louie Family Foundation Scholarship Program**

Amount: $10,000

Eligibility: Un-weighted GPA between 3.7 and 4.0| Minimum SAT of 1300/ACT of 27 (State if you did not take the tests) | Have at least two reference letters from teachers.

Deadline: March 17

Application Link:
https://www.louiefamilyfoundation.org/scholarship-application

- **Black Future Foundation Scholarship**

Amount: $5,000

Eligibility: Black or African-American with a minimum GPA of 3.2 on a 4.0 scale | Residency in the United States; High School Senior; Planning to enroll full-time, in a four-year degree program, at a US accredited, not-for-profit, private or public college or university.

Deadline: January 31

Application Link:
https://sandiegosportsassociation.com/project/bfms/

- **DAR Leo W. and Alberta V. Thomas Utz Scholarship – English**

Amount: $16,000

Eligibility: Scholar with a minimum of 3.24/4.0 GPA, who will be majoring in English.

Deadline: January 31

Application Link: https://www.dar.org/national-society/scholarships/scholarships-1

- **GE-Reagan Foundation Scholarship Program**

Amount: $40,000

Eligibility: U.S. High school seniors with a minimum of 3.0/4.0 GPA | Demonstrate leadership, integrity, drive, and citizenship | Be a U.S. Citizens.

Deadline: January 4

Application Link:
https://www.reaganfoundation.org/education/scholarship-programs/ge-reagan-foundation-scholarship-program/

- **Prudential Emerging Visionaries**

Amount: $15,000

Eligibility: Participants must be individuals between the ages of 14 – 18 | Must be legal residents of the United States or Puerto Rico.

Deadline: November 2

Application Link:
https://www.prudential.com/links/about/emergingvisionaries

- **EPP/MSI Undergraduate Scholarship Program**

Amount: $45,000

Eligibility: Current undergraduate majoring in a STEM field | Students attending Minority Serving Colleges/Universities | At least 3.2/4.0 GPA | Be a U.S. Citizen.

Deadline: January 31

Application Link:
https://www.noaa.gov/office-education/epp-msi/undergraduate-scholarship

- **The Maude and Alexander Hadden Scholarship**

Amount: $20,000

Eligibility: A minimum unweighted GPA of 3.5 on a 4.0 scale | Must be a U.S. Citizen | Demonstrate financial need.

Deadline: March 15

Application Link: http://youth-foundation.org/application/guidelines/

- **Great Khalid Foundation Performing Arts Scholarship**

Amount: $10,000

Eligibility: Minimum of 3.5 GPA | Applicant must Major in Performing Arts | A video performance.

Deadline: March 31

Application Link: https://thegreatkhalidfoundation.org/performing-arts-scholarship

- **Wealth by Health Steps for Change Scholarship**

Amount: $8,000

Eligibility: High school senior with a minimum of 3.5 GPA | Legal resident of the U.S. | Have financial need.

Deadline: May 1

Application Link: https://www.wealthbyhealth.org/steps-for-change-scholarship

- **Licensing International's Scholarship Program**

Amount: $10,000

Eligibility: Scholars interested in a career in brand licensing seeking education in business, e-commerce, marketing, design, engineering, entrepreneurial studies and other brand licensing industry-related programs.

Deadline: January 26

Application Link: https://licensinginternational.org/about/scholarship-program/

- **Harold Johnson Law Enforcement Scholarship**

Amount: $5,000

Eligibility: Students who plan to pursue a career in police work, corrections or other criminal justice fields| Minimum of 2.5/4.0 GPA | Attending or attended high school in the greater San Francisco Bay Area or surrounding areas.

Deadline: February 28

Application Link: https://www.siliconvalleycf.org/scholarships/the-harold-johnson-law-enforcement-scholarship

- **USRA Distinguished Undergraduate Awards**

Amount: $5,000

Eligibility: U.S. citizen or permanent resident and have a minimum cumulative GPA of 3.5

Deadline: August 9

Application Link: https://www.usra.edu/educational-activities-and-opportunities/usra-distinguished-undergraduate-awards

• FSF CASE STUDY SCHOLARSHIP

Amount: $7,500

Eligibility: A minimum of 3.20 GPA | Must be enrolled in a FSF member school | Check website for other requirements.

Deadline: March 15.

Application Link:
https://www.fashionscholarshipfund.org/fsf-case-study-scholarship

• WSIA Derek Hughes Scholarship Program

Amount: $5,000

Eligibility: A minimum of 3.20 GPA | Must be enrolled in college and pursuing a degree in Insurance or business-related program of study.

Deadline: March 5

Application Link:
https://www.wsia.org/wcm/Foundation/Scholarships

• IFMA Foundation Scholarship Program

Amount: $10,000

Eligibility: Undergraduate students enrolled in facility management-related degrees | Have a minimum of 3.2 GPA | Required to attend IFMA's World Workplace Conference.

Deadline: May 2

Application Link:
https://foundation.ifma.org/students-academics/scholarships/

• STEM Stars Actuarial Scholars Program

Amount: $20,000

Eligibility: High school senior/College-bound | Must have a minimum overall GPA of 3.0, or SAT Math: 600+ or ACT 21+ and demonstrate an acumen in Math.

Deadline: April 10

Application Link:
https://actuarialfoundation.org/scholarships/stem-stars/

• IIAR/NRF Founders Scholarship program

Amount: $9,000

Eligibility: A minimum GPA of 3.0 | Must be already enrolled in college and pursuing a STEM degree and completed a specified credit hours.

Deadline: May 31

Application Link:
https://www.iiar.org/arf/ARF_Scholarship/ARF_IIAR_Scholarship.aspx

• NAMI Merit Scholarship

Amount: $5,000 - $10,000

Eligibility: Undergraduates studying Meat or Poultry Science, Animal Science or Culinary Arts and Science | Excellent academic standing is also required.

Deadline: June 14

Application Link:
https://meatscholars.org/

- **Spencer Educational Scholarships**

Amount: $10,000

Eligibility: Scholar must be enrolled in college | Must seek a career in Risk Management, Insurance or Actuarial Science | Be of good academic and extracurricular standing.

Deadline: January 1

Application Link:
https://www.spencered.org/scholarships

- **Ernest F. Hollings Undergraduate Scholarship**

Amount: $19,000 + Other benefits.

Eligibility: A minimum GPA of 3.0 | U.S. Citizen | Currently enrolled in a college/university | Check the website for more details.

Deadline: January 31

Application Link: https://www.noaa.gov/office-education/hollings-scholarship

- **Material Handling Education Foundation, Inc. Scholarship**

Amount: $6,000

Eligibility: Scholars must have at least a 'B' average grade | Must be enrolled in a college/University.

P.S: Check the website for specific requirements for the area of study.

Deadline: January 31

Application Link:
https://www.mhi.org/mhefi/scholarship

- **Udall Scholarship**

Amount: $7,000

Eligibility: The Scholarship Program identifies future leaders in environmental, Tribal public policy, and health care fields | Excellent academic and leadership records.

Deadline: March 2

Application Link:
https://www.udall.gov/ourprograms/scholarship/scholarship.aspx

- **AICPA Foundation Scholarship for Future CPAs**

Amount: $10,000

Eligibility: Applicant must be a U.S. Citizen or permanent resident | Must have a 3.0 GPA | Accounting or related and interested in pursuing a CPA license after graduation.

Deadline: March 15

Application Link:
https://www.thiswaytocpa.com/education/scholarship-search/

- **Dr. W. Wesley Eckenfelder Scholarship**

Amount: $5,000

Eligibility: Applicant must be enrolled in a STEM/Environmental science major | A minimum of 3.0 GPA is required | An essay of at least 250 words.

Deadline: March 31

Application Link:
https://brownandcaldwell.com/careers/eckenfelder-scholarship/

Other Scholarship Titles

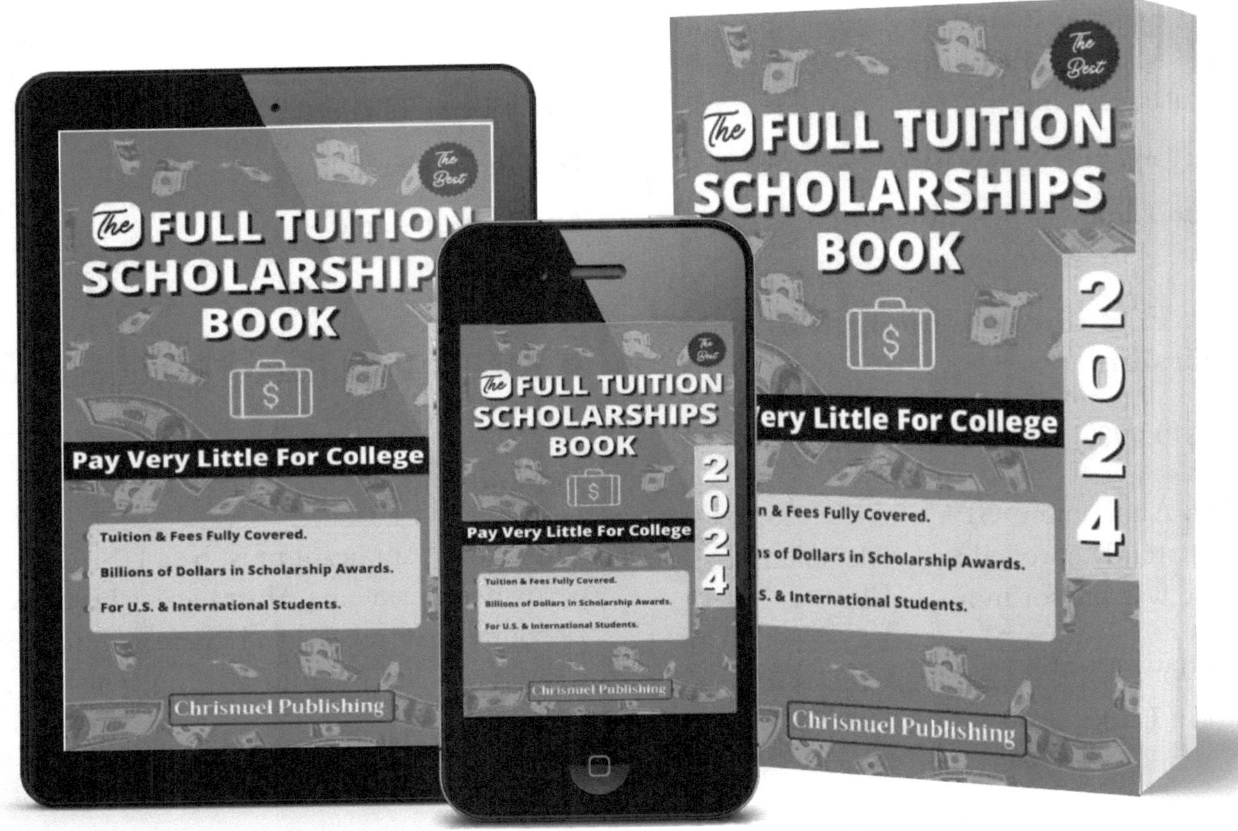

The Full Tuition Scholarships Book: Pay Very Little for College

---

⌘Link to Book:

https://www.amazon.com/s?k=The+full+tuition+scholarships+book

⌘ ENJOY YOUR SCHOLARSHIPS AWARDS !!!

Notes

Notes

Notes

Notes

Made in United States
Troutdale, OR
08/17/2024

22082986R00206